To President Hinsdale
with kind regards
from F. Kindsman

THE KINSMAN FAMILY.

GENEALOGICAL RECORD

OF THE

DESCENDANTS OF

ROBERT KINSMAN,

OF IPSWICH, MASS.

FROM 1634 TO 1875.

COMPILED FOR

Frederick Kinsman

BY

LUCY W. STICKNEY.

BOSTON:
PRINTED BY ALFRED MUDGE & SON,
34 SCHOOL STREET.
1876.

INTRODUCTION.

THIS work was not undertaken with the desire or expectation of showing any marked distinction in the Kinsman family, as History, which notes the progress of events, has never recorded the name prominently in its annals; neither was it undertaken with any hope of sharing in some great estate which might be found without a claimant in the Fatherland, as has been intimated; nor has the idea of compensation for the work, when completed, ever had a moment's consideration: on the contrary, the expenses from the beginning have been incurred with the expectation of pecuniary loss in carrying out the plan, and the result has more than justified this anticipation.

The writer, at a very early period of his life, had a strong desire to know something of his genealogy, and in fact began this work when a boy visiting relatives in Lisbon, Conn., by copying from their old Family Bible the record of his own branch, which extended back to Robert Kinsman, the third of that name in America. This desire was revived and strengthened in after years by an examination of Felt's "History of Ipswich," a book in which frequent mention is made of early members of the family.

Having decided to pursue the inquiry more thoroughly, but living in Ohio, at a distance from where the investigation should begin, the writer first opened a correspondence with Mrs. Louisa Kinsman Holmes, of Ipswich, Mass., and afterwards visited that town, a place of the greatest interest to the Kinsman family, as having been the spot where their first ancestor in America settled on his arrival from England, as well as the home of so many generations of his descendants. Mrs. Holmes was much interested in the subject, and, with her assistance and efficient efforts, so much of the early history of Robert Kinsman of Ipswich, and of his descendants in America, was brought to light, that a short sketch and limited record of the family was prepared, being designed for publication in the "New England Historical and Genealogical Register." This was in the year 1868, and at that time the writer, having become acquainted with Mr. William Low Kinsman, of Salem, Mass., interested him also in the work, and he has rendered valuable aid in its preparation. Having been strongly advised to such a course, we then determined not to publish the Record at that time, but first to have investigations made in England, with the hope of finding there a lineal connection for our emigrant ancestor, Robert Kinsman.

Accordingly Miss Harriet A. Bainbridge, now Mrs. H. A. de Salis, of London, Eng., was employed to make the necessary researches, and the result of her labors will be found in the English Record with which this book commences, and in the Pedigree following. These researches were continued at intervals, with varying prospects of success, during several years, ending only in 1873; but we have finally been compelled reluctantly to abandon the idea of obtaining at present the absolute proofs necessary to establish a *positive connection* for our ancestor, Robert Kinsman, who emigrated in 1634. This result, in view of the importance of the object sought, as well as of the time and labor expended and the expense incurred, is of course a great disappointment; but we are in a measure compensated for it by the remarkably full and excellent Pedigree which we have obtained, dating back to the year 1337.

A careful examination of this, in connection with the English Record, will show that we have found two Roberts, one in Wiltshire and one in Northamptonshire, at the right period of time, each being of the proper approximate age, and both of them apparently unaccounted for in England after 1634; either of whom therefore may have been, and one or the other of whom we believe must have been, the Emigrant whose ancestral line we have endeavored to discover. Although unable to decide positively between the two claimants, and therefore leaving it for each reader to choose for himself, we yet consider the preponderance of evidence, as given in the English Record, to be clearly in favor of the Wiltshire Robert.

Pending the investigation by Miss Bainbridge in England, we concluded that our American Record might be much enlarged and improved by proper effort, and that the attempt ought to be made. We found in the person of Miss Lucy W. Stickney, of Salem, Mass., the energy and experience required, and accordingly she was engaged to carry out this work and prepare the Record for publication. Through her successful efforts it has been greatly extended, and, as far as possible, perfected and completed.

In connection with the Record, we have introduced some interesting historical extracts relating to the times and surroundings of our ancestor at the period of his arrival in America, showing also who were his companions on the voyage from England, and how and where they were finally located; and also giving an idea of the state of public sentiment, and the trials and embarrassments encountered by emigrants, at that time and subsequently.

We do not expect that the Record will be found entirely

free from errors, as the collection and transferrence of so many names and dates, from such various sources, render the liability of mistake necessarily great; besides which, in some instances, words and figures in the letters sent us have been so indistinct that they may have been incorrectly recorded. Believing, however, that it is substantially correct, we hope this work may fill the place for which it was designed, and prove to be a genealogical record by which all the descendants of Robert Kinsman of Ipswich can trace a perfect line back to that worthy ancestor.

If there are any of the family whose names or records, not having been obtained, are omitted here, their correct descent and connection can probably be ascertained, with little difficulty, by means of this Record; any such omissions can be supplied, or corrections made, upon the blank leaves which will be found at the end of this volume, and in case of any such additions or corrections, marginal references to them should be made in the book, at the proper places of connection.

The system of numbering will be readily understood: Kinsman children who have become parents receive a number (at the right hand of the page), and appear again in their proper order, with their families; Kinsmans who have no descendants, and the children of Kinsman mothers bearing another name, are not, as a rule, carried forward.

To all those who have aided in our labors we tender our sincere thanks, hoping that they may find their reward in the completeness of the work that has been accomplished through their assistance.

FREDERICK KINSMAN.

WARREN, OHIO, *January*, 1876.

ENGLISH RECORD.

ENGLISH RECORD.

THE family of Kynesman, Kinnesman, Kingesman, and Kinsman, as it is variously spelled, is of very ancient origin in England.

By reference to the Pedigree, it will be seen that the earliest record found was in 1337, and that there was a continuous line of the family in Northamptonshire, where the main branch flourished, for nearly four hundred years, or till the close of the seventeenth century, when apparently it became extinct.

In Essex, however, a family of Kinsmans flourished till the eighteenth century, and doubtless this family came from the same original stock. As early as 1522, a John Kinnesman lived at Tolleshunt, in that county, and from his Will it is inferred that he was a rich and important man.

In the seventeenth century we find a branch of the Northampton family settled in Devonshire, and their descendants are still living.

From Wills proven at Salisbury and at the Principal Registry, Doctors-Commons, we find a branch of the Kingsman family also in Wiltshire, with records from 1504 to

1647; but owing to the destruction of Registers, the pedigree of their line is not so full and clear as that of the Northampton branch. The Probate Court Records of Salisbury have been well searched, but little has been verified from them, as the Records are not fertile in Kingsman Wills. There are people of the name still living in Wiltshire, but we have failed to obtain from them any information of value.

Our American ancestor left England in 1634.

We begin with the Kynesman family of Northamptonshire.

From Simon Kynesman of Loddington, who married Margaret Zouch, to Robert Kynesman, who married Elizabeth Woodville, there is some uncertainty as to the direct descent or succession, and this is denoted on the Pedigree by the dotted lines. A generation may have been transposed, or missed entirely.

Robert, who married Elizabeth Woodville, is mentioned in the following interesting document: —

"Robert Kynnesman, Inquisitio Post Mortem at Northampton, 28 June, 1 Henry VII (1486). He died 23 Jan. 1 Richard III (1484–5), and William Kynnesman was found to be his heir and aged 8 years 'et amplius.' Held Manor of Lodyngton of William Catesby, Esquire, as of his Manor of Lodyngton, and of William Catesby, Esquire, as of his Manor of Bukley by knights service, which said William Catesby, after the death of Robert Kynnesman, held the Manor and the guardianship of William his son and heir. The said William Catesby granted to Sir William Stoke the wardship of the said William Kynnesman, son and heir of Robert Kynnesman, and of his brother and sister. The said Sir William Stoke granted to Elizabeth, relict of Robert Kynnesman, the charge of the body of the said William Kynnesman, and of his brother and sister."

Of the son William, above mentioned, the following Indenture is found, viz. —

"Indenture recites between William Kynnesman, on the one part, and Maurice Osborne of Kelmarsh, Northamptonshire, of the other part, dates Aug. 16, 9 Henry VIII (1518), agreeing that Mary Poulton, daughter of said Maurice, should after marriage between her and the said William Kynnesman, have the Manor of Lodyngton," etc.

"Also Indenture dated 28 Nov., 13 Henry VIII (1521), between John Ashefelde of Heythorpe, County Oxford, Esquire, of the one part, and the said William Kynnesman on the other part, it was agreed that Robert Kynnesman, son of William Kynnesman, and Cicely, wife of Robert Kynnesman and daughter of the said John Ashefelde, should have sundry messuages," etc.

And the following: "William Kynnesman, Inquisitio Post Mortem at Northampton Castle, 4 Nov., 24 Henry VIII (1532). He died 6 July last (1532), and Robert Kynnesman was found to be his son and heir and aged at his father's death 25 years."

Of George Kinsman, son of William and Alice, of Loddington, the following: —

"19 Nov. 1619, George Kinsman, late of Lodington, Northamptonshire, gentleman, was seized of a messuage etc. in Lodington, and standing in need of, made request to Tristram Bucke and Thomas Asburye als Gascoigne (both being near friends and of alliance unto ye said orator), means to procure the sum of £300, and themselves together with Ferdinand Baud, Esquire, became bound to one Samuel Rubancke." "Purport of the suit is a charge of forcible entry into the premises against certain persons named. Complainant speaks of his wife and children, and of himself, as living in Derbyshire, forty miles away from Lodington."

Frances Kynnsman, born in 1613, the daughter of Harold and Elizabeth, made the following Will, dated 16 Dec. 1639. No proof.

"Fraunces Kynnsman, of Clipston, Northamptonshire, Spinster."

"My mother, Mrs. Elizabeth Kinsman, to see me buried at Broughton near my father."

"To my brother John Kynnsman, £50, and more if need be to set him out of debt."

"To my sister Anne Pettie, a ring."

"To my nephew Henry Collopp, a ring of 10/."

"To Katherine Collopp, and Elizabeth Collopp, my nieces, 20/ each."

"To my brother Pettie, for a pair of gloves, 12*d*."

"To my cozen Katherine Kynnsman, 40/."

"To Johan Goodman, 20/."

"To 6 maids to carry me to church, each a pair of white gloves and white favours."

"To my sister Buswell's servants."

"Residue to my good mother, Mrs. Elizabeth Kynnsman, and make her sole executrix, entreating her to remember my sister Buswell's children."

"Witnesses — John Heselden, William Buswell, Katherine Hulle, Marie Alderman."

Frances Kinsman, in her Will, makes no mention of brothers Richard and Robert. We know that she had such brothers, from the records of Broughton, and Richard was living in Broughton after her Will was made, as will be seen by the following extract from the Royalist Composition Papers, Vol. 35 (2 S.), No. 575: —

"Richard Kinnesman, of Broughton, Northamptonshire, gentleman. His delinquency . . . that he did assist the forces raised against the Parliament, and was comprised within the Articles of Exeter, as by the General's certificate. Since w[ch] he hath been beyond the seas. That he petitioned here the 25th Jan. 1648, whereby he craves the Articles of Exeter. That he is seized of an estate in fee to him and his heirs of a messuage and cottage in Broughton, of the yearly value of £68, whereont is issuing £40 a year, bequeathed by the last will and testament of Harrold Kynnesman the Compounder's father to Elizabeth Kynnesman his mother during her life, as by the s'd Will dated 2 Sept. 1631 appears, w[ch] said Elizabeth is still living. There will remain and come unto him and his heirs, after the dec[e] of the s'd Elizabeth his mother, a messuage etc. in Broughton and other lands in Pitchley of the yearly value of £56. 27 Jan. 1648."

Same volume, No. 581, "a certificate signed by Fairfax, stating that Auditor Kynesman was resident and abiding in Exeter seven months before the surrender of that city and that he ought to have the benefit of the Articles of Exeter," etc. Dated 18 Jan. 1648 [O. S.].

Same volume, No. 583, "Other certificates of Kynesman's residence in Exeter, signed by Jos. Martyn, Jn[o] Colleton, John Wyott, Henry Croone."

Vol. 22 (1 S.), No. 734.

"Richard Kinsman, of Broughton, in Northamptonshire, Gentleman, bound to the sayd Treasurers in £50 ye 10 of February 1648. With condition to pay £27.10/ when the debts for which the sayd fine of £27.10/ was sett, should be recovered. He hath paid £15 in full — 28 Nov. 1649."

About 1644, the civil war between Charles the First and his Parliament began in England. During this struggle, which proved so unfortunate to the monarch, Virginia adhered to the royal cause.

Sir Thomas Fairfax commanded the Parliamentary forces. He blockaded Exeter, and compelled it to surrender upon terms, Feb. 1646. According to Hume, "The soldiers, delivering up their horses and arms, were allowed to disband, and received twenty shillings apiece, to carry them to their respective abodes. Such of the officers as desired it, had passes to retire beyond sea; the others, having promised never more to bear arms, paid compositions to the Parliament and procured their pardon." "These compositions were different, according to the demerits of the person; but, by a vote of the house, they could not be under two years' rent of the delinquent's estate. Journ. 11th of August, 1648. Whitlocke, p. 160."

In "A Perfect Description of Virginia, Printed for Rich'd Wodenoth, at the Star under Peter's Church in Cornhill, London, 1649," which book was reprinted in the Collections of the Massachusetts Historical Society (see Vol. 9, Second Series, page 118), mention is made of a "Richard Kinsman who had resided in Virginia for three or four years, a farmer, and remained in Jamestown in March of 1648."

He was, possibly, the Richard Kinsman of Broughton,[1] who, it will be seen by the certificate of Lord Fairfax before mentioned, was residing in Exeter in July, 1645, and was assisting the forces against the Parliament; and, on its surrender, received a pass "to retire beyond sea," as he mentions that he has "been beyond the seas" in his petition of Jan. 25, 1648 [O. S.], when he returned to Broughton, and craved

---

1 Both Richard of Virginia and Robert of Ipswich may have been of the Broughton family, or both may have been of the Wiltshire family. But Robert's case is not dependent on Richard's.

the Articles of Exeter, and recovered his estates, paying, as will be seen, the fines imposed.

A certificate of the baptism of Robert,[1] the son of Harold and Elizabeth (Golborne) Kinsman, has been received, as follows, the record being an extract from the Register of Baptisms in the Parish of Broughton for the year Sixteen Hundred and Seven: —

"*Roberte ye Sonne of Harold Kinsman was baptised ye sixteenth day of Maye* 1607."

"I, Granville H. Forbes, Rector of Broughton in the County of Northampton, do hereby certify that the above is a true copy.

Witness my hand this eighteenth day of Decr 1872.

GRANVILLE H. FORBES."

"The Kynesman family of Northamptonshire," writes Mrs. de Salis, "was of high standing, as may be inferred from the following facts. Simon Kynesman of Loddington, Northamptonshire, was a member of Parliament in 1420. The same year he obtained a license from the Bishop to celebrate Mass in his own mansion. He was also Sheriff of Northamptonshire in the 9th of Henry V (1422). Harold Kynnesman, baptized at Broughton, Northamptonshire, April 3, 1570, was Vice-Treasurer at Arms in the Irish Wars in the time of Elizabeth, and for his fidelity was recalled to the same office

---

[1] Mrs. de Salis, *née* Bainbridge, in her efforts to trace Robert Kinsman, the ancestor of the Kinsmans of America, offered a reward for a copy of his baptismal register and of his marriage register, in every parish of Northampton, Wiltshire, Somerset, Warwick, and Berkshire, also in Essex, Middlesex, Suffolk, Norfolk, Herts, Oxford, and Lincoln. There were many returns, but this was the only one of any special interest, as approximating the probable age of the emigrant.

2

by King James. Still later, Richard Kinsman, baptized at Broughton, Northamptonshire, Jan. 16, 1602, was Auditor of the Counties of Northampton, Devon, and Cornwall. Another evidence is that the Kinsmans married into the families of the first people in Northampton and the adjacent counties, and bore Coat-Armor from an early period, as it is found described and tricked in Heralds' Visitations."

The Northamptonshire line bore a shield quartering the Arms of three families, as given in the Visitation of 1564: the first quarter, *Per pale azure and gules, three saltires argent;* the second, *Gules, three bulls' heads cabossed argent;* the third, *Gules, a cross fleury argent;* the fourth, the same as the first. Crest, *A buck proper, lodged in fern vert.* The second and third quarterings are the Arms of families with which the Northamptonshire Kinsmans were allied in marriage. The first and fourth quarterings alone, the latter being but a repetition of the first, and the crest, belong to the Kinsmans. No Grant of this coat-of-arms has been found, so that, undoubtedly, it belonged to the family before the College-of-Arms was incorporated (in 1483), and was in existence as far back as 1420, in the time of Simon Kynesman of Loddington, who is styled *Armiger*, or one entitled to Coat-Armor. Our plate of the Kinsman Arms is copied from a seal now owned by a Kinsman of Cornwall in England, who is doubtless a descendant of John Kinsman of Broughton, brother of Richard the Auditor and of Robert.

A description of this shield, interpreting the language of Heraldry, might be given thus: The shield is divided by a perpendicular line into two equal parts (*per pale*), the color of the first half, which would be at the bearer's right hand, being blue (*azure*), and that of the second half being red (*gules*); the figures thereon are three crosses of the pattern called St. Andrew's (*saltires*), and are represented as being of silver (*argent*). The crest is a buck, represented in its natural color (*proper*), and lying down or kneeling but with the head erect (*lodged*), in a bed of green (*vert*) fern.

The Kingsman family of Wiltshire was a branch of the Northampton family, as will be seen by the following Will of one of the Fitzakerlys, or Fazakerlys, who were related, by marriage, to the Northampton Kynesmans.

"In the name of God, Amen. I Rychard Fazakerly, of Warmington, County Northampton, bein of perfett mynde though weak and ill in bodye, and about to goe a jorney to see myne relaçons, doe make this my last Will and Testament in maner and ffourme followynge.

First. I desire that my bodye shal be buryed in Xtian buryiall wher it pleasath Almyhtie God that I shal departe this lyfe, and for my sepulture and braking of the grounde in the churche I will and bequethe 6/8, and I bequethe to the high awlter of the churche of Warmynton 4/7, and also the some of 6/8 for to synge a dirige for the welth of my soule, and I also bequethe to the said churche the some of 6/8 for diryges to be song for the welth of the soules of my fader and moder.

Item. I will and bequethe to Robert my brother, my goblet of siluer and 5 spougnes of siluer.

Item. I will and bequethe to my saide brother Robert, a cup of siluer parcell guilt and a salt of siluer parcell guilt, with couers to them, and 2 paire of ye best sheres.

To my syster Helen ye wyf of my saide brother Robert, 5/7 to buy her a rynge.

Item. I will and bequethe my best gowne to my kinsman Robert Kingesman, of Lodynton, and my dublet of lether to my kinsman John Kingesman, of Sowt Newtone.

Item. I doe alsoe will and bequethe that my kinswoman Isabel Kingesman shal have my ringe with sardonox, as a remembrannce of her gret kindnesse to me a poore synnore when I was in sor affliçon.

And for the residues of any monye I have and my howsehold stuff and my goods movable and unmovable, I will to be equally divided amonge my base childrens, and I do alsoe will and bequethe to my servant Tho. Radleye, 1/.

And I constitute and ordain my kinsman Robert Kingesman and his broder John my kinsman, to be executors of this mee last Will and Testamt. Signed and sealed by me Ric. Fazakerlie this last daye of Septembre in the yere of oure Lorde God one thowsand five hundreth and fower, in the presense of Rob. Wydvile, Maister Sayer, John Howes with other."

From this Will it is clear that Richard Fazakerly calls as "kinsman" not only the Robert Kynesman of Loddington, Northamptonshire, who married Isabel Fitzakerly, his niece, but also Robert's brother John Kingesman, of South Newton, Wiltsihre. This John left the following Will: —

"In the name of God, Amen. In the yere of our lord 1522, the 16 day of Februarie, I John Kyngesman, of South Newton in the countie of Wiltes, being in my perfitte mynde and in good remembrannce, doe make my testament in this maner and fourme.

ffirst and formoste I bequethe my sowle unto Almighty God, to our Lady, and to all the Saintes in Hevyn. My bodie to be buried in the churche of St. Andrewe in South Newton.

Also I bequethe to the Cathedrall churche of Sarum, 3/4.

Item. To the parish churche of St. Andrewe, 5/.

Item. To the high awlter within the same churche, 6/8.

Item. To our lady light, within the same churche, two ewes.

Item. To the parish churche of Wyscheford, 6/8.

Item. To the churche of Stepelforde, 6/8.

Item. To the churche of Wodeforde, 6/8.

Item. I bequethe to the blake freres and to the graye, to every order of them within the citie of Sarum, a quarters whete, for to synge masse and dirige for my soule at the day of my buryinge.

Item. I bequethe to my son Robert, £6.8.4.

To Amye my daughter, £3.6.8.

To Thomas my son, £6.8.4.

To Christian my daughter, £3.6.8.

To Agnes my daughter, £3.6.8.

To Edith my daughter, £3.6.8.

To Anne my daughter, £3.6.8.

To Elizabeth the lady, my daughter, £3.6.8, and that William my sonne shall have the guyding of it to her profite.

Item. to every godchilde that I have, a bushel of barley.

I bequethe to my son Robert 200 shepe to remayne to his moder at the two yeres ende, and she to annser the stock to my Lady. Also that Alyn my servannt a kowe and 20 shepe, half vethers, half ewys. To Edith Stork, a kowe and 5 shepe.

To William Kyngsman, a bullock.

Item. To the Monestery of Whilton, 10/— 5/ of it to the Reparaçons of the churche and the oder 5/ to be devided to the Ladyes at the will of my Lady Abbess, for a dirige and a masse to be songe for the welthe of my soule.

Item. I give the residue of my goodes movable and unmovable, I give and bequethe to Johanne my wyffe, whom I doe make my hole and true executrix, to dispoase for the welth of my soule at hir arbitrement and will.

Also I constitute and ordeyn Sir William my sonne, to be Superuisor of this my Will and Testament, to whome I give and bequethe £6.8.4, for his labour.

Witnesse. Thomas Maister, . . . Martyn, Sir Thomas

Wellys, John Blak of Stoverd, Edmund Herford, with other."

Robert Kingsman of Overton, Wiltshire, the son of this John of South Newton, also left a Will, of which the following is a copy, viz. —

"In the name of God, Amen, the 25 day of Aug. in the yere of oure lord God 1592, and in the 34 of hir Mai'ties raigne. I Robert Kingsman, of Overton in the county of Wilts, yeoman, being of perfitte mynde (the lord be praised therefore) doe make, ordaine this my last Will and Testament, in maner and fourme following.

First. I bequethe my soule into the handes of my lord and Saviour Jesus Christ, who hath redeemed it, and my bodye to be buried in parish churche of Overton.

Item. I give and bequethe Robert Kingsman my 2d sonne, all the goods, chattells, stocks, stores, cattle, implements whatsoever, being, going or feedynge now, uppon the houses, barnes, stables, edifices, landes, meadowes, pastures, and feedinges of the tenement in East Kennett, which I had by lease from Mr. Skillinge.

Also I will and bequethe to said Robert that in respecte of all the wheate growen uppon the said tenement in East Kennett, was brought to Overton, therefore that Richard my oldest sonne shall eare and sowe withe good seede corne, all the grounde which lieth for the next season parcell of the said Robert, as well all the seede of all the wheate as of the barley.

Also I will to the saide Roberte — "various bequestes as to amounts on the tenements of Hoyble in the parish of Calne." He bequeathes also to him "all timber and boards lying about his house at Overton."

To Thomas his youngest son, who was under age, he

bequeathes £13; mentions Thomas Smithe of West Kennett, his brother-in-law, and his son-in-law William Griffin of Belhampton — they to hold some lease for a reasonable sum.

"To Margaret his daughter, £4 of money."

"To Elizabeth his daughter, £3."

"To his loving wife Agnes, and to Robert his sonne, and Richard his eldest sonne, all his debts owing to him, between them to be equally divided."

Also "to his loving wife £100."

Robert Kingsman of Overton, Wiltshire, the second son of Robert and Agnes, above, also left a Will, from which the following items are extracted: —

"Robert Kingsman, of Overton, the elder, yeoman, sicke in body, but in good and perfitt mynde, the 6 day of Aprill, 1647" . . . "desires to be buried in the church of Overton, to which he bequethes 16/."

"To children of my son Richard Kingsman, 20/ apiece."

"To Robert, the sonne of my sonne Robert, the sum of £20 when he shall come to lawful age."

"To children of my son Philip, 20/ apiece."

"To children of my son-in-law Edward Carpenter, 20/ apiece."

"To children of my son-in-law John Newman, 20/ apiece."

"To children of my son-in-law Nathaniell Poole, 20/ apiece."

"To children of my son-in-law Henry Fisher, 20/ apiece."

"To daughter of my son Thomas, and to the child unborn of my son Thomas, 20/ apiece."

"Robert Kingsman to be executor . . . "my kinsman Robert Kingsman, of Overton, yeoman, and Thomas Stevens my kinsman, of Lockbridge, to be overseers." Will proved 26 July, 1647.

From this Will we know that Robert Kingsman of Overton, the second Wiltshire Robert, who died in 1647, left a son, the third Robert; and that the latter had also a son, the fourth Robert, who had not "come to lawful age" in 1647. We also know from other sources that *Robert the Emigrant* had a son Robert, who was born in 1629, and whom we find at a later date in Ipswich, Massachusetts, as a prominent man. We have no dates at all for the third Wiltshire Robert, nor for the Emigrant previous to his leaving England; but the approximate age of the fourth Wiltshire Robert corresponds very closely with that of the Emigrant's son, who must have been seventeen or eighteen years of age in April, 1647, the date of the Will just given. Again, we know from this Will that there was a "son-in-law John Newman," who, being therefore a brother-in-law of the third Wiltshire Robert, might naturally have accompanied him if he went to America. Now, among the fellow-passengers of the Emigrant Robert, there were four Newmans, viz. Thomas, two *Johns*, — one of them the son of Thomas, and the other probably his brother, — and Robert.

As passengers in the "Mary and John," with Robert Kingsman, are also found Thomas Parker, James and Nicholas Noyes, John Woodbridge, Henry Lunt, Richard Kent and others, prominent among the early Puritans of New England. Of Parker, Savage[1] makes the following note: "Thomas Parker, a learned theologian, pupil of the great Archbishop Usher, having passed a short time at Magdalen College, Oxford, . . . finished his preparation for the pulpit at Leyden, and had a school at Newbury in Berkshire, where also he preached; was a bachelor, but stood in place of a father to many divines of the succeeding generation."

Rev. James Noyes and his brother Nicholas were cousins

[1] In his edition of Winthrop's History of New England (vol. i, p. 158).

of Parker; Rev. John Woodbridge was his nephew; and these four men we know to have been natives of Wiltshire. William Elliott, a passenger by the "Hercules" at about the same time, was also from Wiltshire. Parker seems to have been the leader of the company by the "Mary and John," more or less of whom were also from that county, evidently, as is shown by the following extract from "Hubbard's General History of New England": —

"The reverend and learned Mr. Parker was at first called to Ipswich, to join with Mr. Ward; but he choosing rather to accompany some of his countrymen that came out of Wiltshire in England, to that new place, than to be engaged with such as he had not been acquainted withall before; therefore removed with them thither, and settled at Newbury . . ."

Felt, in his History of Ipswich, also has a record of "Rev. Thomas Parker and company out of Wiltshire," arriving at Agawam in May, 1634.

George Smith, M. D., in his "History of Delaware County, Pennsylvania," published in 1862, in the list of early settlers and eminent men, mentions that a "John Kinsman from Fifel in the County of Wilts, England, was settled in Chichester as early as 1684, and was married to Hannah, the daughter of John Simcock, the same year. He was an active member of Chichester Friends' Meeting, and the Monthly Meeting was sometimes held at his house. As a citizen, he held a respectable position in the community. His children were Elizabeth and Hannah, the former of whom married John Dutton in 1704. He died about the year 1701."

It is worthy of notice here that only the Wilts branch of the family spell their name Kingsman (the Northampton line not using a *g*), and in the list of passengers the Emigrant Robert's name is spelled *Kingsman*, although he dropped the *g* after coming to America. There is, also, a noticeable repetition among the American descendants of the Emigrant, for many generations, of some of the old Christian names of the Wiltshire branch. These various facts would seem to furnish strong presumptive evidence that our American ancestor, Robert Kinsman, came from Wiltshire, and was the son of the Robert who died there in 1647. Should future investigation prove this theory, our pedigree is traced to the Northamptonshire family of the fourteenth century, who bore the coat-of-arms already described.

THE ENGLISH PEDIGREE.

The English Pedigree has been obtained from the following sources: Visitations and Grants of Arms at the College of Arms; the Heralds' Visitations at the British Museum in the Harleian Manuscripts, Numbers 1553, 1118, 1138, 1187, 1184, and 1094, and additional manuscripts; the Lansdowne and Egerton Manuscripts; Chancery Proceedings; Close-Rolls; Subsidy Rolls; the Fine Rolls; Escheats; Post-Mortems; Inquisitions; Wills at Principal Registry, Doctors-Commons, including Herts and Essex Wills which are now in that office; the Probate Court Records of Salisbury and Northampton; Parish Registers; State Papers; Royalist Composition Papers; Admiralty Documents; County Histories, both in print and in manuscript; and by correspondence with members of the Kinsman family in England.

AMERICAN RECORD.

ROBERT KINSMAN, THE EMIGRANT.

ROBERT KINSMAN, or Kingsman, the first of the name known in New England, was a passenger in the ship "Mary and John," of London, Robert Sayres master, sailing from Southampton, England, in March, 1634, and arriving in Boston the following May.

The following highly interesting documents, referring to the passengers in this vessel, were published in the "New England Historical and Genealogical Register" for July, 1855, having been communicated by Hon. George Lunt, of Boston, who received them through Mr. Cleveland, of Salem. "They will supply a gap, long bewailed, in the early history of Newbury, by giving us the name of the vessel, in which her first settlers came to this country, in 1634. The list of passengers by the "Mary and John" comprises many well-known names of residents of Newbury and its vicinity, and which also are well known to have been borne by the original planters of that ancient settlement. It will be seen by the Order in Council, that the emigrants were at first 'made staye of, untill further order from their Lordshipps'; who eventually let them go, upon certain conditions, some of which seemed harder to them, perhaps, than they would be now considered."

Extracts from the Records of the Orders in Council: —

"New England — At Whitehall the last of February 1633. Present.

Lop. Arch Bp. of Cant— [William Laud.]

Lo. Keep^r [Sir Thomas Coventry.]

Lo. Privie Seal [Henry Montague, Earl of Manchester.]

Lo. high Chamb^rline [Robert Bertie, Lord Willoughby of Eresby.]

Earle of Kelly [Thomas Erskine, first Earl.]

Lo. [Francis] Cottington

Mr V. Chamb^rline [Sir Thomas Jermyn Kt.]

Mr Compt^r [Sir Henry Vane, Sen.]

Mr Secretary [Sir Francis] Wyndibank

Whereas by a Warr^t bearing date 22nd of this Present the sev^rall ships following bound for New England & now lying in the River of Thames were made staye of untill further order from their L'opps Viz^t. the Clement & Job, The Reformation, The True Love, The Elizabeth Bonadventure, The Sea Flower, *The Mary & John*, The Planter, The Elizabeth & Dorcas, The Hercules & the Neptune.

For as much as the Masters of the said ships were this day called before the Board & several Particulars given them in charge to be performed in their said Voyage, amongst which the said Masters were to enter into several Bonds of One Hundred Pounds a piece to His Maj^stys use before the Clarke of the Councell attendant to observe & cause to be observed & putt in Execuc'on these Articles following vizt.

1. That all & every Person aboard their Ships now bound

for New England as aforesaid, that shall blaspheme or profane the Holy name of God be severely punish't.

2. That they cause the Prayers contained in the Book of Common Prayers establisht in the Church of England to be said daily at the usual hours for Morning & Evening Prayers & that they cause all Persons aboard their said Ships to be present at the same.

3. That they do not receive aboard or transport any Person that hath not Certificate from the Officers of the Port where he is to imbarke that he hath taken both the Oathes of Alleigeance & Supremacy.

4. That upon their return into this Kingdom they Certify to the Board the names of all such Persons as they shall transport together with their Proceedings in the Execuc'on of the aforesaid Articles — Whereunto the said M^{rs} have conformed themselves — It was therefore & for divers other Reasons best known to their Lo^{pps} thought fitt that for this time they should be permitted to proceed on their Voyage, and it was thereupon Ordered that Gabriel Marsh Esqr. Marshalle of the Admiralty & all other His Maj'tys Officers to whom their said Warr^{t} was directed should be required upon Sight hereof to discharge all & every the said Ships & Suffer them to depart on their intended Voyage to New England.

Ex^{t}. JON MEANTYS."

"The names of such Passengers as took the Oathes of Supremacy & Alleigeance to pass for New England in the Mary & John of London Robert Sayres master.

24th Mar 1633

William Trace
John Marshe
John Luff
Henry Traske
William Moudey
Robert Sever
Thomas Avery
Henry Travers
Thomas Sweete
John Woodbridge
Thomas West
Thomas Savery
Christopher Osgood
Phillip Fowler
Richard Jacob
Daniel Ladd
ROBERT KINGSMAN
John Bartlett
Robert Coker
William Savery
John Anthony, *Left behind.*
Stephen Jurden
John Godfrey
George Browne
Nicholas Noyce
Richard Browne
Richard Reynolds
Richard Littlehall
William White
Matthew Hewlett [*Hercules*]
John Whelyer
William Clarke
Robert Neuman
Adrian Vincent

The **26th** day of March

Nicholas Easton
Richard Kent
Abraham Mussey
William Ballard
Matthew Gillett
William Franklin
John Mussey
Thomas Cole
Thomas Parker
James Noyce
John Spencer
William Spencer
Henry Shorte
William Hibbens
Richard Kent
Joseph Myles
John Newman
William Newbey
Henry Lunt
Joseph Pope
Thomas Newman
John Newman

For which we gave certificate, together, with five others whch are said to be left behind to oversee the Chattle to pass in the Hercules vizt.

The names of the Passengers in the Hercules of London, John Kiddey Ma^{r}: for New England —

These six Passengers took their Oathes of Supremacy & Alleigeance the 24th of March and were left behind the Mary & John as intended to pass in ye Hercules — Viz^{t}.

John Anthoney Robert Early William Latcome Thomas Foster William Foster Matthew Hewlett	Cert. the six first to Mt'er· Sayers as intended Secondh to Mr Kiddey to pass in the Hercules —

16th April **1634** —	Nathaniel Davyes
	George Kinge
	Thomas Rider
	William Elliott
	William Fifeilde
18	Henry Phelps —

These Proceedings were Copyed out of an Olde Book of Orders belonging to the Port of South'ton but now remaining at the Custom house in Portsmouth the 6th Day of December 1735 —

p^{r}. THOMAS WHITEHOUSE."

In regard to the dates in the preceding records, as well as those which follow, it is important to bear in mind that they are *Old Style.* "Before 1752 the year was, by the legal method of computation, held to begin on the 25th of March, Lady Day, or Annunciation; in reckoning the months, March was called the first, February the twelfth month, etc." So that the 24th day of March, 1633, according to Old Style, was the last day of that year, and the day following was the first day of the new year, and called the 25th of March, 1634.

To show something of what transpired about the time these emigrants arrived in America, we quote from "Winthrop's

History of New England," by Savage, Vol. I, pp. 158 to 162: —

"The week the court was, [kept at Boston, May 1634,] there came in six ships, with store of passengers and cattle. Mr. Parker, a minister, and a company with him, being about one hundred, went to sit down at Agawam, and divers others of the new comers."

"These ships, by reason of their short passage, had store of provisions left, which they put off at easy rates, viz. biscuit at 20*s*. the hundred; beef at £6 the hogshead, etc."

"The last month (June 1634) arrived here (Boston) fourteen great ships, and one at Salem.

"Mr. Humfrey and the lady Susan, his wife, one of the Earl of Lincoln's sisters, arrived here. He brought more ordnance, muskets, and powder, bought for the public by moneys given to that end; for godly people in England began now to apprehend a special hand of God in raising this plantation, and their hearts were generally stirred to come over.

"Among others, we received letters from a godly preacher, Mr. Levinston, a Scotchman in the north of Ireland, whereby he signified, that there were many good Christians in those parts resolved to come hither, if they might receive satisfaction concerning some questions and propositions which they sent over. Likewise, Mr. Humfrey brought certain propositions from some persons of great quality and estate, (and of special note for piety,) whereby they discovered their intentions to join with us, if they might receive satisfaction therein.

"It appeared further, by many private letters, that the departure of so many of the best, both ministers and Christians, had bred sad thoughts in those behind of the Lord's intentions in this work, and an apprehension of some evil days to come upon England. Then it began now to be apprehended by the archbishops, and others of the council, as a matter of state, so as they sent out warrant to stay the ships, and to call in our patent; but, upon petition of the shipmasters, (alleging how beneficial this plantation was to England, in regard of the Newfoundland fishing, which they took in their way homeward), the ships were at that time released."

"Divers of the ships lost many cattle; but the two which came from Ipswich, of more than one hundred and twenty, lost but seven. None of the ships lost any passengers, but the Elizabeth Dorcas,[1] which, having a long passage, and being hurt upon a rock at Scilly, and very ill victualled, she lost sixty passengers at sea, and divers came sick on shore, who all recovered, (through the mercy of God,) except . . . .

"Mr. Humfrey brought sixteen heifers[2] given by a private friend, viz. Mr. Richard Andrews, to the plantation, viz. to every of the ministers one, and the rest to the poor, and one half of the increase of the ministers' [part] to be reserved for other ministers."

Of these emigrants, the learned English antiquarian, the Rev'd Mr. Hunter, says, that they "consisted very much of persons who though not of the very first rank were yet men of substance and good alliances, ... *will-making families*, families high in the subsidy-books, while some of them, as the Winthrops, were among the principal gentry of the country."

ROBERT KINSMAN, with his fellow-passengers of the "Mary and John," made his way to Agawam, or Ipswich, and his name is found recorded there in 1635.

A grant of land was made to him in 1637, as is shown by

---

[1] In this ship came Henry Sewall, father of the first Chief Justice, of the name of Samuel.

[2] "At that time valuable at £20 per piece." [Hubbard.]

the following, taken from the old records of Ipswich of 1637, called the Commoners' Record.

"Granted to Robert Kinsman by the company of freemen, one house lot, one acre of ground having a house lot now in the possession of Richard Lumpkin on the South, a house lot now in possession of William Avery, on the southeast, John Jackson on the west, the high road leading to the river, on the east end. Also a planting lot six acres lying on the great hill commonly called 'Heartbreak Hill,' having a planting lot of Richard Haffield on the east, a planting of Allen Perley's on the west, a planting of Robert Andrews at the north-east, at the south end the high road leading to Jebaquo (Chebacco). Also thirty-four acres meadow and upland, having Jebaquo river on the east, on the south the land of —— Graves, and the west Daniel Clarkes land. To enjoy all the saide layndes to him, his heirs, and assigns, forever. July 25, 1637."

These land grants were made, subject to the following order, passed May, 1635: —

"No dwelling-house shall be built above a half-mile from the meeting-house in any new plantation, without leave from the Court, except mills and farm-houses of such as have their dwellings in town."

Robert Kinsman's house stood near the place where the South Church of Ipswich now stands.

Of the first settlement of Agawam, or Ipswich, we get the following from Winthrop: —

Jan. 17, 1632–33. "It was agreed, ... that a plantation should be begun at Agawam, (being the best place in the land for tillage and cattle,) least an enemy, finding it void, should possess and take it from us.

"The governour's son (being one of the assistants) was to undertake this, and to take no more out of the bay than twelve men; the rest to be supplied at the coming of the next ships."

March, 1633. "The governour's son, John Winthrop, went, with twelve more, to begin a plantation at Agawam, after called Ipswich."

August 4, 1634. "At the court, the new town at Agawam was named Ipswich, in acknowledgment of the great honor and kindness done to our people which took shipping there, etc.; and a day of thanksgiving appointed, a fortnight after, for the prosperous arrival of the others, etc."

Felt gives this record, in his History of Ipswich: —

"1634, May. Rev. Thomas Parker and company out of Wiltshire, being about one hundred, and other new settlers, take up their abode here [Agawam]."

And "Hubbard's General History of New England" states also: —

"The plantation at Agawam was from the first year of its being raised to a township, so filled with inhabitants, that some of them presently swarmed out into another place, a little further eastward."

The following extract is from the Colonial Records: —

"May 6th, 1635. Quascacunquen is allowed by the court to be a plantation, and it is referred to Mr. [John] Humphrey, Mr. [John] Endicott, captain [Nathaniel] Turner, and captain [William] Trask, or any three of them, to set out the bounds of Ipswich and Quascacunquen, or so much thereof as they can, and the name of the said plantation shall be changed, and shall hereafter be called Newberry.

"Further it is ordered, that it shall be in the power of the court to take order that the said plantation *shall* receive a sufficient company to make a competent towne."

A settlement was commenced that month, and the first emigrants to Newbury from Ipswich are described by Coffin, in his History of Newbury, as going by water through Plum Island Sound, and up the river Quascacunquen [now river Parker]. Thomas Parker, John Woodbridge, James and Nicholas Noyes, and eight or nine more of the "Mary and John" passengers, were among that company. Nicholas Noyes is mentioned as making the first landing.

Robert Kinsman seems to have chosen to remain in Ipswich; but we find no further note of him, until his death. He died in Ipswich, Jan. 28, 1664 [O. S.]. His Will is found on file in the Essex Registry of Probate, and is recorded in Book 1, page 213; the following is a copy of the original:—

"These presents declareth that I, Robert Kinsman of Ipswich, in the county of Essex, being at present sick and weake of Body, but through God's mercy inioyeing my understanding and memory doe make this my last will and testament. first. I doe give my soule into the hands of Jesus Christ, my body to be desently buried in Ipswich burying place. And for my outward estate, I dispose as followeth.

Item. I doe give and bequeath unto my sonn Robert, my Meddow land att Chebacho which he doth now improve to the halfes, payeing unto Isaack & Sarah Ringe, the chilldren of my daughter Mary, ten pound apeece when they come to age, & if either of them dye before they come to age, the surviver to inioy the whole twenty pound.

Item. I give unto my daughter Mary the wife of Usuall Wardell, ten pounds, and to her foure elder children, twenty shillings apeece, Viz't Daniell, Roger, Mary and Susan Ringe.

Item. I give unto my daughter Sarah the wife of Samuell Younglove, my foure acre lott which I exchanged with Samuell Ayres, and to her child or children, which shall be then liveing after her decease.

Item. I give unto my Daughter Hanah, the some of forty pounds.

Item. I give unto my daughter Martha, the wife of Jacob ffoster, the some of thirty pounds.

Item. I give unto my daughter Tabitha Kinsman, my dwelling house and apertenances & land about it, payeing out of it twenty pounds within two yeare after my decease, alsoe I give unto hir my sayd daughter Tabitha my houshould stufe.

Item. I give unto my coussen Richard Nicolls, ten pounds to be payd by my sayd daughter Tabitha, part of the twenty pounds and the other ten pounds to be payd unto my daughter Hanah, by my sayd daughter Tabitha, as part of the forty pounds before given unto her.

Item. I give unto my five daughters each of them a cow and I give unto Mary my daughter ffosters child, my heifer. And I Apoynt my sonn Robert Kinsman and Robert Lord, Sen'r to be my executors of this my last will to see it performed.

Wittnes my hand this 25th of January, 1664.

the marke of
ROBERT [R K] KINSMAN

Signed & declared
by Robert Kinsman to
be his last will and
testament in the presence of

the marke of
EBEN |V| DANE.
ROBERT LORD."

Proved March 28, 1665. Inventory March 28, 1665. Amt. £234.4.0.

HIS CHILDREN:

1. ROBERT, b. 1629: m. Mary Boreman. 1
2. MARY, b. : m. Daniel Rindge; Ursuel Wardwell. 2
3. SARAH, b. : m. Samuel Younglove, Aug. 1, 1660. 3
4. HANNAH, b. : m. William Danford, March 20, 1670; and died without children, Oct. 18, 1678.
5. MARTHA, b. : m. Jacob Foster, Jan. 12, 1658. 4
6. TABITHA, b. : unmarried in 1674.

SECOND GENERATION.

1. ROBERT KINSMAN, son of Robert, born in 1629; married, time not known, MARY BOREMAN, daughter of Thomas (who was Deputy to the General Court in 1636), and Margaret Boreman, of Ipswich.

He "came into full communion" with the church in Ipswich, Feb. 22, 1673; was admitted a Freeman, March 11, 1673-4; chosen a Selectman in 1675; Tithingman 1677; took the Oath of Allegiance, Dec. 11, 1678; Quartermaster, Jan. 1, 1684.

From —— Hull's Account Book, kept in 1675-6, it appears that "Robert Kinsman" received £3 for his services in the Narraganset War; and from the "Records of the Proprietors of Narraganset Township, No. 1, now the Town of Buxton, York County, Maine," by the late Capt. William F. Goodwin, published in 1871, the following is gleaned of the Narraganset War, and of the land bounties given to the descendants of those who served in it: —

"The Narraganset war, under the subtle leadership of King Philip, the ambitious and heroic sachem of Mount Hope, suddenly bursting upon the eastern colonies, in 1675, brought indescribable terror and affliction upon the infant settlements. It is impossible to understand, and much less to describe, in any adequate manner, the misfortunes which this merciless warfare visited upon the feeble settlers of the wilderness. The confederated savages, in the secret conclaves of the forests, under the inspiration of their powerful and relentless chief, had organized the bloody design to utterly extinguish the colonies, and, though defeated in their terrible purpose of extermination, they so far put their sanguinary work into execution, in the brief space of a year, as to have clothed all New England in mourning. Estimates, drawn from official records, show that no less than six hundred of the inhabitants, the flower and strength of the country, either fell in battle, or were murdered by the enemy; and that there were few families, or individuals, who had not lost some near relative in the savage strife. . . . Bancroft, in his account of the 'Narraganset Fort Fight,' says, 'It was resolved to regard the Narragansetts as enemies; and a little before the winter solstice (Dec. 18), a thousand men, levied by the united colonies, and commanded by the brave Josiah Winslow, a native of New England, invaded their territory. After a night spent in the open air, they waded through the snow from daybreak till an hour after noon; and at last reached the cluster of wigwams which a fort protected. Davenport, Gardner, Johnson, Gallop, Siely, Marshall, led their companies through the narrow entrance in the face of death, and left their lives as a testimony to their patriotism and courage. Feeble palisades could not check the determined valor of the white men; and the group of Indian cabins was soon set on fire.'

"When the army was mustered on Dedham plain, in 1675, preparatory to the march against the stronghold of King Philip, a proclamation was made to the troops, in the name of the Government, 'that if they played the man, took the fort, and drove the enemy out of the Narraganset country, which was their great seat, that they should have a gratuity in land besides their wages.'

"The message which the House sent up to the Council urging the claims of these soldiers, and which brought the Board into their views, in 1731, is a state paper of extraordinary dignity and power, presenting the whole merits of the case in language of the greatest dignity and propriety. It sets forth the hardships and perils incurred in storming the fort in the depth of winter, and the pinching wants they afterwards underwent in pursuing the Indians that escaped through a hideous wilderness, famously known throughout New England ever afterwards as 'the Hungry March'; and that until this brave though small army did thus 'play the man' and take the fort, the whole country was filled with distress; and the inhabitants trembled even in the capital Boston itself.

"These Narraganset officers and soldiers, who, in the language of the message already mentioned, are characterized as . . . the best men of the province, the fathers and sons of some of her greatest and best of the families, commenced effort to secure the promised land bounty, as early as 1685."

"The list [of claimers] was, in due time, finally completed, and in April, 1733, presented, numbering eight hundred and forty; and thereupon it was ordered that five additional townships be granted under the same conditions as in the case of the two already bestowed. This order passed without controversy between the House and Council, and received the signature of Governor Belcher."

"The grantees, eight hundred and forty in number, met on Boston Common, in the autumn of 1733, according to order of the Court, and entered into due organization. Seven independent associations, each embracing one hundred and twenty members, were formed; and a Joint Committee of twenty-one members, three from each sub-division, was appointed to assign the townships."

The grants were assigned Oct. 17, 1733, and Narraganset,

Number One, (now Buxton, Me.,) on Saco River, was assigned to Philemon Dane and one hundred and nineteen others, the Company from Ipswich and vicinity.

From the Massachusetts Court Record, Feb. 11, 1733, is taken the following "Action of the General Court on the Plats of two Narraganset Townships between Saco and Presumpscut rivers: — Plats were presented by a Committee of the General Court of two Townships for the Narraganset Soldiers, contiguous to each other, lying between Saco River and Pesumpscot River, each of the Contents of Six Miles Square with an allowance to that next Saco River of thirteen hundred acres for Ponds & of Seven hundred Acres formerly granted to Hill & others and with an allowance to that next Pesumpscot River of twelve hundred acres for Ponds, & of Five hundred acres formerly granted to Tyng & others; Which Tracts are bounded as follows; viz, BEGINNING at Saco River at the Head of Biddeford, & running North East by the Needle twelve Miles by the Head of Biddeford, Scarboro' and Falmouth till it comes to Pesumpscot River, & then bounded by Pesumpscot River, & running up the same till it makes seven miles & one quarter of a Mile on a strait Course North 33° 00′ West, then running nine miles & fifty rods South West till it comes to Saco River, & then bounded South Westerly by Saco River till it comes to the Head of Biddeford afore Said; the dividing Line between the two Townships, begins on the Line next on the Head of the Townships seven miles & one quarter of a Mile to the North East of Saco River and runs North 33° 00′ West by the Needle, & extends seven miles and one Quarter of a Mile.

"In the House of Representves Read and ORDERED that these Plans be accepted, & that the Lands set forth in the Plat Number One be and hereby are confirmed unto One hundred and twenty of the Original Grantees, their Heirs and assigns: viz, THAT SOCIETY of them of which Philemon Dane & others were appointed a Committee for regulating Ipswich Society &c. so called at a General meeting of the Grantees in Boston, the Sixth of June last, as by the Grantees Votes and Orders may appear PROVIDED the Plat contains no more than the Contents of Six miles Square of the unappropriated Land (exclusive of the former Grants & allowances within mentioned) & that it does not interfere with any former Grant:—In Council; Read and Concur'd;—

"Consented to, J. BELCHER—"

"At a Leagal meeting of the Narraganset Soldiers belonging to a Township Caled No. 1 Laying on the East Side of Saco River in the County of York," Aug. 1, 1733: "m^r^ Philemon Dain Was Chosen Colector to Gather the money that is to be Paid by the Grauntees or their Representatives: claiming in Ipswich List . . . and m^r^ Jonathan Fellows of Ipswich, Treasurer."

It was also "Voted that Each Grauntee or there Leagal Representative Shall Pay ten Shillings towards defraying the Charges that have allready arisen or that may hereafter arise in bringing forward the Settlement of Said Township," etc.

March 19, 1734–5, a Committee was "Chosen and Impowared to Lay out one hundred and Twenty three Lots in Said Township no Lot to Exceed Twenty acres and to make Return of their doings on or before the middle of June Next

"at the above Sd meeting Voated that Each Propriator pay Twenty Shillings to the Colectors Chosen at the Last meeting & by them paid to the Treasurers belonging to Sd Propriators

"at the above Sd meeting Voated that the Treasurers pay fifty pounds to the Comittee Chosen to Lay out Said Lots to Inable them to prosceed in that Service and take their Recept their for"

"Persuant to the Vote of the Narraganset Propriators belonging To the Township Called No 1 Laying on the East Side of Saco River — We the Subscribers have laid out one hundred & Twenty three Lots in Said Township and Laid out ways to Each Lot as by the Plan herewith Exhibited may at Large apear. . . .

	JOHN HOBSON	
Dated November 17th	SAMLL CHASE	Committee"
Anno 1735 —	JAMES CHUTE	
	PHILEMON DANE	

"Joseph Kinsmon on the Right of his father Robert Kinsmon — No. 19 on a Raing of Lots known by the letter D."

"The Lots Known by the Letter D are Twenty Rods wide and the ways Running Southeast and North West are Eight Rods wide."

July 19, 1738, "Pelatiah Kinsman" was, with others, "fully Impowared to prosecute any person or persons that Shall Cut or Carrey of any wood or Timber from any of Said Propriators undevided Land."

Oct. 13, 1738, a Second Division of Lots was made, and Joseph Kinsman, on the original Right of Robert Kinsman, drew a lot on Range D. No. 16.

On the 1st day of Feb. 1742–3, an appointed committee "Sold the originall Right of one Joseph Kinsman unto one John Kinsman at a Publick Vendue as Said Kinsman was the highest bidder Said Right was Sold for thirty Pounds (old tenor)"

Narraganset Township Number One, in the County of York, was incorporated July 14, 1772, as the Town of Buxton.

As this Robert Kinsman took a prominent part, being one of the Selectmen, in the resistance of Ipswich, in August,

1687, to the arbitrary and unlawful taxes imposed by Andros, an account of that controversy may prove interesting.

Sir Edmund Andros had returned to America, after an absence in England of nearly six years, arriving at Boston December 19, 1686, and bearing a commission from King James, as Governor of all New England; the Charter of Massachusetts having been declared vacated, October 23, 1684. Being thus clothed with full powers, he at once inaugurated a series of measures of the most obnoxious and oppressive character.

Palfrey says: — "From the earliest period of New England, towns had their executive magistracy; they held meetings as often as occasion arose for deliberation on matters of common concern; they taxed themselves, and made other orders, for the maintenance of their roads, their schools, and their poor; and, when a Colony tax was imposed by the General Court, each town, having received notice of the proportion which it was to contribute, proceeded, by its municipal officers, to assess the sum on its inhabitants. There was now no General Court; the Governor in Council imposed taxes; and the first act of his administration required a compulsory assessment of them by Commissioners and Selectmen.

"It was not to be expected that privileges so important and so long enjoyed should be withdrawn without creating dissatisfaction and disturbance. At length the time arrived, that had been specified in the Act for its provisions to go into effect. A warrant came from the Treasurer for each town to choose a Commissioner to act with the Selectmen, in assessing upon its citizens the sum at which the town was rated. Several towns of Massachusetts, including every town but three in Essex County,[1] refused to proceed to the election which was ordered.

[1] Viz. Salem, Newbury, and Marblehead.

"The proceedings of the government against Ipswich, then perhaps the second town in the Colony, attracted particular attention at the time, and will serve for a specimen of the encroachments of the Governor and Council, on the one hand, and of the course and the consequences of resistance to it, on the other."

The following is an extract from an old pamphlet (without date) entitled "A Narrative of the Miseries of New England, By Reason of an Arbitrary Government Erected there": —

"Sir *Edmund Andross* caused a Tax to be leavied of a Penny in a Pound on all the Towns then under his Government: And when at *Ipswich* and other places, the *Select Men* (as they are there stiled) voted, That in as much as it was against the Common Priviledges of *English* Subjects, to have money raised without their own Consent in an Assembly or Parliament; That therefore they would petition the King for liberty of an Assembly before they made any Rates; the said Sir *Edmund Andross* caused them to be Imprisoned and Fined, some 20*l.* some 30*l.* and some 50*l.* as the Judges, by him instructed, should see meet to determine; Yea, and several Gentlemen in the Country were Imprisoned and bound to their Good Behaviour, upon mere suspition, that they did Incourage their Neighbours not to comply with these *Arbitrary Proceedings.*"

Palfrey adds: "So vigorous a course of proceeding as this, was decisive. Unless the country was prepared for violent measures of redress, submission was unavoidable. Men who possessed the confidence of their fellow-citizens, and were fit to take the lead in public movements, could not be expected to persevere in a course of opposition, at once fruitless to the public, and ruinous to themselves. The towns succumbed."

But this submission was not final; after suffering under the tyranny of Andros for more than two years, the people finally revolted, and succeeded in effecting the bloodless overthrow of his government, in April, 1689, and in February of the next year, he was sent to England, a prisoner.

1689, Dec. 24th. Ipswich votes, "That the Rev. John Wise and the Selectmen draw up the town's abuses with respect to the rates taken and the calumnies cast upon the town and persons, who have suffered by the late Government in Sir Edmund Andros' rule, and present them to the town next lecture-day after lecture."

In "The Revolution in New England Justified," printed in 1691, we find the following Affidavits: —

"Complaints of great wrongs done under the Ill Government of Sir *Edmund Androsse* Governour in *N. E.*, in the year 1687.

"We *John Wise*, *John Andrews*, *senior*, *Robert Kinsman*, *William Goodhue*, *junior*, all of *Ipswich* in *New England*, in the County of *Essex*, about the 22d day of *August*, in the year above named, were with several principal Inhabitants of the Town of *Ipswich* met at Mr. *John Appletons*, and there discoursed and concluded that it was not the Towns Duty any way to assist that ill method of raising Money without a general Assembly, which was apparently intended by abovesaid Sir *Edmund* and his Council, as witness a late Act issued out by them for such a purpose. The next day in a general Town-Meeting of the Inhabitants of *Ipswich*; We the above named *John Wise*, *John Andrews*, *Robert Kinsman*, *William Goodhue* with the rest of the Town then met (none contradicting) gave our assent to the vote then made.

The ground of our trouble, our crime was the Copy transmitted to the Council, *viz.* At a Legal Town meeting *August* 23. Assembled by vertue of an Order from *John Usher*, Esq: Treasurer for choosing a Commissioner to join with the Select men, to assess the Inhabitants according to an Act of his Excellency the Governour and Council for laying of rates; the Town then considering that the said Act doth infringe their Liberty, as free born English Subjects of His Majesty by interfering with the Statute Laws of the Land, by which it was Enacted that no Taxes should be Levied upon the Subjects without consent of an Assembly chosen by the Freeholders for assessing of the same, they do therefore vote that they are not willing to choose a Commissioner for such an end without said priviledge; and moreover consent not that the Select-men do proceed to lay any such rate until it be appointed by a general Assembly concurring with the Governour and Council. We the complainants with Mr. *John Appleton* and *Thomas French* all of *Ipswich* were brought to answer for the said vote out of our own County, thirty or forty miles into *Suffolk*, and in *Boston* kept in Goal, only for contempt and high misdemeanors as our *Mittimus* specifies, and upon demand, denied the priviledge of an *Habeas Corpus*, and from Prison overruled to answer at a Court of *Oyer* and *Terminer* in *Boston* aforesaid. Our Judges were Mr. *Joseph Dudley* of *Roxbury* in *Suffolk* in *New-England*, Mr. *Stoughton* of *Dorchester*, *John Usher* of *Boston*, Treasurer, and *Edward Randolph*. He that officiates as Clerk and Attorny in the case is *George Farwel*.

The Jurors only twelve men and most of them (as is said) Non-freeholders of any Land in the Colony, some of them Strangers and Forreigners, gathered up (as we suppose) to serve the present turn. In our defence was pleaded the repeal of the Law of Assessment upon the place. Also the *Magna Charta* of *England*, and the Statute Laws that secure the Subjects Properties and Estates, *&c*. To which was replied by one of the Judges, the rest by silence assenting, that we must not think the Laws of *England* follow us to the ends of the Earth, or whither we went. And the same person (*John Wise* abovesaid testifies) declared in open Council upon examination of said *Wise*;

Mr. *Wise* you have no more priviledges left you, than not to be sold for Slaves, and no man in Council contradicted. By such Laws our Trial and Trouble began and ended. Mr. *Dudley* aforesaid Chief Judge, to close up the debate and trial, trims up a speech that pleased himself (we suppose) more than the people. Among many other remarkable Passages, to this purpose, he bespeaks the Jury's obedience, who (we suppose) were very well preinclined, *viz.* I am glad, says he, there be so many worthy Gentlemen of the Jury so capable to do the King service, and we expect a good Verdict from you, seeing the matter hath been so sufficiently proved against the Criminals. Note, the evidence in the case as to the substance of it, was that we too boldly endeavored to persuade ourselves we were English Men, and under priviledges; and that we were all six of us aforesaid at the Town meeting of *Ipswich* aforesaid, and as the Witness supposed, we assented to the foresaid Vote, and also that *John Wise* made a Speech at the same time, and said we had a good God, and a good King, and should do well to stand for our Priviledges—Jury returns us all six guilty, being all involved in the same Information. We were remanded from Verdict to Prison, and there kept one and twenty days for Judgement. There with Mr. *Dudley's* approbation, as Judge *Stoughton* said, this Sentence was passed, *viz.*

"*John Wise*, suspended from the Ministerial Function, fine fifty pound, money, pay cost, a thousand pound bond for the good behaviour one year.

"*John Appleton* not to bear Office, fine 50*l.* money, pay cost, a thousand pound for the good behaviour one year.

"*John Andrews* not to bear Office, fine 30*l.* money, pay cost, five hundred pound bond for the good behaviour one year.

"*Robert Kinsman* not to bear Office, fine twenty pound money, pay cost, five hundred pound bond for the good behaviour one year.

"*William Goodhue* not to bear Office, fine twenty pound money, pay cost, five hundred pound bond for the good behaviour one year.

"*Thomas French* not to bear Office, fine 15*l*. Money, pay cost, 500*l*. bond for the good behaviour one year.

"The Total Fees of this case upon one single Information demanded by *Farewell* abovesaid, amount to about a hundred and one pound seventeen shillings, who demanded of us singly about sixteen pound nineteen shillings six pence, the cost of Prosecution, the Fines added made up this, *viz.* Two hundred eighty and six pounds seventeen shillings, money.

Summa Totalis 286*l*. 17*s*.

"To all which we may add a large account of other Fees of Messengers, Prison charges, Money for Bonds and Transcripts of Records, exhausted by those ill men one way and another to the value of three or fourscore pounds, besides our expence of time and imprisonment.

"We judge the Total charge for one Case and Trial under one single Information involving us six men abovesaid in expence of Time and Moneys of us and our Relations for our necessary Succour and Support to amount to more, but no less than 400*l*. Money.

"Too tedious to illustrate more amply at this time, and so we conclude. *John Wise*, *John Andrews*, Senior, *William Goodhue*, Junior, *Thomas French*, these four persons named, and *Robert Kinsman*.

"These four persons first named appeared the twentieth day of *December*, and *Robert Kinsman* appeared the one and twentieth day of *December*, 1689, and gave in their Testimony upon oath before me *Samuel Appleton* Assistant for the Colony of the *Massachusetts* in *New-England*."

Felt says: "This narration was drawn up at the request of the government, which succeeded that of Andros, so that it might be sent to England among the charges against him.

Several years afterwards, the town made up the loss which the narrators incurred, as previously described. . . .

"No town was probably more glad than Ipswich, that Andros was constrained to relinquish his authority by the threatening attitude of the people in Boston and the vicinity. The occasion of so sudden a change was, that news arrived, that the Prince of Orange had landed in England to put down the sway of James II, whose officers in Massachusetts had rendered themselves obnoxious to most of the colonists. Had William failed in this enterprise, there would probably have been a reaction upon our fathers as oppressive, as what they experienced after favoring Cromwell and then falling into the hands of restored and avenging Royalty."

Although by their sentence, the complainants were condemned not to bear office, yet the good people of Ipswich, after the recall of Andros, elected John Wise as a Deputy to the General Court in 1689, and Robert Kinsman in 1692.

Robert Kinsman was confirmed as Quartermaster in Capt. Thomas Wade's Company in 1691; and he had a seat appointed to him "at the table" in the meeting-house, 1700.

Quartermaster Robert Kinsman, of Ipswich, gives by Deed of Gift dated March 21, 1698–9, to his son Joseph, "his now dwelling house, out-houses, barne, stable, orchard, yard and half his common right on ye commons of Ipswich, and ye feild about ye house or home lott, about 14 acres of tillage and mowing ground, be it more or less as bounded one end by ye common, ye south side by John Brown's land, the other end by pasture land, and the other side of the highway yt. leads to Chebaccho . . . also pasture land about twenty acres more or less . . . also all the lower field and marsh belonging to it bounding East on Haffills Creek, except 4 acres of tillage land lying next to Mr Rogers' land

. . . Except what preveledges s'd parent hereby reserves during his natural life and the life of his wife, that he may leave at his decease yt. part of his building called ye old house, upper and lower room, providing for a wife if he should marry again," etc. etc.

To his son Robert Kinsman, he gives "the one half of his comonages and common rights in and on the commons of Ipswich, also about 40 acres of pasture, mowing and marsh ground, bounded easterly by Haffills Creek . . . also four acres of tillage land in ye lower field (before excepted) . . . also about 10 acres of salt marsh ground called ye low marshes . . . also a parcell of marsh ground and upland at Chebaccho, containing about 14 acres more or less as bounded southerly by Chebaccho river . . . Half ye common right — except a reserve during his present life and the life of his widow." — [Essex Deeds 13 : 129–131.]

Robert Kinsman, senior, of Ipswich, yeoman, gives by Deed of Gift dated April 15, 1701, to his two grandsons, the sons of his son Thomas Kinsman, of Ipswich, deceased, viz. Stephen and Thomas Kinsman, "a certain parcel of upland and meadow, with a dwelling house, in Ipswich, bounded Northerly and Westerly by land of Isaac Fellows, and South-Easterly by ye common, and Southerly by land that Thomas Kinsman abovesaid, late deceased, bought of ye town of Ipswich . . . . after they arrive to 21 years . . . . Stephen paying to his eldest sister, Elizabeth Kinsman, £20 at or before three years after he becomes 21 years of age, and Thomas paying to Mary Kinsman, their youngest sister, £20 at or before he is 21 years of age." — [Ibid 14 : 117.]

In the ancient Burial-Ground of Ipswich is a gravestone bearing the following inscription : —

"Here lieth buried ye body of Quarter Master Robert Kinsman who died February ye 19, 1712. Aged 83 years."

He left a Will, which is found on file in the Essex Registry of Probate, and is recorded in Book 10, page 260; the following is a copy of the original: —

"In the Name of God, Amen. I, Robert Kinsman, Senr. of Ipswich, in ye County of Essex in New England, Glazier, being aged, & not knowing how soon it may please God to take mee out this world, yet thro' God's Goodness of perfect mind & memory, & being willing to settle yt small estate yt I have not yet Disposed off by Deed of Gift to my two sons, Joseph & Robert, & my Grand sons, ye sons of my son Thomas Kinsman Dec[d], I make & ordaine this & no other to be my Last Will & Testament, & Dispose of my person & estate in manner & fforme, following.

I give & comend my soul to God, who gave it mee, hopeing & beleiving yt thro' ye meritts of Christ Jesus my blessed Saviour, to obtaine a Glorious Resurrection to Life Eternall, and my Body to be Decently buryed att ye Discretion of my Executors & Overseers hereafter named. As to my outward estate, I will yt all my just & honest Debts & funerall charges be payd & Discharged by my Executors hereafter named in convenient time after my Decease. I give to my two sons Joseph & Robert Kinsman, all my Glazeing Tools, Husbandry, and Carpenter Tools, of all sorts, to be equally Divided between them. I also give them my ffowling peice, & all with what they already have had by Deed, to be their portion, and they, equally to pay all my Debts & ffunerall Expences.

I give to my Daughter, Sarah Perkins, who stayed longest with me, my Bed in ye great chamber, with all ye furniture belonging to it.

I give to my Daughter, Unice Burnam, my chest of draws.

I give to my five Daughters, Mary, Sarah, Joanna, Margarett & Unice, all my moveable estate of household goods & Debts yt shall be due att my Decease, and all my quick stock of all sorts & kinds whatsoever, as cattle, sheep, & horse kind, except what I hereafter in this my will, shall be Disposed of, & also my crane, tramells & hooks, equally to be Divided among them five.

I give to my son Pelatiah, but ten shillings beside what I have given him already.

Item. I give unto my maid Eliz[a] Dingey, five good sheep if shee abide with mee till my Decease, otherwise I give but three good sheep.

Item. In consideration, my son Joseph Kinsman haveing had many priviledges & advantages which my son Robert hath not had, I see cause to give him no more, but I give my son Robert twenty pounds out of what he was to pay after my Decease, & to be Deducted from his sisters equally.

Item. I constitute, ordaine & appoint my said two sons Joseph & Robert Kinsman to be Joynt Executors, to this my Last Will & Testament, & I desire my well respected ffreinds, Deacon Nath'll Knowlton, & Daniel Rogers of Ipswich, to be Overseers, to see this my Will fullfilled.

In confirmation that this is my Last Will and Testament, I ye above said Robert Kinsman, Doe hereunto sett my hand & seale, this twenty fourth day of August, Anno Dom. 1710, in ye ninth of her Majesties Reigne Anne of Great Brittaine, &c Queen.

ROBERT KINSMAN [Seal]

Signed, sealed, published
& Declared in presence of
DANIEL ROGERS
NATH[LL] KNOWLTON
JOHN POTTER"

Proved March 12, 1712–13.

THEIR CHILDREN:

1. MARY, b. Dec. 21, 1657.
2. SARAH, b. March 19, 1659: m. Jacob Perkins. **5**
3. THOMAS, b. April 15, 1662: m. Elizabeth Burnham. **6**
4. JOANNA, b. April 25, 1665: m. Nathaniel Rust, Feb. 22, 1684. He served in the expedition against Canada, 1690. At a town-meeting holden in Ipswich, Dec. 28, 1704, it was "voted to give Nathaniel Rust, Jun[r], in behalf of his father Quarter Master Kinsman, two acres of land by his house in Chebacco up ye hill . . . which land is accepted in full satisfaction for ye loss and damage ye s'd Kinsman sustained under Sir Edmund Androse Government."

   Administration on his estate was granted to his widow Johannah Rust, Oct. 15, 1711, and the inventory of the estate of "Lieut Nathaniel Rust, Jun., late of Ipswich, deceased, who dyed Sept. 9, 1711," was taken Oct. 18, 1711. Amount £193.6.6; and Johannah Rust, administratrix, made oath to the truth of it, Oct. 22, 1711. [Essex Probate, 10 : 184.]
5. MARGARET, b. July 24, 1668.
6. EUNICE, b. Jan. 24, 1670: m. Nathaniel Burnham. **7**
7. JOSEPH, b. Dec. 20, 1673: m. Susanna Dutch; Sarah Peabody. **8**
8. ROBERT, b. May 21, 1677: m. Lydia Moore; Rebecca Burley. **9**
9. PELATIAH, b. Nov. 10, 1680: m. Sarah Cumbey. **10**

---

2. MARY KINSMAN, daughter of Robert (p. 34), married DANIEL RINDGE. He was of Roxbury, 1639; removed to Ipswich before 1648. His Will dated Feb. 3, 1661; proved March 25, 1662; on file; recorded Essex Probate, 1 : 152.

She married for her second husband, URSUEL WARDWELL, May 3, 1664. He was born April 7, 1639, son of William and Alice Wardwell, of Boston.

HER CHILDREN BY DANIEL RINDGE:

1. MARY, b.
2. SUSANNA, b. Her uncle Robert Kinsman, of Ipswich, was appointed her guardian, May 2, 1669, when she is called Susanna, daughter of Daniel Rindge, of Ipswich, deceased. She calls Ursuel Wardwell her father-in-law. [Essex Deeds, 3 : 129.]
3. DANIEL, b. 1654: m. Hannah Perkins. She d. July 9, 1684. He d. Nov. 30, 1738, æ. 84. Styled Captain on gravestone.
4. ROGER, b. June 19, 1657: m. Sarah Shatswell, June 9, 1684.
5. SARAH, b. Aug. 7, 1659: (m. Joseph Andrews, Feb. 16, 1680?)
6. ISAAC, b. : m. about 1693, Elizabeth, daughter of John and Mary (Roper) Dutch. She d. May 3, 1700. He was

published, July 21, 1700, to Widow Elizabeth Kinsman, whom he married. (See p. 53.)

HER CHILDREN BY URSUEL WARDWELL:

7. Abigail, b. Oct. 27, 1665.
8. Alice, b. Dec. 27, 1667.
9. Hannah, } twins, b. September, 1677.
10. Mary, }

---

3. SARAH KINSMAN, daughter of Robert (p. 34), married in Ipswich, Samuel Younglove, Aug. 1, 1660. He was born in England in 1634, sailed for New England with his parents, Samuel and Margaret Younglove, in the "Hopewell," Thomas Babb, master, Sept. 11, 1635; settled in Ipswich; admitted Freeman 1671; took the Oath of Allegiance in 1678 (when he is called 40 years of age?).

THEIR CHILDREN:

1. Sarah, b. July 5, 1663: m. John Shatswell, June 20, 1684.
2. Samuel, b. Oct. 3, 1665: died in infancy.
3. Mary, b. March 17, 1668: m. Jacob Rowell, April 29, 1690.
4 Samuel, b. July 27, 1671: served in the expedition against Canada under Capt. Stephen Cross, and died on his passage home in 1690.
5. Mercy, b. May 25, 1676.
6. John, b. Aug. 29, 1677.

---

4. MARTHA KINSMAN, daughter of Robert (p. 34), married in Ipswich, Jacob Foster, Jan. 12, 1658. He was born in England, 1635, the son of Reginald and Judith Foster. Resided in Ipswich; was one of its Selectmen, 1697. She died Oct. 15, 1666. Deacon Jacob Foster died July 9, 1710, in the 75th year of his age. [Gravestone.]

THEIR CHILDREN:

1. Judith, b. Oct. 12, 1659: d. Jan. 27, 1659-60.
2. John, b. 1660: d. in infancy.
3. Jacob, b. May 15, 1662: d June, 1662.
4. Mary, b. : d. Jan. 11, 1666-7, mentioned in her grandfather Robert Kinsman's Will. (See p. 33.)
5. Sarah, b. Aug. 3, 1665: m. John Caldwell, May 1, 1689. He d. Feb. 7, 1721-2. She d. July 11, 1721-2.

THIRD GENERATION.

5. SARAH KINSMAN, daughter of Robert and Mary (p. 50), born in Ipswich, March 19, 1659; married, there, JACOB PERKINS. Resided in Ipswich.

His Will dated Ipswich, Nov. 10, 1705; proved Dec. 3, 1705; on file; recorded Essex Probate, 8:217; mentions wife Sarah and eight children.

THEIR CHILDREN:

1. MARY, b. Aug. 2, 1685: d. in infancy.
2. ELIZABETH, b. May 8, 1687: m. William Leatherland, of Ipswich; pub. Oct. 23, 1708.
3. JACOB, b. Jan. 3, 1690: m. Elizabeth Kinsman; pub. March 6, 1713.
4. EUNICE, b. March 14, 1691: not mentioned in father's Will, 1705.
5. JOHN, b. Oct. 17, 1693: (m. Elizabeth Endicott, of Boxford; pub. 15, 1, 1718?)
6. SARAH, b. Dec. 26, 1696: (m. John Leighton; pub. 4, 10, 1714?)
7. MARY, b. Nov. 26, 1698: (m. Jonathan Burnham; pub. March 17, 1710?)
8. HANNAH, b. July 24, 1701: (m. Benjamin Newman, Jr.; pub. Oct. 5, 1723?)
9. JUDITH, bapt. Nov. 4, 1705: (m. Joseph Burnham; pub. 5, 3, 1716?)
10. ELISHA, birth or baptism not found on record, but mentioned as a son in father's Will, 1705.

---

6. THOMAS KINSMAN, son of Robert and Mary (p. 50), born in Ipswich, April 15, 1662; married, there, ELIZABETH BURNHAM, July 12, 1687, the daughter of Deacon John Burnham, Senior, of Ipswich.

He took the Oath of Allegiance in 1678, and died intestate, at Ipswich, July 15, 1696. Administration on his estate was granted Nov. 12, 1696, to his widow Elizabeth. He left £142.14.4. His debts were £79.5.12. The remainder was to be divided, one third to the widow forever, and one third of the real estate during her natural life, after her decease to be divided among her children. Stephen, the eldest son, to have a double portion. Elizabeth, Thomas, and Mary, each a single portion. [Essex Probate, 5 : 76, 141.]

His widow married Isaac Rindge, of Ipswich; published July 27, 1700. He was the son of Daniel and Mary (Kinsman) Rindge. (See p. 50.)

THEIR CHILDREN:

1. Stephen, b. about 1688: m. Lucy Kimball; Lydia Kimball. **11**
2. Elizabeth, b. about 1690: m. Jacob Perkins. **12**
3. Thomas, b. April 3, 1693: is of Ipswich, mariner, in a deed dated Jan. 3, 1714, when he sells to his brother Stephen. (See p. 62.)
4. Mary, b. Oct. 14, 1695: m. Thomas Waite, Jr. **13**

---

7. EUNICE KINSMAN, daughter of Robert and Mary (p. 50), born in Ipswich, Jan. 24, 1670; married Nathaniel Burnham.

Eunice, widow of Nathaniel Burnham, late of Boxford, deceased, made her Will at Boxford, May 16, 1749; proved April 2, 1750; on file; recorded Essex Probate, 29 : 91.

THEIR CHILDREN:

1. Nathan, b. Sept. 19, 1700.
2. Nathaniel, b. Sept. 19, 1701.
3. Eunice, b. Feb. 12, 1703: m. John Day.
4. Phebe, b. Feb. 3, 1705: perhaps the dau. who m. Nath'l Cross.
5. Sarah, bapt. 1, 30, 1712: m. Coole Smith.

---

8. JOSEPH KINSMAN, son of Robert and Mary (p. 50), born in Ipswich, Dec. 20, 1673; married Susanna Dutch. She was born in Ipswich, 1674, the daughter of John and Mary (Roper) Dutch. In the old Burial-Ground of the First Parish of Ipswich, stands a stone to her memory, bearing the following inscription: "Here lyes Buried the

Body of Mrs. Susanna Kinsman, wife to Lieut. Joseph Kinsman, who departed this Life, Novr 9th Ann^{o} Dom^{y} 1734. Ætatis Suæ 60."

He married, second, SARAH PEABODY, of Boxford, April 27, 1736.

May 8, 1705, Joseph Kinsman, of Ipswich, glazier, buys of his brother Robert Kinsman, Jr., of Ipswich, farmer, 4 acres of land in Ipswich, the home field of his farm. [Essex Deeds, 17 : 104.]

For his father Robert Kinsman's services in the Narraganset War, 1675, there was granted to Joseph, as his heir, Nov. 24, 1735, land in Narraganset Number One, now Buxton, Me., which he sold, Feb. 1, 1742–3, to his son John Kinsman.

His Will is on file in the Essex Registry of Probate, and is recorded in Book 24, page 232; the following is a copy of the original: —

"In the name of God, Amen. The twenty eight day of November Anno Dom: 1737. I, Joseph Kinsman of Ipswich, in ye County of Essex, Within his Majesties Provience of ye Mass^{tts} Bay in New England, Yeoman, Being now growen into years and under some decays of body, but yet through ye Mearcy and goodness of God, of sound & disposing minde and memory, and calling to mind ye Mortality of my body, and ye uncertainty of this transitory life, and knowing not how soon God shall call mee hence by death; and therefore desireous according to my duty to sett things in order before I go hence; Do make this my Laste Will & Testament in maner & form following. That is, first and principally, I committ my soul to God that gave it mee, hopeing for, & expecting ye free pardon & remission of all my sins, through ye death & sufferings and merrits of Jesus Christ my only Saviour & Redeemer, and to obtain an inheritance amoungst those that are sanctified. And my body I committ to ye earth att death, to be decently buried at ye discretion of my executors herein after mentioned. And touching my worldly estate, which it hath pleased God to bless mee with I dispose of it in ye following manner.

Imperimis My Will is that all my just debts to any pearsons due togather with my funerll charges shall first be paid and discharged in convenant time after my decease, by my executors.

Item. My Will is that Sarah my loveing wife shall have fivefty pound paid to her out of my estate by my executors after my decease according to the contract I maide with her before Marraige, and also all ye houshould stuffe that she brought with her which was hers before I had her, and all her plate, and also all her bonds, bills or book debts that were due or owing to her before I had her, or have become due since by vertue of the same: Furthermore my Will is that all and every peart of ye contract before mentioned maide with my wife before Marraige, be fullfiled by my executors according to ye true intent and meaning of the same.

Item. I give and bequeath to John Kinsman my son, all ye land whereon the house & barn standeth, with ye house and barn thats now in his possession, with all ye land that I bought of my brother Robert Kinsman. That is to be understood, his homestead with all ye common rightes adjoyning to it, that did belonge to a south eaight so called and allso a nine accor right lying in a pastor called Browns & Kinsmans pastor. The which right also belonged to a south eaight, and hes to enjoy ye same according to ye quite clames that wee[v] alredy given to each other, and also all my righte and interst that I have in Wilderness hill pastor so called, ye which also belonged to a South Eaight, and also three accors and one halfe of ye salt meadow, lying and being att an island called Hoveys Island, and also another pearsell of salt meadow lying in Argilly so called, ye same salt meadow that I bought of Capt. John Choate Esq[r]. And allso all my righte and interest in Jefferys Neck, ye same that I bought of Fitts, Fellows and Perkins; and also one third pearte of my low salt meadow, and also one third pearte of my thach lots, and also one third peart of my wood land that lyes on ye southarly side of Jabaco ponds. And also all ye wood standing or lying on booth my lower islands, That I bought of my brother Robert Kinsman. The which wood hee shall and may have liberty to take off from ye said land, hee or his heirs, att his or their owen pleasuer, and ye above said premises that are given to my son John Kinsman are free to him or to his assigns, hee or his heirs or administrators paying ye several sumes hereafter mentioned in this my last will, for him to pay his pearte off.

Item. I give and bequeath to Pelatiah Kinsman my son, The one halfe of my now dwelling house, and also ye one halfe of my barnes, and also ye one halfe of my homestead, and also ye one halfe of all my lands and meadows & woodlands within ye townshipe of Ipswich (That I have not given to my son John Kinsman), all ye above said premises that I have given in this my last Will to my son Pelatiah Kinsman are free to him or to his assigns. Hee or his heirs, or administrators, paying ye several sumes hereafter mentioned for him to pay his pearte off.

Item. I give and bequeath to Benjamin Kinsman my son the one halfe of my now Dwelling House; and also ye one halfe of my Barn, and also ye one halfe of my homestead, and also ye one halfe of all my lands and meadows & wood lands within ye Townships of Ipswich (That I have not given to my son John Kinsman) all ye above said premises that I have given in this my last Will to my son Benjamin Kinsman, are free to him or to His assigns, Hee or his hiers or administrators, paying ye several sumes hereafter mentioned for him to pay his pearte off.

Item. I give and bequeath to John Kinsman & to Pelatiah Kinsman & to Benjamin Kinsman, my three sons all my stock of cattel & other creatures, and all my husbandry tools and also all my Bonds, Bills, or Book debts or any other debt thats dew or owing to mee att my decese to be equally divided amongst them three.

Item. I give and bequeath to Nathaniel Kinsman my son ye full and just sume of two hundred and fivefty pounds in money in or as Bills of this Provience now passing. To be paide to Him or to his hiers or assigns within the terme of ye time of three years after my decease, by my executors hereafter to be mentioned.

Item. I give and bequeath to Susannah How & to Eunice Wells and to Sarah Wells and to Elizebeth Brown & to Hannah Wallis & to Martha Denies my six daughters, or to their heirs, all my houshould stuff, within doors, that I have not allredy given away in this my Laste Will to be equally divided amoungst them, or amoungst theire heirs.

Item. I give and bequeath to Susannah How, and to Eunice Wells, & to Sarah Wells & to Elizebeth Brown, & to Hannah Wallis and to Martha Denies my six daughters or to theire heirs, the full and just sume of five pounds to each of my six daughters, To be paid to them or to theire heirs in or as bills of this Provience now passing of ye Ould Tenour. Besides what I have already given to them, to be paid to them by my executors in six years time after my decease and not before.

Furthermore in this my Last Will and Testament I do constitute and appointe & ordain John Kinsman & Pelatiah Kinsman & Benjamin Kinsman my three well beloved sons to be ye soul executors of this my last will and testament; and my Will is that if Devine Providence shall call mee out of this life before Benjamin Kinsman my youngest son shall arive to ye age of twenty one years, Then, and if it should so happen, my Will is and I do appionte John Kinsman and

Pelatiah Kinsman my two sons to be overseers to Benjamin Kinsman, to act and do for him as overseers in all things, and for him in and about ye trust in him and them reposed, untill he arive to ye age of twenty one years: My will is that my three sons whome I have named executors for this my Last Will and testament, Do each of them pay thiere equal pearte of ye sevriel Legacies and sumes mentioned in this my Last Will for them to pay.

And I do hereby utterly, disallow, revoke and disannul all and evrey other former Testaments, Wills, Legacies and Bequests & Executors by mee in any ways before named, willed and bequeathed ratifying and confirming this and no other to be my last will and testament. In witness whereof I have hereunto sett my hand and seal ye day and yeare above written.

Signed, Sealed, Published, Pronounced and Declared by ye said Joseph Kinsman as his last Will and Testament in ye presence of us ye subscribers.

THOMAS NORTON.
ANDREW BURLEY. JOSEPH KINSMAN. [Seal]
THOMAS NORTON, JUN."

Proved May 25, 1741.

His widow, Sarah Kinsman, made her Will, Aug. 13, 1752; proved Dec. 8, 1756; on file; recorded Essex Probate, Book 34, page 87.

HIS CHILDREN BY SUSANNA DUTCH:

1.	SUSANNAH,	b. Feb. 16, 1700:	m. Increase How; John Smith.	**14**
2.	JOSEPH,	b. Sept. 15, 1701:	d. Nov. 18, 1724.	
3.	EUNICE,	Twins,	m. Moses Wells	**15**
4.	SARAH,	b. June 23, 1705:	m. Nathaniel Wells.	**16**
5.	ELIZABETH,	b. Nov. 11, 1707:	m. William Browne, Jr.	**17**
6.	JOHN,	Twins,	m. H. Burnham; E. Perkins.	**18**
7.	HANNAH,	b. Nov. 21, 1709:	m. Robert Wallis.	**19**
8.	MARTHA,	b. July 13, 1712:	m. Thomas Dennis.	**20**
9.	NATHANIEL,	b. Dec. 5, 1714:	m. A. Robinson; D. Parsons.	**21**
10.	PELATIAH,	b. Feb. 5, 1715:	m. Jane Farley.	**22**
11.	BENJAMIN,	b. April 26, 1719:	m. Elizabeth Perkins.	**23**

9. ROBERT KINSMAN, son of Robert and Mary (p. 50), born in Ipswich, May 21, 1677; married LYDIA MOORE, of Boston, April 3, 1700. She died without issue. He married, second, REBECCA BURLEY, June 28, 1705. She was born March 29, 1683, the daughter of Cornet Andrew and Mary (Conant) Burley, of Ipswich, and great-grand-daughter of Roger Conant, one of the earliest settlers of Massachusetts, 1624.

Feb. 18, 1720–1, he is of Ipswich, yeoman, and, with wife Rebecca, sells to his brother Joseph Kinsman, Sen'r, of Ipswich, yeoman, his house and lands in Ipswich. [Essex Deeds, 40 : 17.] Oct. 28, 1721, he is of Norwich, Ct., with wife Rebecca. [Ibid. 73 : 25.]

He removed with his family to what was then called Norwich, Ct., and settled in that part of the town known as Newent Society in Lisbon. Miss Caulkins, in her history of Norwich, says, "Robert Kinsman was admitted an inhabitant Dec. 5, 1721. He was one of the Selectmen in 1725 and 1728. He died June 7, 1761, and his wife died Nov. 11, 1775."

He left a Will, of which the following is a copy: —

"Know all men by these presents that I, Robert Kinsman, of Norwich, in the county of New London, and Colony of Connecticut in New England, considering the mortality of my body . . . have thought fit now in my right understanding and memory to settle and dispose of my worldly goods and estate by this my last will and testament in the following manner and form:

Imprimis. My just debts and funeral charges being paid, I give and bequeath to my beloved wife Rebeckah Kinsman, one third part of my personal estate to be hers forever, and over and above that I further give to her one of my horses or mares which she shall choose, and tackling suitable and the value of eighty pounds old tenor, out of my personal estate and the improvement of one half of my dwelling house during her widowhood and the improvement of one third part of my real estate during her widowhood, and the value thereof if she shall find it necessary for her comfortable subsistence during her natural life.

Item. I give to my daughter Mary Little twenty five pounds to be paid to her out of my estate.

Item. I give and bequeath to my grandchildren (viz.) Benjamin Burnam, Susannah Burnam, Joanna Burnam and Ester Burnam, the children of my Daughter Mary Little, one hundred and sixty pounds (old tenor) that is to say Forty pounds to each of my said grandchildren above named to be paid to them by my two sons Robert and Jeremiah equally.

Item. I give to my daughter Margaret Marsh to be hers forever one hundred and twenty five pounds (old tenor) the which with what I have already given to her, I judge to be the full of her portion of my estate, and to have it paid to her by my two sons abovenamed equally within two years after my decease.

Item. I give and bequeath to my two sons (viz.) Robert and Jeremiah, all my lands and buildings, to them, their heirs and assigns forever (they allowing to my said wife Rebeckah the improvement as above willed unto her, and also paying the legacies to my children, and grand children, as is above willed to them), which lands and buildings are to be equally divided to and between them my two sons, the which with what I have already given to them by deed in lands which they possess, I judge to be the full of their portion of the estate.

Item. My will is that all the legacies above given by this my last will shall be paid in old tenor, bills of credit, or equivalent, and further my will is and I do order it so, and it must be observed that if either of my grandchildren above named shall die and leave no heir of his or her body lawfully begotten before he or she hath received the portion above given, that then such childs portion shall be equally divided to and among the survivors of my grandchildren above named.

Finally. I do make, constitute, and appoint my beloved and faithful wife Rebekah, sole executrix of this my last will and testament. I do hereby solemnly revoke, make null and void, all other and former wills, testaments, and bequests by me heretofore made, Ratifying and allowing this and no other to be my last will and testament.

In witness whereof I have hereunto put my hand and seal, the sixth day of September in the year 1750.

Signed, sealed, published, pronounced and declared by the said Robert Kinsman to be his last will and testament, in presence of us the subscribers

SAMUEL LATHROP
JOSHUA HATCHERS — ROBERT KINSMAN.
JOHN PERKINS"

Proved the fourth day of July, 1761.

HIS CHILDREN BY REBECCA BURLEY:

1. REBECCA, b. Aug. 15, 1706: d. Dec. 17, 1719. [Gravestone, Ipswich.]
2. MARY, b. Jan. 20, 1707–8: m. Benj. Burnham; —— Little. **24**
3. JOANNA, b. July 11, 1710: d Dec. 19, 1729, and was the first interred in the family burying-ground at (then Norwich, now) Lisbon, Ct.
4. ROBERT, b. May 3, 1713: m. in Boston (but called of Norwich, Ct.), Bethiah Doggett, Sept. 27, 1749. He d. Dec. 16, 1788. He may have had a son Pelatiah who d. April 2, 1797, aged 47 years, and was buried in Copp's Hill burial-ground in Boston, where a stone stands to his memory.
5. MARGARET, b. May 25, 1718: m. —— Marsh.
6. JEREMIAH, b. Feb. 28, 1719: m. Sarah Thomas. **25**

10. PELATIAH KINSMAN, son of Robert and Mary (p. 50), born in Ipswich, Nov. 10, 1680; married in Boston, by Rev. Cotton Mather, to SARAH CUMBEY, July 1, 1708.

He was Sailing Master of the ship "Hopewell," in 1706.

He was a member of the New North Church in Boston (founded March, 1712), and in 1720 remonstrated against the settlement of Peter Thacher as Pastor. He probably withdrew with others and founded the Society at the New Brick. [See "History of Boston," by Samuel G. Drake, p. 546.] Will of Pelatiah Kinsman, of Boston, in New England, mariner, dated Jan. 6, 1715–16; proved May 22, 1727. "Calling to mind the dangers of the seas," he gives all his property to his "dearly beloved wife Sarah Kinsman," and appoints her executrix. [Suffolk Probate Files.]

His widow, Sarah Kinsman, was married in Boston, by the Rev. Peter Thacher, to Zechariah Hubbard, May 18, 1732.

FOURTH GENERATION.

11. STEPHEN KINSMAN, son of Thomas and Elizabeth (p. 53), born about 1688; married LUCY KIMBALL; published Nov. 24, 1711. She was born in Ipswich, Sept. 19, 1693, the daughter of Caleb and Lucy (Edwards) Kimball, and died Feb. 22, 1715–16, aged 23. [Gravestone, Ipswich.]

He married, second, LYDIA KIMBALL; published Nov. 19, 1716. She was probably born in Ipswich, Sept. 14, 1694, the daughter of Richard and Lydia (Wells) Kimball, and died October, 1762.

Jan. 3, 1714, he is of Ipswich, a weaver, and buys of his brother Thomas Kinsman, of Ipswich, mariner, house and lands, which had been given to the said Thomas by his grandfather Robert, and part of that which his father Thomas bought of the town of Ipswich, and he had received at his death. [Essex Deeds, 33 : 5.]

Dec. 19, 1729, he is of Ipswich, and buys of his sisters, Elizabeth, the wife of Jacob Perkins, and Mary, the wife of Thomas Waite, Jr., their right in the estate of their father Thomas Kinsman, late of Ipswich, deceased. [Ibid. 56 : 277.]

He is styled Sergeant. He died in Ipswich, Dec. 8, 1756, leaving a Will, dated Dec. 28, 1751; proved Dec. 27, 1756; recorded Essex Probate, 34 : 95.

HIS CHILDREN BY LUCY KIMBALL:

1.	STEPHEN,	b. March 15, 1713:	d. in infancy.	
2.	THOMAS,	b. Feb. 13, 1715:	m. Mary Tilton.	**26**

HIS CHILDREN BY LYDIA KIMBALL:

3.	STEPHEN,	b. March 30, 1718:	m. Elizabeth Russell.	**27**
4.	DANIEL,	bapt. Oct. 23, 1720:	m. Mary Perkins.	**28**
5.	JEREMIAH,	bapt. May 3, 1725:	m. Sarah Harris.	**29**
6.	LYDIA,	bapt. Aug. 10, 1729:	m. Ephraim Adams, April 6, 1749.	

---

12. ELIZABETH KINSMAN, daughter of Thomas and Elizabeth (p. 53), born in Ipswich about 1690; married there JACOB PERKINS; published March 6, 1713.

He was born in Ipswich, Jan. 3, 1690, the son of Jacob and Sarah (Kinsman) Perkins. (See p. 52.)

Resided in Ipswich, where children were baptized. She died there, Sept. 26, 1732, in the 43d year of her age. [Gravestone.]

THEIR CHILDREN:

1.	JACOB,	bapt. May 8, 1715:	(m. Mary Fuller; pub. Feb. 9, 1739?)
2.	FRANCIS,	bapt. July 28, 1717:	d. in infancy.
3.	ELIZABETH,	bapt. Oct. 26, 1718:	d. in infancy.
4.	LUCY,	bapt. Oct. 16, 1720:	d. Oct. 30, 1726, æ. 6.
5.	FRANCIS,	bapt. June 28, 1724:	(m. Martha Quarles; pub. Oct. 17, 1747?)
6.	ELIZABETH,	bapt. Aug. 14, 1726:	d. Aug. 25, 1726.
7.	LUCY,	bapt Aug. 12, 1727:	d. Feb. 9, 1727-8.
8.	LUCY,	bapt. Aug. 25, 1728:	d. March 6, 1728-9, æ. 7 months.
9.	DANIEL,	bapt. Sept. 19, 1731:	d. Sept. 29, 1731.

13. MARY KINSMAN, daughter of Thomas and Elizabeth (p. 53), born in Ipswich, Oct. 14, 1695; married there THOMAS WAITE, JR.; published 10 m. 14 d. 1717. Resided in Ipswich. Mary, wife of Thomas Waite, deceased in Ipswich, Aug. 4, 1771. His Will dated March 12, 1773, he "being advanced in age"; proved June 28, 1774; on file; recorded Essex Probate, 50: 171.

THEIR CHILDREN:

1.	MARY,	bapt. Oct. 12, 1718:	living unmarried, 1777.
2.	THOMAS,	bapt. March 27, 1720:	d. March 3, 1753.
3.	ELIZABETH,	bapt. May 27, 1722:	not living, March 12, 1773.
4.	SUSANNA,	bapt. Oct. 16, 1726:	living unmarried, 1777.
5.	HANNAH,	bapt. Feb. 2, 1728:	living unmarried, 1777.
6.	LUCY,	bapt. Aug. 1, 1731:	living unmarried, 1777.
7.	SARAH,	bapt. May 27, 1733:	m. Wm. Baker; pub. May 18, 1754.
8.	DANIEL,	b.	living, March 12, 1773.
9.	STEPHEN,	bapt. Oct. 30, 1737:	drowned, April 29, 1762.
10.	EUNICE,	bapt. Sept. 30, 1739:	m. Rob. Stocker; pub. Nov. 22, 1761.

---

14. SUSANNAH KINSMAN, daughter of Joseph and Susanna (p. 58), born in Ipswich, Feb. 16, 1700; married INCREASE HOW; published Aug. 10, 1723. He resided in Ipswich, and died Jan. 29, 1754. She married, second, Capt. JOHN SMITH, Jan. 28, 1762.

HER CHILDREN BY INCREASE HOW:

1.	SARAH,	bapt. July 12, 1724:	d. Sept. 4, 1724.
2.	SUSANNAH,	bapt. Feb. 13, 1725:	m. Samuel Swazey, Feb. 10, 1747-8.
3.	ELIZABETH,	bapt. March 7, 1730:	m. Thomas Boardman; pub. May 23, 1747.
4.	JOSEPH,	bapt. Sept. 4, 1737:	m. Eliz'th Berry; pub. Dec. 9, 1758.
5.	JOHN,	bapt. Nov. 4, 1744:	d. Aug. 2, 1752.

---

15. EUNICE KINSMAN, daughter of Joseph and Susanna (p. 58), born in Ipswich, June 23, 1705; married MOSES WELLS; published Nov. 20, 1724. He was born in Ipswich, March 16, 1701, the son of Nathaniel and Mary

Wells. Resided in Ipswich. Eunice, wife of Ensign Moses Wells, died March 23, 1767.

THEIR CHILDREN:

1. JOHN, b. Nov. 12, 1725.
2. MOSES, bapt. Dec. 21, 1727: m. Mary Harris.
3. BEMSLEY, bapt. April 26, 1730: m. Widow Ruth Andrews, Dec. 13, 1759, and d. April 14, 1770.
4. JOSEPH, bapt. June 18, 1732.
5. EUNICE, bapt. Feb. 1, 1735: (m. her cousin, Wm. Browne, Jr.?)
6. LUCY, bapt. June 24, 1739: (m. Jeremiah Lord, Jr.?)
7. AARON, bapt. April 10, 1742: (m. Mary Wallis?)

---

16. SARAH KINSMAN, daughter of Joseph and Susanna (p. 58), born in Ipswich, June 23, 1705; married NATHANIEL WELLS; published July 7, 1723. He was born in Ipswich, April 24, 1699, the son of Nathaniel and Mary Wells. Resided in Ipswich. Sarah, wife of Capt. Nathaniel Wells, died July 5, 1772, in 67th year. [Gravestone.] His Will made July 3, 1789; proved June 7, 1790; on file; recorded Essex Probate, 60: 239.

THEIR CHILDREN:

1. SARAH, bapt. Sept. 27, 1724: m. Nathaniel Lord, 3d; pub. Feb. 27, 1746.
2. ELIZABETH, bapt. July 10, 1726: m. Capt. Adam Smith.
3. MARY, bapt. June 16, 1728.
4. SUSANNA, bapt. May 3, 1730: m. Ephraim Smith.
5. LYDIA, } Twins, { d. 7 m. 9 d. 1732.
6. LUCY, } bapt. Aug. 27, 1732: { d. 7 m. 13 d. 1732.
7. NATHANIEL, bapt. May 26, 1734: m Lucy Goodhue.
8. LYDIA, bapt. Feb. 15, 1735: m. her cousin, Samuel Wallis.
9. ABIGAIL, bapt. April 2, 1737: (m. John Kinsman, Feb. 9, 1758?)
10. HEPZIBAH, bapt. June 11, 1740: m. Nehemiah Patch.
11. SIMEON, bapt. Aug. 22, 1742: living, July 3, 1789.
12. HANNAH, bapt Aug. 4, 1745: m. John Friend.
13. JOHN, bapt. May 22, 1748: living, July 3, 1789.

17. ELIZABETH KINSMAN, daughter of Joseph and Susanna (p. 58), born in Ipswich, Nov. 11, 1707; married WILLIAM BROWNE, JR.; published Jan. 1, 1726. He was probably the one baptized in Ipswich, 12 m. 3 d. 1711, the son of Samuel and Martha Brown. Resided in Ipswich.

THEIR CHILDREN:

1. LUCY, bapt. July 6, 1729.
2. WILLIAM, bapt. Aug. 8, 1731: (m. his cousin, Eunice Wells, and d. April 22, 1759?)
3. SUSANNA, bapt. March 3, 1733.
4. MEHETABEL, bapt. Aug. 31, 1740.
5. EBENEZER, bapt. Oct. 14, 1744.
6. JAMES, bapt. Nov. 30, 1746.

---

18. JOHN KINSMAN, son of Joseph and Susanna (p. 58), born in Ipswich, Nov. 21, 1709; married HANNAH BURNHAM, Jan. 31, 1733. She was born in Ipswich, 7th of 2d month, 1717, the daughter of James and Sarah (Rogers) Burnham, and died May 31, 1753, aged 37. [Gravestone, Ipswich.] He married, second, ELIZABETH (Fellows) PERKINS, the widow of Joseph Perkins, of Ipswich; published Dec. 9, 1753. She survived him.

June 7, 1758, he, with wife Elizabeth, sells half the homestead of her late husband, to James Perkins, of Ipswich. [Essex Deeds, 106 : 183.] July 4, 1759, they sell land to his son, John Kinsman, of Ipswich. [Ibid. 109 : 56.] Oct. 18, 1760, he is of Ipswich, yeoman, and deeds to his son, James Kinsman, of Ipswich, husbandman, house and lands in Ipswich. Witnessed by his daughter, Hannah Kinsman. [Ibid. 110 : 133.]

He is styled Captain, was a wealthy farmer of Ipswich, and a man of some note. He died leaving a Will, dated June 7, 1783; proved March 7, 1785; on file; recorded Essex Probate, 57 : 179.

HIS CHILDREN BY HANNAH BURNHAM:

1. HANNAH,	bapt. June 1, 1735:	d. April 20, 1737.	
2. JOHN,	bapt. Aug. 21, 1737:	m. A. Wells; M. Appleton.	**30**
3. JAMES,	bapt. May 13, 1739:	m. Mary Boardman.	**31**
4. HANNAH,	bapt. June 27, 1741:	m. James Perkins.	**32**
5. JOSEPH,	bapt. May 22, 1743:	d. Nov. 6, 1762.	
6. SARAH,	bapt. Oct. 20, 1745:	m. William Appleton.	**33**
7. SAMUEL,	bapt. July 19, 1747:	m. Martha Smith.	**34**
8. JONATHAN,	bapt. Jan. 17, 1749-50:	m. H. Burnham; S. Bemont.	**35**
9. MARTHA,	bapt. Jan. 19, 1752:	m. Samuel Gilman.	**36**

---

19. HANNAH KINSMAN, daughter of Joseph and Susanna (p. 58), born in Ipswich, Nov. 21, 1709; married there ROBERT WALLIS, Dec. 25, 1735. He was born in Ipswich, May 20, 1704, the son of Samuel and Anna Wallis. Resided in Ipswich. He died June 21, 1775, aged 72. His widow died Dec. 9, 1792, aged 83. [Gravestones.]

THEIR CHILDREN:

1. ROBERT, bapt. Oct. 10, 1736: m. Eunice Brown, and d. Jan. 9, 1824, aged 87. She d. Nov. 27, 1813, aged 77.
2. SAMUEL, bapt. July 2, 1738: m. his cousin, Lydia Wells.
3. HANNAH, bapt. Sept. 14, 1740: m. Pelatiah Brown.
4. JOSEPH, bapt. March 27, 1743: d. March 31, 1743.
5. SARAH, bapt. May 13, 1744: m. —— Friend.
6. JOHN, bapt. March 19, 1746.
7. JOSEPH, bapt. May 28, 1749.
8. DENISON, bapt. Feb. 16, 1755.

---

20. MARTHA KINSMAN, daughter of Joseph and Susanna (p. 58), born in Ipswich, July 13, 1712; married there THOMAS DENNIS, May 11, 1732. He was born in Ipswich, Sept. 29, 1701, the son of Thomas and Elizabeth Dennis. Resided in Ipswich. Martha, wife of Capt. Thomas Dennis, died April 21, 1761. Col. Thomas Dennis died March 6, 1771. Will dated Feb. 19, 1771; proved March 25, 1771; on file; recorded Essex Probate, 46: 270.

THEIR CHILDREN:

1. THOMAS, bapt. Nov. 25, 1733: (m. Mary Leatherland?)
2. MARTHA, b. Aug. 27, bapt. Aug. 31, 1735: m. Benjamin Lamson, March 14, 1765.
3. LYDIA, bapt. April 24, 1737: m. Nathaniel Heard.
4. SARAH, bapt. May 20, 1739: d. young.
5. JOHN, bapt. May 3, 1741: (m. Salome Hodgkins?)
6. JOSEPH, bapt. May 22, 1743: (m. Hannah Rogers?)
7. NATHANIEL, bapt. Jan. 27, 1744: d. in infancy.
8. NATHANIEL, bapt. May 24, 1747.
9. SARAH, bapt. Sept. 17, 1749: m. John Farley.
10. DAVID, bapt. June 23, 1751.

---

21. NATHANIEL KINSMAN, son of Joseph and Susanna (p. 58), born in Ipswich, Dec. 5, 1714; married ANNA ROBINSON, Feb. 11, 1741, the daughter of Capt. Andrew and Rebecca (Ingersoll) Robinson, of Gloucester. He married, second, DORCAS PARSONS, Nov. 22, 1787, who survived him.

He resided in Gloucester, where all his children were born. The following obituary of him is taken from the "Salem Gazette" of July 28, 1797:—

"Died at Gloucester, that worthy servant of God and the Church, Deacon Nathaniel Kinsman, after a short but painful illness, in the 83d year of his age. He well supported thro' life the moral, the Christian, the social and domestic characters, with that of a good federal citizen, and died in a good old age."

HIS CHILDREN BY ANNA ROBINSON:

1. ANNA, b. June 16, 1743: m. —— Kent; John Hopkinson, and lived and died in Exeter, N. H.
2. NATHANIEL, b. Oct. 5, 1745: m. Abigail Eveleth. **37**
3. DANIEL, b. March 23, 1748: probably died before 1807.
4. MARY, b. June 9, 1751: m. Wm. Dane, and d. in Gloucester.

5. SIMEON, b. Nov. 21, 1752: m. in Boston, Jane Mecom, Feb. 13, 1800. He was a ship-master, and died in Boston, January, 1818, aged 66 years. Had no children.
6. WILLIAM, b. Aug. 9, 1754: m. Anna Lyman; Abigail Low. **38**
7. BENJAMIN, b. Dec. 29, 1757: d. in infancy.
8. JOSEPH, b. Feb. 25, 1759: d. in infancy.
9. BENJAMIN, b. May 27, 1760: probably died before 1807.
10. JUDITH, b. Jan. 7, 1762: m. Capt. Thomas Parsons; pub. Nov. 24, 1780; resided in Boston, and died in 1847.
11. SUSANNA, b. Aug. 30, 1763: probably died before 1807.
12. JOHN, b. Aug. 7, 1766: m. in Gloucester, Hannah Procter; pub. Dec. 8, 1798, the dau. of Joseph and Elizabeth Procter. He was a mariner of Gloucester, and died there March 24, 1829. His widow was living in 1838.

---

22. PELATIAH KINSMAN, son of Joseph and Susanna (p. 58), born in Ipswich, Feb. 5, 1715; married JANE FARLEY. She was baptized in Ipswich, Nov. 6, 1726, the daughter of Michael and Hannah (Emerson) Farley.

June 14, 1750, he is of Ipswich, and, with wife Jane, sells one half of a Fulling Mill, part of the estate of their father Michael Farley, late of Ipswich, who deceased March 7, 1748. [Essex Deeds, 96 : 124.]

She died in Ipswich, April 2, 1791, aged 64. He died there, Oct. 6, 1796. [Gravestones.]

THEIR CHILDREN:

1. MICHAEL, bapt. April 6, 1746: m. S. Treadwell; M. Knowlton. **39**
2. NATHANIEL, bapt. March 20, 1747: m. P. Treadwell; E. Choate. **40**
3. JANE, bapt. March 11, 1749: m. Mark Haskell; pub. Mar 3, 1798.
4. SUSANNA, bapt. July 7, 1751: m. David Dennis, July 1, 1779.
5. EUNICE, bapt. Sept. 17, 1752: d. unm. Sept. 17, 1832.
6. MOSES, } Twins, { m. L. Cogswell; S. Cogswell. **41**
7. AARON, } bapt. July 7, 1754: { m. Hannah Howe. **42**
8. ISRAEL, bapt. Aug. 15, 1756: mariner, of Ipswich, Aug. 5, 1786; died unmarried.
9. LUCY, bapt. March 26, 1758: m. Richard D Jewett. **43**
10. PELATIAH, bapt. May 18, 1760: d. in infancy.
11. HANNAH, bapt. Aug. 25, 1764: d. Oct. 9, 1786.
12. PELATIAH, bapt. Nov. 2, 1766: d. Oct. 4, 1776.
13. MERCY, bapt. Nov. 2, 1766: d. unm. Sept. 22, 1836.

23. BENJAMIN KINSMAN, son of Joseph and Susanna (p. 58), born in Ipswich, April 26, 1719; married ELIZABETH PERKINS; published Dec. 27, 1740. She was probably baptized in Ipswich, Nov. 27, 1720, the daughter of Robert and Elizabeth (Douton) Perkins. He removed from Ipswich to Cornwallis, Nova Scotia, in 1760, and June 3, 1763, when he is of "Cornwallis, Nova-Scotia, husbandman," with "wife Elizabeth," he sells to John Calef, of Ipswich, physician, his land in Ipswich. [Essex Deeds, 114: 51.]

"The Township of Cornwallis contained about 100,000 acres of land which was granted July 21, 1761, to proprietors chiefly from Connecticut, invited by Proclamation in the last year of the reign of George II, and after the expulsion of the French. Each proprietor was entitled to a right for himself and half right for his family, each right consisted of a town lot of 3 acres, a farm lot of 40 acres, and 700 acres of wilderness land. It appears from this grant that there was an earlier one, which, not fully securing the grantees in their rights and shares therein, was returned: the one on file being a substitute for the first." On this list appears the name of "Benjamin Kinsman."

He died in Cornwallis in 1794. His widow died in 1806.

THEIR CHILDREN:

1.	ELIZABETH,	b. Oct. 20, 1741.		
2.	BENJAMIN,	b. Nov. 3, 1743:	m. Hannah Pelton.	**44**
3.	NATHANIEL,	b. Aug. 13, 1745:	married.	
4.	ROBERT,	b. May 27, 1747:	m. Jerusha Bill; Mehitable Rand.	**45**
5.	EBENEZER,	b. June 2, 1750:	d. June 17, 1750.	
6.	EBENEZER,	b. Aug. 10, 1751:	m. —— Cogswell.	**46**
7.	SUSANNA,	b. June 17, 1753:	m. Capt. Ebenezer Wheaton.	
8.	JOSEPH,	b. Dec. 16, 1760:	married.	
9.	MARY,	b. Aug. 13, 1763.		

24. MARY KINSMAN, daughter of Robert and Rebecca (p. 61), born in Ipswich, Jan. 20, 1707–8; married BENJAMIN BURNHAM, of Norwich, Ct., April 20, 1727. He was born in Ipswich, Dec. 21, 1696, the son of Lieut. Thomas and Esther Burnham. He died Oct. 15, 1737. His widow married a Mr. LITTLE, as the Will of her father shows that at his decease she was Mary Little.

HER CHILDREN BY BENJAMIN BURNHAM:

1. BENJAMIN, b. Feb. 9, 1729: the grandfather of Jedediah Burnham, of Kinsman, Ohio. He died May, 1799.
2. SUSANNAH, b. June 20, 1731: m. —— Pettingell.
3. JOANNA, b. May 30, 1733: m. Dr. Joseph Perkins, of Lisbon, Ct.; 2d, Pember Caulkins, of New London, Ct.
4. ESTHER, b. March 24, 1736: m. —— Smith.

---

25. JEREMIAH KINSMAN, son of Robert and Rebecca (p. 61), born in Ipswich, Feb. 28, 1719; married SARAH THOMAS, March 19, 1752.

She was born in Marshfield, Mass.; was a sister of Gen. John Thomas, one of the first generals appointed by the Continental Congress, and a descendant of John Thomas, who in 1635 came to Plymouth in the ship "Hopewell," a boy fourteen years of age, and remained in the family of Gov. Edward Winslow until after his majority.

She died Sept. 23, 1798.

Captain Kinsman was a farmer of Lisbon, Ct.; prominent as a business man; active in all works of public interest. Among many public movements that engaged his attention was the building of the Old Newent Church. The Society resolved to build a new meeting-house about the year 1770, and secured a subscription for that purpose. He, as principal manager of the enterprise, commenced the work, and finding it at the time extremely difficult to procure suitable lumber in the vicinity, and money being very scarce, collected a quantity of farm products from the subscribers, such as pork, beef, grain, etc., and shipped it to Maine in charge of Robert Avery, as supercargo, to exchange for pine lumber.

Avery performed his mission with satisfaction, and returned to Norwich, landing his cargo of lumber, which was conveyed, by farmers and others having teams, to the place of destination, and the church was in due time completed.[1]

Of this church, an extract is given from Miss Caulkins' "History of Norwich."

"He (Rev. Levi Nelson) preached his half-century sermon in 1854. Only one of the thirty-eight members who received him as their pastor in 1804, was then living; but of the ordination choir, four were present and united in singing again the same hymns that formed a part of the original service. The old Kirtland[2] Church was then extant, seated in decaying dignity upon gently rising ground, with its barrack-like row of sheds spread out at the side like wings. The outside of the edifice had been covered and re-covered, as the *wear and tear* of years demanded, but no tool or painter's brush, under pretence of improvement or repair, had invaded the interior since it was first completed. The impression produced on the mind upon entering, was that of homely, stern solemnity. The pulpit was high and contracted, with a sounding-board frowning over it, and a

---

[1] The Rev. David Hale was ordained, June, 1790, and occupied this church until 1803. He was a brother of the accomplished and chivalrous Capt. Nathan Hale, who was executed as a spy on Long Island, by order of Sir William Howe; and father of David Hale, so well known as proprietor and editor of the "Journal of Commerce."

[2] Should be *Benedict*, I think, as the Rev. J. Benedict was the first divine that occupied it. The old Kirtland Church was situated some distance south of this location. F. K.

seat for the deacons in front of it, below. The pews were square, with high partitions; the galleries spacious, with certain seats more elevated than others for the tything-men or supervisors of behavior. This venerable structure is believed to be the last specimen of the old New England sanctuary that lingered in the nine-miles-square. It was demolished when about eighty-eight years of age, and its place supplied by a new church, dedicated Sept. 15, 1858."

Miss Caulkins names Jeremiah Kinsman, with others, as the leading patriots of the town of Norwich in 1767.

He died June 24, 1811, leaving a Will, of which the following is a copy: —

"I, Jeremiah Kinsman of Lisbon, in the county of New London, & state of Connecticut, being of perfect mind and memory, do make and ordain this my last will and testament in manner following.

Imprimis. I give and bequeath to my son John Kinsman, his heirs & assigns forever, all my land with buildings thereon standing, which I purchased of Samuel Starr and Samuel Clift situate on the south-easterly side of the highway or county road leading by my house to Canterbury. I also give my said son John, Fifty pounds lawful money to be paid by my executor hereinafter named, in six months after my decease.

Item. I give and bequeath to my son Jeremiah Kinsman and his heirs & assigns forever, all my lands & real estate situate in the town of Plainfield, & also a lot of land in Canterbury, situate on the easterly side of Quinabaug River, which my brother Robert Kinsman purchased as part of the estate of Charles Davenport & which my s'd brother died seized of. I also give my said son Jeremiah, thirty pounds lawful money, to be paid by my executor hereafter named, within six months after my decease.

Item. I give and bequeath to my daughter Joanna Fanning, one hundred & ninety pounds lawful money, to be paid by my executor hereafter named, in six months after my decease.

Item. And lastly I give and bequeath to my son Thomas Kinsman & to his heirs & assigns forever, all the residue of my estate both real & personal which I shall die possessed of, and order him to pay the aforesaid sums of money to my other children, out of the estate given him by this will, and my will is that in case a negro man named Prince, who was owned by my brother Robert Kinsman in his life time, shall ever become chargable, so that any part of my estate, disposed of by this will, should by law be liable for the support of s'd Prince, it is my will that my three sons before mentioned should jointly defray the expense thereof, so that my sons John & Jeremiah shall pay one half the expense thereof, & my son Thomas the other half thereof.

And I do hereby constitute my son Thomas Kinsman sole executor of this my last will & testament, and I also order and direct, as part of my last will & testament, that my debts & funeral expenses be paid by my said executor, out of that part of my estate given to him, so that the legacies given my other children be not diminished by the payment thereof.

Signed, sealed, published & delivered this 23d day of October, A. D. 1798, by the said Jeremiah Kinsman, as his last will & testament in presence of us.

BELA PECK.
NATHAN JOHNSON.
ASA SPALDING."

JEREMIAH KINSMAN.

Proved July 7, 1801.

THEIR CHILDREN:

1. JOHN, b. May 7, 1753: m. Rebecca Perkins. **47**
2. JOSEPH, b. Jan. 15, 1755: d. March 5, 1777.
3. JOANNA, b. Nov. 19, 1756: m. Frederick Fanning, a merchant of Jewett City, Ct. She died without issue, July 7, 1819.
4. JEREMIAH, b. July 12, 1759: m. Sarah Douglas. **48**
5. THOMAS, b. Aug. 31, 1764: d. Feb. 12, 1765.
6. THOMAS, } Twins, b. Dec. 14, 1767: m. Polly Tracy. **49**
7. SARAH, } Twins, b. Dec. 14, 1767: m. Frederick Perkins, a farmer of Lisbon, Ct. She died without issue, April 10, 1798.

FIFTH GENERATION.

26. THOMAS KINSMAN, son of Stephen and Lucy (p. 63), born in Ipswich, Feb. 13, 1715; married MARY TILTON, published April 25, 1745, the daughter of David and Anne Tilton, of Ipswich.

He resided in Hamilton, and died April 7, 1779. His widow died Aug. 18, 1806, aged 93.

THEIR CHILDREN:

1. MARY, bapt. March 30, 1746: d. unm. Jan. 16, 1826.
2. RACHEL, bapt. July 12, 1747: m. —— Kelham, and died in Hamilton, Jan. 24, 1836.
3. JEMIMA, bapt. June 17, 1750: m. Jas. Browne, Jr., Jan. 1, 1782.
4. THOMAS, b. May 27, 1753: m. Martha Knowlton. **50**
5. LUCY KIMBALL, bapt. May 16, 1756: d. Dec. 9, 1773.
6. WILLIAM, b. July 22, 1760: m. Esther Knowlton. **51**

---

27. STEPHEN KINSMAN, son of Stephen and Lydia (p. 63), born in Ipswich, March 30, 1718; married ELIZABETH RUSSELL, April 10, 1739.

He was living in Ipswich, with wife Elizabeth, as late as Oct. 23, 1767.

THEIR CHILDREN:

1. STEPHEN, b. March 17, 1739-40: m. Elizabeth Caryl. **52**
2. NATHAN, bapt. Oct. 4, 1741: m. M. Wheeler; E. Shattuck. **53**
3. AARON, bapt. Aug. 21, 1743: m. Rose Burnham; Mary Hall. **54**
4. ISAAC, bapt. Dec. 15, 1745.
5. ELIZABETH, bapt. April 10, 1748.
6. LYDIA, bapt. June 24, 1750: m. Francis Knight, of Manchester, Jan. 21, 1768; 2d, Mr. Sessions.
7. EBENEZER, bapt. May 24, 1752: died in infancy.
8. EUNICE, bapt. Dec. 22, 1754.
9. EBENEZER, bapt. Feb. 19, 1758: was probably the clergyman of the Baptist denomination, who, after several years of useful labor as a licentiate in Maine, was ordained pastor of the church in Limerick, County of York, Maine, in October, 1796; resigned in 1807. He was still residing and preaching there in 1819.
10. EPHRAIM, bapt. Jan. 11, 1761: m. Mary Hall. **55**
11. SARAH, bapt. Jan. 16, 1763.
12. ABIGAIL, bapt. Jan. 16, 1763.

One of the daughters of this family, it is said, married a Mr. Carr, and settled in Newport, N. H., and had Sally, who married James Riddle, and settled in Grafton, N. H.

---

28. DANIEL KINSMAN, son of Stephen and Lydia (p. 63), born in Ipswich; baptized there Oct. 23, 1720; married MARY PERKINS, Jan. 23, 1740. She was probably baptized in Ipswich, March 10, 1722-3, the daughter of Robert and Elizabeth (Douton) Perkins.

He probably died in Ipswich, March 11, 1746, and his widow may have married ABRAHAM CARTER, of Gloucester, Aug. 23, 1750.

THEIR CHILDREN:

1. DANIEL, bapt Sept. 20, 1741: d. July 28, 1742.
2. DANIEL, bapt. May 13, 1744: m. Abigail Morse. **56**
3. LUCY, bapt. Aug. 24, 1746: pub. to Ebenezer Trask, of Gloucester, April 8, 1768.

---

29. JEREMIAH KINSMAN, son of Stephen and Lydia (p. 63), born in Ipswich; baptized there May 3,

1725; married Sarah Harris, Jan. 21, 1743. She died Sept. 19, 1805, aged 79. He resided in Ipswich, and died March 3, 1818, leaving a Will dated Nov. 30, 1805; proved June 2, 1818; on file; recorded Essex Probate, 93 : 71.

THEIR CHILDREN:

1. Sarah, b. : m. Capt. John Andrews, Dec. 18, 1766; resided in North Yarmouth, Me., where she died at an advanced age.
2. Dorothy, b. : m. Joseph Adams, of Gloucester, Sept. 19, 1774. She died, aged 91 years.
3. Jeremiah, b. Oct. 6, 1748: m. Martha Andrews; L. Campbell. **57**
4. William, b. Aug. 27, 1752: m. Anna Brown. **58**
5. Mehetable, b. about 1757: m. John Burnham, Nov. 23, 1780, son of John, of Ipswich; removed to Enfield, N. H. He d. April 17, 1847. She d. April 18, 1847.

---

30. JOHN KINSMAN, son of John and Hannah (p. 67), born in Ipswich; baptized there Aug. 21, 1737; married Abigail Wells, Feb. 9, 1758. She was probably baptized in Ipswich, April 2, 1737, the daughter of Ensign Nathaniel and Sarah (Kinsman) Wells.

July 4, 1759, he is of Ipswich, and buys land of his father John Kinsman and Elizabeth his wife. [Essex Deeds, 109 : 56.] Dec. 14, 1759, he is of Ipswich, Junior, and buys a pew in the Rev. Mr. Walley's meeting-house in Ipswich. [Ibid. 115 : 177.][1]

His wife deceased, and he married, second, Margaret Appleton, June 3, 1773.

---

[1] From the Essex Registry of Deeds, it appears that, May 24, 1760, John Kinsman of Ipswich, and wife Mary, sell land in Ipswich. [Book 115 : 160.] Also, Jan. 21, 1772, John Kinsman, Jr., of Ipswich, yeoman, and wife Martha, buy land in Ipswich. [Book 131 : 162.]

And the Town Records of Ipswich state that Hannah, wife of John Kinsman, died Dec. 23, 1772.

But there seems to be no John Kinsman, in our Record, who will answer for a husband to either the Mary, or Martha, or Hannah above; so that, if these names and dates are correct, they must refer to one or more Johns, of whom we have no other account.

May 7, 1784, he, with wife Margaret, sells land, etc., to Moses Kinsman of Ipswich. [Ibid. 142 : 173.]

He died in Ipswich, June 2, 1785, aged 48. [Gravestone.] His Will, dated May 14, 1784, proved July 4, 1785, is on file, and recorded Essex Probate, 57 : 246; by it he gives all his property to his wife Margaret. When presented for probate, it was stated that he was late an inhabitant of Newburyport.

His widow Margaret married Daniel Thurston, of Rowley, Dec. 2, 1789 or 1790, and she deceased about 1817.

HIS CHILDREN BY ABIGAIL WELLS:

1. JOHN, b. Nov. 7, 1762: bapt. Nov. 21, 1762.
2. JAMES, b. July 22, 1764.

---

31. JAMES KINSMAN, son of John and Hannah (p. 67), born in Ipswich; baptized there May 13, 1739; married MARY BOARDMAN, Nov. 6, 1760. She was probably baptized in Ipswich, Dec. 6, 1730, the daughter of Capt. John and Abigail (Choate) Boardman.

Administration on the estate of James Kinsman, late of Ipswich, deceased, intestate, was granted to his widow, Mary Kinsman, Jan. 12, 1763. [Essex Probate, 40 : 82.]

April 20, 1763, Mary Kinsman, of Ipswich, widow, one of the children and legatees of Capt. John Boardman, of Ipswich, deceased, sells her interest in her father's estate. [Essex Deeds, 110 : 127.]

March 20, 1765, she sells to John Kinsman, of Ipswich, gentleman. [Ibid. 113 : 182.]

(She married, second, Samuel Bragg; published Aug. 17, 1765; and resided, Sept. 30, 1784, in Dover, N. H.)

THEIR CHILD:

1. MARY, b. Dec. 18, 1761: m. in Dover, N. H., James Remick, Sept. 10, 1782. She is mentioned in her grandfather John Kinsman's Will of 1783.

32. HANNAH KINSMAN, daughter of John and Hannah (p. 67), born in Ipswich; baptized there June 27, 1741; married there JAMES PERKINS, Oct. 28, 1762. Resided in Ipswich. She died Oct. 6, 1771. He was undoubtedly the James Perkins who was baptized in Ipswich, May 23, 1736, the son of Joseph and Elizabeth (Fellows) Perkins, as the latter, when a widow, married John Kinsman (**18**), father of this Hannah. (See p. 66.)

THEIR CHILDREN:

1. JAMES, bapt. Aug. 14, 1763: m. Martha Patch; pub. Feb. 7, 1780, when he is called of "Dammas-Cotta."
2. JOSEPH, b. Aug 20, 1765.
3. JOSEPH, bapt. Feb. 7, 1768.
4. ISAAC, bapt. Sept. 23, 1770.

---

33. SARAH KINSMAN, daughter of John and Hannah (p. 67), born in Ipswich; baptized there Oct. 20, 1745; married WILLIAM APPLETON; published April 21, 1764. He was born in Ipswich, 1737, the son of John and Lucy (Boardman) Appleton, and died Aug. 9, 1807. His widow died Jan. 12, 1809.

THEIR CHILDREN:

1. WILLIAM, bapt. June 30, 1765: m. Anna Bowditch. She d. June, 1795, aged 23. He m., 2d, Tamesin Abbot, July 23, 1797. She d. Jan. 27, 1850 He resided in Salem, and d. Sept. 1822, leaving no issue.
2. SARAH, bapt. Jan. 4, 1767: m. David Choate, of Gloucester, July 18, 1789.
3. LUCY, bapt. Nov. 13, 1768: m. —— Baker.
4. HANNAH, b. Aug. 16, 1770: m. Daniel Wallis, Jr., Oct. 13, 1791, and d. Dec. 26, 1851.
5. ELIZABETH, b. : d. Sept. 29, 1775.
6. MARY, b. 1772: m. Ebenezer Bowditch, of Salem. and d. May 23, 1819. He d. July 17, 1830.

34. SAMUEL KINSMAN, son of John and Hannah (p. 67), born in Ipswich; baptized there July 19, 1747; married MARTHA SMITH, Nov. 30, 1769.

May 7, 1784, Samuel Kinsman, of Ipswich, and wife Martha, sell to John Kinsman, Jr., of Ipswich, land in Ipswich and woodland in Manchester. [Essex Deeds, 142 : 72.]

He died in Ipswich, Dec. 29, 1806, leaving a Will dated March 25, 1803; proved Feb. 3, 1807; on file; recorded Essex Probate, 75 : 3. His widow died Dec. 10, 1820, aged 68.

THEIR CHILDREN:

1. MARTHA, bapt. June 23, 1771: m. Stephen Boardman, June 2, 1791; 2d, Elias Haskell, of Gloucester, Sept. 21, 1812.
2. BETSEY, bapt. July 7, 1776: m. John Wells, Jr., Dec. 15, 1796.
3. SAMUEL, bapt. Aug. 7, 1785: m. Hannah Pearson, Nov. 5, 1809. She d. Sept. 5, 1859, aged 75 years, 6 months. He d. April 8, 1860. [Gravestones.]

---

35. JONATHAN KINSMAN, son of John and Hannah (p. 67), born in Ipswich, Jan. 14, 1749–50; baptized there Jan. 17, 1749–50; married HANNAH BURNHAM. She was born in Ipswich, May 18, 1755, the daughter of Isaac and Hannah Burnham, and died in Parsonsfield, Me., Sept. 4, 1795. He married, second, SUSANNA (Williams) BEMONT, in 1796. She died in Athens, Me., in the autumn of 1829.

He was educated at Brown University, Rhode Island; was a man of good business qualifications; engaged in various pursuits. He became a proprietor in a township of land in Maine; called it "Kinsmantown," where he settled in 1798. The town was afterwards incorporated as Athens, Me. He was a Justice of the Peace at Parsonsfield, York County, Me., in 1788. Is styled Colonel. He died in Athens, Me., April 27, 1825.

HIS CHILDREN BY HANNAH BURNHAM:

1. Hannah Burnham, b. Dec. 1773: m. William Paine. **59**
2. Salome, b. Sept. 7, 1775: m. Hardy Merrill. **60**
3. Betsey, b. Sept. 27, 1778: m. Thomas O. Fox. **61**
4. Joseph, b. Jan. 21, 1780: m Eliza Page. **62**
5. Jonathan, b. June 1782: m. Abigail Cass. **63**
6. Mary, b. Oct. 10, 1784: m. John B. Brown. **64**
7. John, b. Feb. 21, 1790: m. Mrs. Anne Bodwell. **65**
8. Daniel, b. March 10, 1792, in Parsonsfield, Me.; went to New York City; m. Letitia Burger, became wealthy, and died without issue, Jan. 13, 1868.
9. Isaac B., b. Oct. 1794, in Parsonsfield, Me.; went to Ohio in 1822, and in 1824 took the stump in the unsuccessful canvass for General Jackson; in 1825 he went to Opelousas, La. Living Aug. 19, 1840.

---

36. MARTHA KINSMAN, daughter of John and Hannah (p. 67), born in Ipswich; baptized there Jan. 19, 1752; married Capt. Samuel Gilman, Sept. 16, 1779. She died Oct. 19, 1809. He resided in Exeter, N. H.; was born March 15, 1752, and died Aug. 29, 1838.

THEIR CHILDREN:

1. Sarah, b.
2. Jonathan, b. April 27, 1784: d. June 7, 1809.
3. John K., b. Aug. 14, 1787: resided in Newburyport.
4. Martha, b. Feb. 21, 1789: d. in Virginia, 1864.
5. Lydia, b. May 11, 1791: m. Joseph Boardman; she died Feb. 2, 1832.
6. Hannah, b. May 15, 1794: living, a widow, in Virginia, 1869.
7. Samuel Kinsman, b. May 2, 1796: m. Lucy Dummer, April 24, 1821; resided in Hallowell, Me.

---

37. NATHANIEL KINSMAN, son of Nathaniel and Anna (p. 68), born in Gloucester, Oct. 5, 1745; married there Abigail Eveleth, May 17, 1770. They resided in Gloucester as late as April 24, 1823.

THEIR CHILDREN:

1. Abigail, b. : d. aged 18 years.
2. Mary, bapt. Nov. 9, 1777: m. Capt. William Allen; resided in Gloucester, where she died in 1807, leaving two children.
3. Anna, b : m. Capt. Nathaniel Smith; resided in Derry, N. H.; died, leaving two children.
4. Susan, b. April 13, 1780: d. unm. Aug. 2, 1862.
5. Sally, b. : d. aged 22 years.
6. Charlotte, b. : d. aged 11 years.

---

38. WILLIAM KINSMAN, son of Nathaniel and Anna (p. 69), born in Gloucester, Aug. 9, 1754; married Anna Lyman. She was born Jan. 22, 1759, and died in Gloucester, September, 1802, where all her children were born. He married, second, Abigail Low, December, 1804. She was the widow of John Low; her maiden name Hall. She died December, 1809, aged 47.

He enlisted in Gloucester, in Capt. Nathaniel Warner's Company, Little's Regiment, and served as a Sergeant in the Battle of Bunker Hill. He was also in other service, and rose to the rank of Lieutenant. He was a ship-master, and died in Vassalborough, Me., Nov. 23, 1823.

HIS CHILDREN BY ANNA LYMAN:

1. William, b. Dec. 26, 1779: d. Nov. 2, 1784.
2. Joseph, b. Dec. 18, 1781: m. Rhoda Webber. 66
3. Nancy, b. June 14, 1785: d. Feb. 26, 1789.
4. William, } Twins, b. April 9, 1788: { d. Oct. 14, 1795.
5. Eliza Ann, } { m. William Hales, of Boston, Jan. 1, 1812. He died in Roxbury, April, 1847. Had no children. She is living in Boston.
6. Mary, b. Sept. 15, 1795: d. Oct. 7, 1795.
7. Nathaniel, b. Dec. 6, 1797: d. Nov. 28, 1800.
8. Anna, b. Jan. 12, 1800: d. Dec. 29, 1800.
9. Henry Allen, b. April 5, 1802: m. Ednah Jewett. 67

39. MICHAEL KINSMAN, son of Pelatiah and Jane (p. 69), born in Ipswich; baptized there April 6, 1746; married SARAH TREADWELL; published Nov. 19, 1768. She died in Ipswich, Feb. 4, 1782, aged 35 years 11 months 17 days. [Gravestone.] He married, second, MARY KNOWLTON, Dec. 15, 1783. He died in Ipswich, Nov. 25, 1795.

(His widow married David Dennis, of Nobleborough, Me.; published April 22, 1809.)

HIS CHILDREN BY MARY KNOWLTON:

1. BETSEY, b. : m. Aaron Blaney, Jr.; resided in Bristol, Me.
2. PELATIAH, b. Jan. 11, 1785: d. April 18, 1807.
3. MARY, b. June 16, 1787: m. Henry Little, Jr.; resided in Newcastle, Lincoln County, Me.
4. ISRAEL, b. June 8, 1789: was a merchant of Salem, for a time; removed to Philadelphia, Pa., about 1817; married there Oct. 28, 1817, Elizabeth Walker, and continued there until 1844, when he removed to New York City, and became President of the Parkhurst Manufacturing Company (for making Wool and Cotton Gins), in which office he remained until 1849. He died in New York, Jan. 10, 1862.
5. SARAH, b. Oct. 5, 1791: m. David Dennis, Jr.; resided in Nobleborough, Me.
6. MICHAEL, b. Sept. 18, 1794: removed to Philadelphia, Pa.; was a merchant there in 1821; m. Elizabeth ——. He died without issue. She was his widow in 1844, and was living in 1865.

---

40. NATHANIEL KINSMAN, son of Pelatiah and Jane (p. 69), born in Ipswich; baptized there March 20, 1747; married PRISCILLA TREADWELL, March 12, 1772. She was baptized in Ipswich, March 5, 1748, the daughter of John and Priscilla (Burnham) Treadwell, and died Jan. 10, 1786. He married, second, ELIZABETH CHOATE, Dec. 31, 1786. She died July 18, 1834, aged 77.

He was a farmer of Ipswich, and died June 30, 1807.

HIS CHILDREN BY PRISCILLA TREADWELL:

1. PRISCILLA, b. Oct. 6, 1773: m. Thomas Hodgkins, Aug. 27, 1795; settled in Portland, Me.; had children, and both died there.
2. NATHANIEL, b. Nov. 24, 1775: m. Deborah Webb. **68**
3. HANNAH, b. Dec. 8, 1777: m. John P. Bartlett, of Portland, Me., where she d. May 25, 1857, leaving children.
4. MICHAEL, b. Aug. 9, 1780: d. Dec. 12, 1781.
5. MICHAEL, b. April 3, 1783: d. at sea, unmarried, Feb. 11, 1800.

HIS CHILDREN BY ELIZABETH CHOATE:

6. JOHN C., b. July 5, 1789: m. Anna Lord. **69**
7. ELIZABETH, b. July 1, 1791: d. March 1, 1804.
8. MARY, b. Jan. 7, 1795: d. unm. Aug. 6, 1820.
9. MARTHA, b. Feb. 2, 1798: d. unm. Dec. 16, 1821. At the age of twelve, she wrought a sampler, containing her father's family record, as taken from the old family Bible. A running vine and handsomely wrought flowers form the border. It is carefully preserved in a frame by her brother, John C., who also has another sampler, worked by his mother in 1775.

---

41. MOSES KINSMAN, son of Pelatiah and Jane (p. 69), born in Ipswich, July 6, 1754; baptized July 7, 1754; married LUCY COGSWELL, Sept. 28, 1780. She died Nov. 29, 1804, aged 46. He married, second, SUSANNA COGSWELL, Dec. 21, 1809. She died Jan. 10, 1841, aged 75. He resided in Ipswich, and died March 24, 1836. [Gravestones.]

HIS CHILDREN BY LUCY COGSWELL:

1. LUCY, b. Oct. 14, 1781: m. Aaron Cogswell. **70**
2. JOSEPH, b. March 14, 1783: m. Eunice Brown. **71**
3. MARY, b. Dec. 13, 1785: m. Bemsley Smith, Oct. 6, 1811.
4. HANNAH, b. Oct. 14, 1787: m. Ephraim Brown, Oct. 6, 1811.
5. ELIZABETH, b. April 15, 1789: m. Capt. Winthrop Boardman, Dec. 28, 1824, and d. Aug. 4, 1861.
6. FARLEY, b. Nov. 18, 1790: m. Jerusha Norwood. **72**
7. SUSANNA ELWELL, b. July 6, 1793: d. Sept. 24, 1808.
8. ABIGAIL ELWELL, b. Nov. 3, 1796: m. Capt. Winthrop Boardman, Jan. 30, 1821, and d. June 28, 1823.
9. MOSES, b. Oct. 17, 1798: m. Jane Kinsman, Dec. 31, 1834, daughter of Aaron and Hannah (Howe) Kinsman; he d. May 7, 1862.

42. AARON KINSMAN, son of Pelatiah and Jane (p. 69), born in Ipswich, July 6, 1754; baptized July 7, 1754; married HANNAH HOWE. She died March 3, 1860, aged 89 years 4 months. He resided in Ipswich, and died Oct. 3, 1836. [Gravestones.]

THEIR CHILDREN:

1. NATHANIEL, b. Oct. 17, 1795: m. Joanna Brown. **73**
2. HANNAH, b. Dec. 31, 1796: d. Dec. 14, 1869.
3. JANE, b. July 19, 1799: m. Moses Kinsman, Dec. 31, 1834, the son of Moses and Lucy (Cogswell) Kinsman. He d. May 7, 1862. His widow resides in Ipswich.
4. CHARLOTTE, } Twins, b. March 29, 1801: m. Elisha Brown. **74**
5. CLARISSA, } Twins, b. March 29, 1801: unmarried; residence, Ipswich.
6. AARON, b. June 26, 1804: unmarried; residence, Ipswich.

43. LUCY KINSMAN, daughter of Pelatiah and Jane (p. 69), born in Ipswich, March 7, 1758; baptized there March 26, 1758; married RICHARD DUMMER JEWETT, Dec. 25, 1791. They resided in Ipswich, where he died Jan. 15, 1825, and his widow died Nov. 28, 1837.

THEIR CHILDREN:

1. RICHARD D., b. Sept. 8, 1792: sailed from Boston the 15th of December, 1813, for New Orleans, and from thence for France, in the schooner "Milo," of Boston, Burnham, master; was never heard from afterward.
2. MARY, b. March 17, 1794: d. Nov. 7, 1794.
3. MARY, b. April 13, 1796: d. May 6, 1797.
4. ISRAEL, b. March 24, 1799: m. Sally Averill, July 23, 1820.

---

44. BENJAMIN KINSMAN, son of Benjamin and Elizabeth (p. 70), born in Ipswich, Nov. 3, 1743; baptized there Nov. 6, 1743; married HANNAH PELTON. He removed with his father to Cornwallis, Kings County, Nova Scotia, where he died in 1817. His widow, Hannah Kinsman, died about 1824, aged probably 84 years.

THEIR CHILDREN:

1.	Ruby,	b.	: m. Stephen Porter.	
2.	Wealthy,	b.	: m. Francis West.	
3.	Achsa,	b.	: m. Samuel Gore.	
4.	Perkins,	b.	: d. in infancy.	
5.	Hannah,	b.	: d. in infancy.	
6.	Jeremiah,	b.	: m. Lavinia Clark.	75
7.	Hannah,	b.	: m. James Moore.	
8.	Jerusha,	b.	: m. George Jackson.	
9.	Eunice,	b.	: m. Robert Sharp.	
10.	Benjamin Avery,	b. Dec. 2, 1787	: m. Mary English; ——— ——.	76

---

45. ROBERT KINSMAN, son of Benjamin and Elizabeth (p. 70), born in Ipswich, May 27, 1747; baptized there May 30, 1747; removed with his father to Cornwallis, Kings County, Nova Scotia, and there married Jerusha Bill, Dec. 9, 1773. She died in 1781 or 1782. He married, second, Mehitable Rand. They had seven children, and she died in June, 1844. He died May 12, 1820.

HIS CHILDREN BY JERUSHA BILL:

1.	Amos,	b. Sept. 18, 1774	: m. Abigail Chase.	77
2.	Sarah,	b. Sept. 21, 1776	: m. Jedediah Ells.	
3.	Lydia,	b. Nov. 4, 1778	: m. Wilmot Osborne.	
4.	James,	b. Dec. 14, 1780	: m. Dorothy Chase.	78

HIS CHILDREN BY MEHITABLE RAND:

5.	Melatiah,	b. Aug. 13, 1783	: m. Rhoda Wright.	79
6.	Elizabeth,	b. Feb. 3, 1785	: m. Major John Fuller.	
7.	Jerusha,	b. Sept. 10, 1786	: m. William Jordan.	
8.	Samuel,	b. Aug. 30, 1788	: m. Hannah Bishop in 1816. She d. in 1846. He m., 2d, Eunice White in 1847. Resides in St. John, New Brunswick.	
9.	Mary,	b. June 24, 1790	: m. Peter Woodworth, and died July 13, 1817.	
10.	Theodorus,	b. June 11, 1792	: m. Hannah Kinsman; E. North.	80
11.	Ephraim,	b. Oct. 1, 1794	: d. March 7, 1810.	

46. EBENEZER KINSMAN, son of Benjamin and Elizabeth (p. 70), born in Ipswich, Aug. 10, 1751; baptized there Aug. 11, 1751; removed with his father to Cornwallis, Nova Scotia, in 1760; married, it is presumed, a Miss COGSWELL, and resided in Cornwallis.

THEIR CHILDREN PROBABLY WERE:

1.	JOHN,	b.	: m. Sarah Holton.	**81**
2.	BETSEY,	b.	: m. David Borden; —— Horton.	
3.	EZEKIEL,	b.	: m. Mary Neshert.	**82**
4.	DANIEL,	twins, b.	: m. Mary Tupper.	**83**
5.	ADOLPHUS,	twins, b.	: never married.	
6.	OLIVE,	b.	: m. William Masters.	
7.	ANN,	b.	: m. John Lemont.	
8.	EBENEZER,	b.	: m. Mary Ells.	**84**

---

47. JOHN KINSMAN, son of Jeremiah and Sarah (p. 75), born in Norwich (now Lisbon), Ct., May 7, 1753; married REBECCA PERKINS, Oct. 4, 1792. She was born Sept. 29, 1773, the daughter of Capt. Simon and Olive (Douglas) Perkins, of Lisbon, Ct.[1]

At the age of 23 years, on a call from Gov. Trumbull for nine regiments, in 1776, he is found enrolled as an Ensign in a company of Connecticut Militia, marching to New York, to take position under General Washington, in the defence of his country.

His company, being a part of Col. Jedediah Huntington's regiment, was soon mustered into service, and took an active and prominent part in the great Battle of Long Island. He was there, with many of his companions in arms, taken a prisoner of war, and placed in the hands of the Hessian soldiers. Thrust into prison in the prison-ships (of which history gives a detailed account), he remained for some time

---

[1] For her ancestry, see N. E. Hist. Gen. Register, vol. 14, page 116.

in close confinement, suffering from filth, vermin, and hunger, nearly to starvation, by which his health became impaired, and he never entirely recovered. By some means he and two of his companions, Charles Fanning and Anthony Bradford, were released from the prison-ship on parole, and allowed to mess together in a room in the city of New York. From the "Independent Chronicle," printed at Boston, Sept. 19, 1776, is taken the following: "A List of the Names of the Officers that are Prisoners with the Enemy, and have by Flag of Truce, sent for their Baggage and Cash." "Of Col. Huntington's Regiment, Ensign Kinsman." And from the "Continental Journal and Weekly Advertiser," printed at Boston, May 8, 1777: "Fish-Kill, April 20. To the Printer. Head Quarters, Morris-Town, April 10, 1777. Sir. His Excellency General Washington desires that the following gentlemen may be informed through your paper, that they are exchanged, and at liberty to enter into the service again. I am &c. G. Johnston, A. D. C." Among the gentlemen mentioned, was "Ensign John Kinsman."

While in New York, he acquired a knowledge of the hatting business, that induced him, immediately on his release and return home, to embark in that business. He at once established a shop, placed in it an experienced workman, Mr. Capron, as foreman, purchased a stock of goods, and devoted his time to the care of the store, furnishing the shop, and making sales of the products. He supplied the army largely with hats, and the trade generally proved to be successful, and was continued in Connecticut, with his farm, until after the war.

In 1797 he was elected a Representative to the State Legislature, where he was continued three years. In that connection, he became acquainted with the officers and stockholders of the Connecticut Land Company, and made extensive purchases of those lands.

In 1799 he first went to Ohio, to explore his lands; subsequently he fixed upon a township (16,600 acres) which he had purchased (with other lands), now known as Kinsman, in Trumbull County, Ohio, then a wilderness, for his future residence; built houses, store, and saw-mill, and moved his family to that location in 1804, and cleared and occupied a large farm.

He was a man of great energy and activity in business, was appointed a Justice of the Peace under the Territorial Government, and an Associate Judge under the State Government, and was also prominent in the County organization. He was one of the main projectors and the largest subscriber to the stock of the "Western Reserve Bank," the first bank established in Northern Ohio.

His life and business were marked by great activity and toil; he rode often on horseback to Connecticut and to Philadelphia, to purchase goods, and over many parts of the Connecticut Western Reserve, to look after the new settlements, and the sale of his land; frequently camping out at night, with nothing but an extra blanket to cover him.

His time was so constantly devoted to the progress and improvement of the early settlements, that he exerted himself beyond the powers of endurance, and sank under the care and fatigue of a life too laborious for his constitution, and died Aug. 17, 1813, aged 60 years. He died intestate, leaving a large estate, which was administered upon by his brother-in-law, Gen. Simon Perkins.

Mrs. Kinsman died May 27, 1854, aged 80 years. She was a devoted Christian, a member of the Congregational Church, gave largely of her means during her widowhood to the educational and religious enterprises of the day, and contributed to the building of a house of worship for the church in Kinsman, of which she was a member, giving a parsonage, with land, and a liberal endowment.

THEIR CHILDREN:

1.	John,	b. Sept. 20, 1793:	m. Mrs. Jane W. Cass.	**85**
2.	Joseph,	b. March 8, 1795:	d. June 17, 1819.	**86**
3.	Rebecca,	b. Nov. 24, 1796:	d. in Lisbon, Ct., Oct. 26, 1797.	
4.	Sarah,	b. Dec. 7, 1798:	d. Jan. 13, 1807.	
5.	Olive Douglas,	b. Oct. 4, 1800:	m. George Swift.	**87**
6.	Thomas,	b. Aug. 20, 1804:	m. Sophia Burnham.	**88**
7.	Frederick,	b. March 4, 1807:	m. O. D. Perkins; C. G. Pease.	**89**
8.	Joanna,	b. Oct. 19, 1808:	d. Sept. 19, 1809.	
9.	Daughter,	b. June 13, 1813:	d. July 11, 1813.	

---

48. JEREMIAH KINSMAN, son of Jeremiah and Sarah (p. 75), born in Norwich, Ct., July 12, 1759; married Sarah Douglas, of Plainfield.

He was a farmer of Plainfield, Ct., and one of the leading men of the township; was elected a Representative to the State Legislature in 1804, 1805, and 1827. He died Jan. 1, 1832.

THEIR CHILDREN:

1.	Susannah,	born and died.		
2.	Sarah,	b. Feb. 17, 1785:	m. Capt. Roswell Adams.	**90**
3.	Joanna,	b. Oct. 21, 1790:	m. Benjamin Bacon.	**91**

---

49. THOMAS KINSMAN, son of Jeremiah and Sarah (p. 75), born in Norwich, Ct., Dec. 14, 1767; married Polly Tracy, Oct. 15, 1802. He was a prominent citizen and farmer of Lisbon, Ct., and in 1819 was elected a Representative to the State Legislature. He died without issue, Sept. 21, 1861, aged 94 years.

SIXTH GENERATION.

50. THOMAS KINSMAN, son of Thomas and Mary (p. 75), born in Ipswich, May 27, 1753; married MARTHA KNOWLTON, October, 1778.

He resided in Hamilton, and died May 24, 1786. In the settlement of the estate of his mother, Widow Mary Kinsman, late of Hamilton, Oct. 6, 1806, Robert Dodge gives his receipt for their portion, in behalf of the children ot Thomas Kinsman, deceased, late of Nobleborough, Lincoln County, Me. (His widow, Martha Kinsman, married Dr. Thomas Flint, of Nobleborough, Me.)

THEIR CHILDREN:

1. MARTHA, bapt. Sept. 21, 1783: m. Winthrop Allen; resided in Farmington, Kennebec County, Me.
2. ELIZABETH, b. March 27, 1785: m. Benjamin Flint, Feb. 23, 1808. They resided in Brooklyn, N. Y., where she died without issue, Sept. 9, 1842.

---

51. WILLIAM KINSMAN, son of Thomas and Mary (p. 75), born in Ipswich, July 22, 1760; married ESTHER KNOWLTON, March 8, 1785. She was born September, 1761, the daughter of Samuel and Esther (Dean) Knowlton.

He resided in Hamilton, where he died July 17, 1806, aged 46. His widow died Aug. 21, 1807, aged 46.

THEIR CHILDREN:

1. SAMUEL,	b. Oct. 22, 1785:	m. Rachel Carter.	**92**
2. MARY,	b. Oct. 2, 1787:	m. Ephraim Annable.	**93**
3. THOMAS,	b. June 22, 1789:	m. Sally Patch.	**94**
4. WILLIAM,	b. Dec. 13, 1791:	m. Hannah Shatswell.	**95**
5. ESTHER,	b. July 1, 1793:	m. Moses Sanborn.	**96**
6. INFANT SON,	b. Aug. 8, 1797:	d. Aug. 26, 1797.	
7. EBENEZER,	b. Oct. 21, 1799:	d. Jan. 6, 1816.	
8. MARTHA,	b. Oct. 21, 1801:	d. Oct. 1, 1804.	
9. ELMINA,	b. Dec. 29, 1804:	m. Ezekiel Roberts.	**97**

52. STEPHEN KINSMAN, son of Stephen and Elizabeth (p. 76), born in Ipswich, March 17, 1739–40; baptized there same month; married, in Hopkinton, Mass., ELIZABETH CARYL, Dec. 9, 1762. She was born May 20, 1745, the daughter of Benjamin Caryl, Jr.

He removed from Ipswich to Hopkinton, where all his children were born. He and his wife were admitted to the Congregational Church there, Jan. 15, 1786, and he was elected Deacon, Sept. 28, 1786.

He followed his brother Ephraim to Springfield, N. H., in November, 1793, and remained there for a time; then removed to Grafton, N. H., where he died December, 1819. His widow survived him for many years, dying at the age of 98.

THEIR CHILDREN:

1.	LYDIA,	b. Sept. 16, 1763:	m. John Morrill.	**98**
2.	AARON,	b. June 27, 1765:	m. Polly Mellen.	**99**
3.	BETSEY,	b. May 27, 1767:	m. Jason Walker.	**100**
4.	ISAAC,	b. June 12, 1769:	m. Mary Murray.	**101**
5.	ASA,	b. Nov. 18, 1771:	m. Susan Murray.	**102**
6.	JOHN,	b. March 8, 1774:	m. Susan Lumbard.	**103**
7.	STEPHEN,	b. April 19, 1777:	d. July 18, 1778.	
8.	LUCY,	b. March 11, 1779:	d. Sept. 28, 1794.	
9.	JERUSHA,	b. Jan. 3, 1782:	d. Dec. 5, 1784.	
10.	MOSES,	b. March 6, 1784:	m. Abigail Wood.	**104**

---

53. NATHAN KINSMAN, son of Stephen and Elizabeth (p. 76), born in Ipswich; baptized there Oct. 4, 1741; married MERCY WHEELER; married, second, in Littleton, N. H., ELIZABETH SHATTUCK, Sept. 6, 1772, the daughter of Stephen and Elizabeth (Robbins) Shattuck. He was a hatter in Concord, N. H., where most of his children were born. In 1782 he removed to Landaff (then a part of Lincoln), N. H., where he was a farmer and physician, and lived at the foot of Mount Kinsman, a mountain named for him. His second wife died June 14, 1798, aged 54. He married, third, a Widow CHAPIN.

He was in the French War in 1756, and taken prisoner; and was, probably, the Nathan Kinsman who served at Annapolis, N. S., from Nov. 2, 1759, to June 7, 1760, in Capt. Daniel Fletcher's Company, Col. Frye's Regiment. [Mass. Archives, 98 : 158.]

He died Feb. 8, 1822, aged 80.

HIS CHILDREN BY MERCY WHEELER:

1. NATHAN, b. April 22, 1767 : d. April 15, 1776.
2. MERCY, b. April 10, 1769 : d. in infancy.

HIS CHILDREN BY ELIZABETH SHATTUCK:

3. STEPHEN, b. Aug. 14, 1773 : m. Ruth F. Osgood. **105**
4. PETER, b. Aug. 3, 1775 : d. March 21, 1776.
5. NATHAN, b. Nov. 14, 1777 : m. Eliza Dafforne. **106**
6. PETER, b. Nov. 23, 1779 : m. Mary Raymond. **107**
7. MARTHA, b. Oct. 9, 1781 : m. Nathan Robbins. **108**
8. TIMOTHY, b. Aug. 17, 1783 : m. Lucy S. Abbott. **109**

---

54. AARON KINSMAN, son of Stephen and Elizabeth (p. 76), born in Ipswich; baptized there Aug. 21, 1743; married ROSE BURNHAM, Dec. 5, 1765. He married, second, in Medford, MARY HALL, of that place, Dec. 26, 1775.

He removed from Ipswich to Concord, N. H., about 1770. Was Captain of one of the Companies in Col. (afterwards Gen.) Stark's Regiment, at the Battle of Bunker Hill. Afterwards styled Colonel, of Hanover, N. H. He died in 1810.

HIS CHILDREN BY ROSE BURNHAM:

1. AARON, bapt. Oct. 12, 1766 : m. Hannah Crane; Ann Willis. **110**
2. ABIGAIL, b. : m. James Wheelock, of Hanover, N.H.; pub. July 16, 1786, in Concord, N. H. Probably the grandson of Rev. Dr. Eleazer Wheelock, first President of Dartmouth College.
3. MARY, b. : m. Thomas S. Sparhawk. **111**

55. EPHRAIM KINSMAN, son of Stephen and Elizabeth (p. 76), born in Ipswich, Jan. 9, 1761; baptized there Jan. 11, 1761; married in Concord, N. H., MARY HALL. She was born Jan. 18, 1761, and died in 1845.

He purchased land and settled in Springfield, N. H., where most of his children were born. Is styled Captain. He afterwards went to Williamstown, Vt., where he died June, 1817, or April, 1818.

THEIR CHILDREN:

1. MARY, b. Oct. 22, 1777: m. Moses Reed. **112**
2. WATSON, b. 1779: d. in Hanover, N. H., July 4, 1801, aged 22 years.
3. SARAH, b. June 23, 1781: m. Moses Dickerson. **113**
4. ABIGAIL, b. : m. Samuel Fowler, of New Hampshire, and died in New York State.
5. ISAAC, b. May 18, 1783: m. Matilda Knapp. **114**
6. JAMES HALL, b. March 11, 1786: m. Sarah Robinson. **115**
7. AARON BODON, b. Dec. 25, 1789: m. O. Martin; J. G. Webster. **116**
8. EPHRAIM, b. May 2, 1792: m. R. Dow; S. W. Daniels. **117**
9. NEWELL, b. June 21, 1795: m. Leonora Lamb. **118**
10. WILLIS, b. July 17, 1798: m. Fannie Warren. **119**

---

56. DANIEL KINSMAN, son of Daniel and Mary (p. 76), born in Ipswich; baptized there May 13, 1744; married in Hopkinton, ABIGAIL MORSE, April 7, 1768.

May 21, 1765, he gives his receipt to his uncle, Jeremiah Kinsman, for £43.6.8, a legacy given him by his grandfather, Stephen Kinsman. [Essex Probate, 42 : 85.]

He soon after removed to Hubbardston, Worcester County, Mass., where his children were born, and his wife died, aged about 63 years.

In 1807 he settled in Shrewsbury, Rutland County, Vt., where he died Dec. 12, 1818, aged 74.

THEIR CHILDREN:

1.	SAMUEL,	b. March 1, 1769:	m. Kezia Newton.	120
2.	DANIEL,	b. :	d. unm. in Shrewsbury, Vt.	
3.	DAVID,	b. :	m. Abigail Putnam.	121
4.	LUCY,	b. :	m. Nahum Forbes, of Westborough.	
5.	ABIGAIL,	b. :	m. John Hemenway, of Framingham.	
6.	JOSEPH,	Twins,	m. Kezia Bangs.	122
7.	JOHN,	b. Aug. 14, 1782:	m. Eunice Merritt; A. Merritt.	123
8.	JAMES,	b. July 7, 1783:	m. Nancy Miller.	124

---

57. JEREMIAH KINSMAN, son of Jeremiah and Sarah (p. 77), born in Ipswich, Oct. 6, 1748; married MARTHA ANDREWS, Nov. 16, 1769. She was born Feb. 1, 1749, the daughter of John and Martha Andrews, and died April 11, 1810. He married, second, in New Ipswich, N.H., LYDIA CAMPBELL, May 7, 1812. She died Sept. 24, 1857, aged 98 years 8 months.

He was a soldier of the Revolution, and served fifteen months and twenty-six days, travelling five hundred and thirty-five miles. He lived in Ipswich during the war; afterwards removed to Fitchburg, Mass., where he died March 11, 1828.

HIS CHILDREN BY MARTHA ANDREWS:

1.	MARTHA,	b. Sept. 11, 1770:	d. unm. Aug. 27, 1868.	
2.	LYDIA,	b. July 7, 1772:	m. Ephraim Gibson.	125
3.	JEREMIAH,	b. Aug. 19, 1775:	m. Olive Messinger.	126
4.	DANIEL,	b. March 30, 1778:	m. Lucy Monroe; Hannah Carr.	127
5.	MARY,	b. Feb. 2, 1781:	d. unm. Jan. 5, 1859.	
6.	LUCY,	b. Aug. 15, 1783:	m. Silas Lawrence.	128
7.	JOHN,	b. April 24, 1786:	m. Nancy Sherwin.	129
8.	SALLY,	b. April 7, 1790:	d. unm. Oct. 31, 1863.	
9.	ASA,	b. March 30, 1793:	m. Martha Stone; H. Burnap.	130

58. WILLIAM KINSMAN, son of Jeremiah and Sarah (p. 77), born in Ipswich, Aug. 27, 1752; baptized there, by Rev. John Cleveland of Essex, May 4, 1764; married ANNA BROWN, daughter of Lieut. Jacob and Anna (Quarles) Brown.

He enlisted in Capt. Parker's Company of Newburyport, Col. Moses Little's Regiment, and was in the Battle of Bunker Hill. Afterwards was a Revolutionary pensioner. He died in Ipswich, Sept. 30, 1843, aged 91 years, leaving a Will dated Dec. 20, 1827; proved Nov. 7, 1843; recorded Essex Probate, 112 : 227.

His descendants, at the time of his decease, were more than one hundred in number. His widow died April 16, 1849, aged 91 years.

THEIR CHILDREN:

1.	ANNA,	b. May 27, 1773:	m. Benjamin Potter.	**131**
2.	WILLIAM,	b. Sept. 4, 1776:	m. Sarah Brown.	**132**
3.	JACOB B.,	b. April 9, 1779:	m. Bethiah Dodge.	**133**

---

59. HANNAH BURNHAM KINSMAN, daughter of Jonathan and Hannah (p. 81), born in Ipswich, December, 1773; baptized there Feb. 27, 1774; married WILLIAM PAINE. Resided in Brownfield, Me., where he died Nov. 11, 1821, aged 50. She died in Conway, N. H., June 16, 1856.

THEIR CHILDREN:

1. CATHARINE, b. July 21, 1794: m. John Wedgewood, of Parsonsfield, Me.; d. September, 1859, leaving children.
2. BETSEY, b. June 16, 1796: m. Simeon Eaton; had eleven children. He d. July 28, 1862. She is still living.
3. JOSEPH, b. Feb. 3, 1804: m. ——; d. Jan. 3, 1871, in Brownfield, Me., leaving children.

60. SALOME KINSMAN, daughter of Jonathan and Hannah (p. 81), born in Ipswich, Sept. 7, 1775; baptized there Oct. 8, 1775; married HARDY MERRILL. He was born in Newbury, Oct. 18, 1774; settled in Parsonsfield, Me., where he died. She also died there Jan. 10, 1864.

THEIR CHILDREN:

1. JOSEPH, b. Dec. 3, 1795: m. Hannah F. Burbank; Mrs. Mercy Leavitt.
2. ISAAC, b. March 1, 1798: m. Hannah E. McDonald; d. June 17, 1871.
3. SALOME, b. Nov. 29, 1800: m. David Mudgett.
4. HENRY, b. Dec. 30, 1802: m. Rebecca Merrill; Adeline Bray.
5. ABIGAIL, b. May 21, 1805: m. James Moore.
6. HANNAH, b. Sept. 21, 1807: m. Gilman L. Bennett.
7. LOUISA, b. Aug. 14, 1810: m. Silas Moulton; has deceased.
8. REBECCA, b. April 27, 1813: m. Abner Kezar; Sylvanus Bangs.
9. SAMUEL, b. Sept. 2, 1815: m. Elizabeth R. Knapp; Mrs. Rebecca M. Merrill.

---

61. BETSEY KINSMAN, daughter of Jonathan and Hannah (p. 81), born in Gilmanton, N. H., Sept. 27, 1778; married THOMAS O. FOX, Oct. 17, 1792. He was born in Gilmanton, N. H., Nov. 15, 1769, the son of John and Anna (Holland) Fox.

They settled in Parsonsfield, Me., where five of their children were born; then removed to Athens, Me., where he died July 7, 1842, and she died Jan. 11, 1854.

THEIR CHILDREN:

1. SALLY, b. Feb. 26, 1793: m. John Hight, March 18, 1813; residence, Harmony, Me.
2. HANNAH, b. June 8, 1795: m. Hovey French, Nov. 25, 1828; residence, Canaan, Me.
3. JONATHAN K., b. Sept. 27, 1798: m. Sophia Judkins, July 1, 1824; d. in Palmyra, Me., Aug. 7, 1844.
4. THOMAS, b. April 20, 1800: m. Eliza Cass, Aug. 25, 1829; residence, Athens, Me.
5. ALVAH, b. Oct. 20, 1803: residence, Athens, Me.
6. JOHN K., b. June 2, 1813: m. Rachel Dearborn, Aug. 1, 1856; d. in Athens, Me., Jan. 11, 1871.
7. AARON B., b. July 5, 1815: m. Esther Drew, Dec. 6, 1847.

62. JOSEPH KINSMAN, son of Jonathan and Hannah (p. 81), born in Exeter, N. H., Jan. 21, 1780; married ELIZA PAGE, Jan. 12, 1820. She was born April 29, 1790, the daughter of Capt. Enoch and Elice (Cilly) Page.

He accompanied his father to Maine, and became one of the proprietors of Athens; was twice a member of the State Legislature; was an extensive land-owner on the Penobscot and Kennebec Rivers in the State of Maine, and a large lumber dealer; was also engaged in agriculture. He was, for many years, Brigadier General of the State. Resided in Cornville, Me., where all his children were born, and where he died Dec. 25, 1857. His widow survives him.

THEIR CHILDREN:

1. JOSEPH CHARLES THIOT, b. Feb. 7, 1821: m. C. E. Dow. **134**
2. ENOCH JEWETT, b. Sept. 22, 1822: d. Dec. 19, 1844, when a medical student of Bowdoin College.
3. JOSIAH BURNHAM, b. April 29, 1824. **135**
4. HANNAH FRANCES JOSEPHINE, b. June 30, 1826.
5. CLYMENE ANN M., b. April 5, 1830: d. March 12, 1834.
6. RUEL DANIEL, b. July 1, 1833: d. March 8, 1834.

---

63. JONATHAN KINSMAN, son of Jonathan and Hannah (p. 81), born in Exeter, N. H., June, 1782; married ABIGAIL CASS, March, 1806, the daughter of Capt. Moses Cass, of Cornville, Me.

He died in Dresden, Me., May, 1808.

THEIR CHILD:

1. JONATHAN BURNHAM, b. May 22, 1807: m. Elizabeth Bodwell. **136**

---

64. MARY KINSMAN, daughter of Jonathan and Hannah (p. 81), born in Saco, Me., Oct. 10, 1784; married

John Burnham Brown, April 5, 1818. He was born in Ipswich, Sept. 12, 1779, and died there June 17, 1868. She died in Ipswich, June 11, 1867.

THEIR CHILDREN:

1. Mary Kinsman, b. Jan. 11, 1819: m. Manasseh Brown, of Ipswich, Dec. 15, 1836; d. July 15, 1851.
2. Lucy, b. Dec. 10, 1820: m. Wilder J. Mellen, May 9, 1854.
3. John A., b. Sept. 28, 1822: unm.; residence, Chicago.
4. Emeline, b. July 17, 1824: d. Feb. 7, 1825.
5. Emeline F., b. May 30, 1827: unm.; residence, Ipswich.
6. Hannah B., b. April 18, 1831: m. Theodore F. Cogswell, Oct. 27, 1854; residence, Ipswich.

---

65. JOHN KINSMAN, son of Jonathan and Hannah (p. 81), born in Saco, Me., Feb. 21, 1790; married Mrs. Anne Bodwell, March 16, 1816. She was the widow of Capt. Bodwell, of Somersworth, N. H.; her maiden name Brewster. He was a farmer of Athens, Me., where he died Dec. 9, 1866.

THEIR CHILDREN:

1. John Brewster, b. May 9, 1817: d. Nov. 16, 1840.
2. Mary, b. May 7, 1819: m. Rodney R. Hathorne; had seven children.
3. Maria, b. April 11, 1821: d. July 8, 1827.
4. Maria L., b. Jan. 8, 1825: m. William Leavitt, July 9, 1856; had five children.

---

66. JOSEPH KINSMAN, son of William and Anna (p. 82), born in Gloucester, Dec. 18, 1781; married Rhoda Webber, March 8, 1810, the daughter of Ignatius Webber, of Gloucester. He resided in Gloucester until 1832; then removed to Portland, Me. He died Jan. 2, 1857. She died Dec. 22, 1866, aged 76.

THEIR CHILDREN:

1.	JOSEPH,	b. Nov. 16, 1812:	d. April 28, 1814.	
2.	RHODA,	b. Dec. 20, 1814:	m. Capt. Henry Thurston.	**137**
3.	JOSEPH,	b. Jan. 7, 1819:	m. Lucinda Jordon.	**138**
4.	WILLIAM H.,	b. Jan. 14, 1821:	m. E. A. Hosack; R. G. Varney.	**139**
5.	ALLEN,	b. Aug. 10, 1823:	d. Sept. 25, 1824.	
6.	JOHN,	b. Sept. 25, 1828:	m. R. Hedman; Clara Walker.	**140**
7.	GEORGE,	b. Aug. 18, 1830:	m. Sarah S. Trowbridge.	**141**

---

67. HENRY ALLEN KINSMAN, son of William and Anna (p. 82), born in Gloucester, April 5, 1802; married in Salem, EDNAH JEWETT, June 23, 1830. His widow resides in Boston.

THEIR CHILD:

1. ELIZA A. H., b. : m. Edward R. Kimball, of Boston, 1848, and has a son, Henry Thurston, b. in Boston, Sept. 21, 1857. Mr. Kimball d. Nov. 17, 1869, and his widow resides in Boston.

---

68. NATHANIEL KINSMAN, son of Nathaniel and Priscilla (p. 84), born in Ipswich, Nov. 24, 1775; baptized there Dec. 3, 1775; married DEBORAH WEBB, March 10, 1797. She was born in Salem, Nov. 15, 1768, the daughter of Capt. Stephen and Mary (Manning) Webb.

He was a ship-master, and died in Salem, Nov. 17, 1808. His widow died there Feb. 5, 1850.

THEIR CHILDREN:

1.	NATHANIEL,	b. Feb. 6, 1798:	m. Rebecca Chase.	**142**
2.	MICHAEL,	b Feb. 24, 1800:	d. Sept. 12, 1801.	
3.	JOSHUA,	b. Aug. 12, 1801:	m Mary Brown.	**143**
4.	ELIZABETH,	b. Dec. 14, 1804:	m. John A. Southwick.	**144**
5.	MARY ANN,	b Jan. 3, 1807:	d. Sept. 5, 1830.	

69. JOHN CHOATE KINSMAN, son of Nathaniel and Elizabeth (p. 84), born in Ipswich, July 5, 1789; baptized there Sept. 6, 1789; married ANNA LORD, the daughter of Nathaniel and Lucy (Smith) Lord, of Ipswich.

He was a ship-master for thirty years, his family residing in Ipswich; removed to Salem in August, 1838, and engaged in business in Boston. She died in Salem, Feb. 21, 1874, aged 85 years 1 month 7 days. He is living in Salem.

THEIR CHILDREN:

1. JOHN, b. Sept. 3, 1810: m. Nancy B. Fogg; M. Lord. **145**
2. ELIZABETH, b. July 31, 1812: m. James L. Wells, of Charlestown, May 20, 1832.
3. LUCY ANN, b. Aug. 22, 1814: m. Nathaniel Pulsifer, Sept. 3, 1838; d. Feb. 21, 1844.
4. SUSAN CHOATE, b. Jan. 5, 1817: m. Israel Crafts, of Manchester, Oct. 19, 1834; d. Jan. 11, 1861.
5. NATHANIEL, b. June 6, 1819: m. Clarissa R. Hodgkins; Mary Kimball; Phebe S. Parker. **146**
6. MARY, b. Sept. 4, 1821: d. Sept. 23, 1821.
7. MARY, b. Nov. 24, 1822: m. Henry W. Farley; residence, Oswego, Ill.
8. MARTHA, b. May 14, 1829: d. June 11, 1845.

---

70. LUCY KINSMAN, daughter of Moses and Lucy (p. 84), born in Ipswich, Oct. 14, 1781; married AARON COGSWELL, May 20, 1802. Resided Essex, Mass., where she died, a widow, Oct. 22, 1874.

THEIR CHILDREN:

1. AARON, b. Feb. 21, 1807: m. Hannah B. Stacy, Feb. 21, 1837. Residence, Ipswich.
2. ALBERT, b. Oct. 9, 1810: m. Elizabeth Edwards, Dec. 25, 1849. Residence, Essex.
3. LUCY, b. July 14, 1813: m. Aaron L. Burnham; residence, Essex.
4. JONATHAN, b. March 5, 1820: unm.; residence, Essex.

71. JOSEPH KINSMAN, son of Moses and Lucy (p. 84), born in Ipswich, March 14, 1783; married EUNICE BROWN, May 18, 1809. They resided in Ipswich. He died May 30, 1855. She died July 18, 1855, aged 81.

THEIR CHILDREN:

1. JOSEPH, b. June 24, 1811: m. Mary E. Brown; Hannah S. Pert. **147**
2. ASA, b. Sept. 5, 1814: m. Caroline A. Parsons, May 1, 1858; has no children; residence, Ipswich.
3. EUNICE, b. Sept. 3, 1818: m. John Brown, Sept. 10, 1840.

---

72. FARLEY KINSMAN, son of Moses and Lucy (p. 84), born in Ipswich, Nov. 18, 1790; married in Gloucester, JERUSHA NORWOOD, March 27, 1823. He died in Gloucester, Sept. 26, 1825. Administration on his estate was granted to his widow Jerusha Kinsman and William Whipple, Esq., both of Gloucester, Nov. 15, 1825. [Essex Probate, 47 : 22.] They had one child that died in infancy. She has also deceased.

---

73. NATHANIEL KINSMAN, son of Aaron and Hannah (p. 85), born in Ipswich, Oct. 17, 1795; married JOANNA BROWN, Dec. 16, 1828. She was born in Ipswich, April 12, 1798, the daughter of Tristram and Joanna (Baker) Brown, and died July 28, 1832. He resided in Ipswich, and died July 18, 1864.

THEIR CHILDREN:

1. JOANNA, b. Oct. 25, 1829.
2. ABIGAIL, b. Oct. 9, 1831: m. Joseph Marshall. **148**

74. CHARLOTTE KINSMAN, daughter of Aaron and Hannah (p. 85), born in Ipswich, March 29, 1801; married ELISHA BROWN, July 1, 1840. He was born in Gloucester, Nov. 3, 1796, the son of Elisha and Martha Brown.

They resided in Ipswich, where she died March 29, 1860.

THEIR CHILDREN:

1. EVERETT KINSMAN, b. April 24, 1841: m. Margueretta Wilson, Nov. 24, 1870; residence, Ipswich.
2. CHARLOTTE ANNA, b. Jan. 17, 1843.
3. ELISHA NEWTON, b. June 18, 1845: m. Eliza Ann Philbrook, Nov. 30, 1871; residence, Ipswich.

---

75. JEREMIAH KINSMAN, son of Benjamin and Hannah (p. 86), born in Cornwallis, Kings County, N. S.; married there LAVINIA CLARK.

THEIR CHILDREN:

1. HENRY, b. : m Elizabeth Parker; had two children. She has deceased. He resides in Billtown, Cornwallis, N. S.
2. MARY ANN, b. : m. Daniel Mills; residence, Billtown.
3. LAVINIA, b. : m. Joshua Spicer; residence, Berwick, Cornwallis, N. S.
4. GIDEON, b. : unm.; residence, Billtown.
5. SARAH ALICE, b. : m. Major Messinger; residence, Bridgetown, Annapolis County, N. S.

---

76. BENJAMIN AVERY KINSMAN, son of Benjamin and Hannah (p. 86), born in Cornwallis, N. S., Dec. 2, 1787; married there MARY ENGLISH, Feb. 21, 1811. She was born Dec. 19, 1790, the daughter of Joel and Sarah (Lee) English, and died Nov. 14, 1830. Resided in Cornwallis. After the death of his wife, he went to Philadelphia, Pa.; married and had three children born there.

HIS CHILDREN BY MARY ENGLISH:

1.	Amarine,	b. April 1, 1812:	m. Charles Rumsey.	
2.	Danson,	b. April 23, 1813:	m. Eliz'th A. Douglas.	**149**
3.	Mary L.,	b. Feb. 23, 1815:	m. John P. Crowe.	**150**
4.	Sarah Jane,	b Feb. 6, 1817:	m. Joseph Rumsey.	
5.	Eunice,	b. March 10, 1819:	d. unmarried.	
6.	Eliza,	b. July 28, 1821:	m. William Douglas.	
7.	Avery Benjamin,	b. Feb. 12, 1824:	m. Ann M. Whitman.	**151**
8.	William Grandison,	b. March 15, 1826:	m. Sarah A. Porter.	**152**
9.	Lee English,	b. May 5, 1828:	m. Sarah Newcomb.	**153**

---

77. AMOS KINSMAN, son of Robert and Jerusha (p. 86), born in Cornwallis, Kings County, N. S., Sept. 18, 1774; married Abigail Chase, April 11, 1800, the daughter of Joseph and Hannah Chase. Residence, Cornwallis.

THEIR CHILDREN:

1. Joseph Charles, b. Jan. 10, 1803: m. Sarah Martin. **154**
2. Lydia, b. Jan. 21, 1805: m. Matthew Paton, Oct. 31, 1854. He was born in Scotland, May 3, 1800.
3. Esther, b. Jan. 4, 1807: m. Benjamin Burgess. **155**
4. Mary Jane, b. Nov. 18, 1808: m. Johnston Patterson. **156**
5. Olivia Ann, b. March 12, 1811: m. Isaac H. Newcomb. **157**
6. Hannah, b. March 14, 1813: m. Elias Calkins. **158**
7. Robert, b. Jan. 26, 1816.
8. Joshua, } Twins, b. Aug. 11, 1819: m. Mary A. Caldwell. **159**
9. David, } Twins, b. Aug. 11, 1819: m. Rachel Stronach, April 27, 1870; residence, Cornwallis, N. S.
10. Benjamin, b. June 5, 1821: m. Mary A. Burgess. **160**

---

78. JAMES KINSMAN, son of Robert and Jerusha (p. 86), born in Cornwallis, N. S., Dec. 14, 1780; married Dorothy Chase, April 5, 1804. She was born in Cornwallis, Nov. 22, 1784, the daughter of Stephen and Dorothy (Cone) Chase, and died Dec. 29, 1851. He resided in Cornwallis, and died Dec. 30, 1861.

THEIR CHILDREN:

1.	JETHRO,	b. June 2, 1805:	m. Rebecca Tupper.	**161**
2.	REBECCA,	b. Oct. 10, 1808:	m. William Foote.	**162**
3.	JERUSHA,	b. July 1, 1810:	d. July 1, 1811.	
4.	EPHRAIM,	b. Sept. 21, 1812:	m. Eunice Borden.	**163**
5.	ESTHER,	b. Aug. 31, 1815:	m. Nelson Patterson.	**164**
6.	THEODORUS,	b. Nov. 18, 1817:	m. Roxana Borden.	**165**
7.	JERUSHA,	b. Sept. 9, 1825:	m. Hugh Patterson.	**166**

---

79. MELATIAH KINSMAN, son of Robert and Mehitable (p. 86), born in Cornwallis, N. S., Aug. 13, 1783; married RHODA WRIGHT, March 10, 1809.

They resided in Cornwallis, where he died Dec. 14, 1830.

THEIR CHILDREN:

1.	JERUSHA,	b. Oct. 20, 1810.	
2.	TIRZA,	b. Sept. 13, 1812:	m. Elijah Caufield.
3.	ORSON O.,	b. Aug. 12, 1814.	
4.	MELATIAH,	b. Nov. 13, 1816.	
5.	JOHN N.,	b. Aug. 9, 1820.	
6.	SARAH M.,	b. Aug. 13, 1825:	m. —— Edgar; residence, Oskaloosa, Ia.

---

80. THEODORUS KINSMAN, son of Robert and Mehitable (p. 86), born in Cornwallis, N. S., June 11, 1792; married HANNAH KINSMAN, Sept. 29, 1818. She was born in Cornwallis, N. S., Nov. 22, 1798, the daughter of Ezekiel and Mary (Chase) Kinsman, and died April

24, 1828. He married, second, ESTHER NORTH, May 13, 1829. She was born in Cornwallis, N. S., Jan. 4, 1800, the daughter of William and Lois (Strong) North, and died Sept. 19, 1858.

They resided in Cornwallis, where he died Dec. 31, 1870.

HIS CHILDREN BY HANNAH KINSMAN:

1. MARY, b. Aug. 23, 1819: m. Kinsman Fuller, of Horton, Kings County, N. S., and died without issue, June 5, 1859.
2. REBECCA, b. March 31, 1821: m. Albert Chase, of Cornwallis, 1842.
3. MELATIAH, b. June 26, 1823: m. Margaret A. Parker; residence, Cornwallis, N. S.
4. SAMUEL, b. Feb. 28, 1825: m. Wilhelmina Rockwell; residence, Cornwallis, N. S.

HIS CHILDREN BY ESTHER NORTH:

5. OLIVIA ANN, b. March 4, 1830: m. John Rand. **167**
6. WILLIAM HENRY, b. July 11, 1832: graduated from Claverack Academy, in Claverack, Columbia County, N. Y., about 1857; studied law; admitted to practice in Council Bluffs, Ia.; when the war broke out, joined the army, rose to the rank of Colonel of the 23d Iowa Infantry, and fell in battle near Vicksburg, Miss., May 18, 1863, in Grant's army.
7. ROBERT N., } Twins, b. Dec. 11, 1834: m. Eliza A. Robinson. **168**
8. EZEKIEL N., } Twins, b. Dec. 11, 1834: m. Eliz'th Scribner. **169**
9. HANNAH ELIZABETH, b. Nov. 14, 1836: m. Henry Pineo. **170**
10. CHARLOTTE, b. Sept. 3, 1839: m. David Burgess. **171**
11. THEODORUS, b. June 21, 1843: residence, Cornwallis, N. S.

---

81. JOHN KINSMAN, son of Ebenezer? (p. 87), born in Nova Scotia; married SARAH HOLTON, of Northfield, Mass. When young he went to Orford, N. H., to reside with his aunt, the widow of Gove Spooner, of Vermont, where he remained until about 1830, when he moved to Thetford, Vt.

THEIR CHILDREN:

1. Samuel, b. : m. Mary Ann Jones, of Portsmouth, N. H.; second, Elizabeth H. Lyman, of Fitchburg. He lived in Lowell for many years, but died in Thetford, Vt., about 1865.
2. Caleb, b. : m. Eliza Benson. **172**
3. Sarah, b. : m. Feneman I. Howard, of Thetford, Vt.
4. Martha, b. : m. Uriel Hosford, of Thetford, Vt.
5. Mary, b. : m. Mason O. Mann, of Orford, N. H.
6. Elizabeth, b. : m. John Spalding, May 1, 1833. He was born Aug. 2, 1809; died in Pepperell, Mass., Feb. 11, 1860. She married, second, Samuel F. Warren, Feb. 7, 1872; residence, Townsend Harbor, Mass.
7. Joanna, b. : m. Cummings S. Taylor, of E. Thetford, Vt.
8. John, b. : m. Julia A. ——. **173**

---

82. EZEKIEL KINSMAN, son of Ebenezer? (p. 87), born in Cornwallis, N. S.; married Mary Neshert, and resided in Billtown, Cornwallis.

THEIR CHILD:

1. Daughter, b. : m. —— Caldwell, High Sheriff of Kings County, N. S.; residence, Billtown.

---

83. DANIEL KINSMAN, son of Ebenezer? (p. 87), born in Cornwallis, N. S., twin with Adolphus; married Mary Tupper, and resided in Billtown, Cornwallis.

THEIR CHILDREN:

1. Ephraim.
2. Jerusha.
3. Alpheus.
4. Ezekiel.

84. EBENEZER KINSMAN, son of Ebenezer? (p. 87), born in Cornwallis, N. S.; married MARY ELLS; lived Upper Dyke Village, Cornwallis.

THEIR CHILDREN:

1.	SARAH,	b.		: unm. 1870.	
2.	CATHARINE,	b.		: m. James Burbige.	
3.	ADOLPHUS,	b.	1811	: m. Rebecca Whiting.	174
4.	MEHITABEL,	b.		: m. George Morton.	
5.	JERUSHA,	b.		: m. John Kinsman.	
6.	LEMUEL,	b.		: m. Anna T. Newcomb; has no children; resided Cornwallis 1874.	
7.	JOHN,	b.			
8.	EBENEZER,	b.		: m. —— Rockwell.	
9.	THOMAS,	b.		: m. —— McFall.	

---

85. JOHN KINSMAN, son of John and Rebecca (p. 90), born in Lisbon, Ct., Sept. 20, 1793, and removed with his parents to Kinsman, O., in the summer of 1804. He married Mrs. JANE WILLIAMS CASS, April 28, 1846. She was the widow of John Jay Cass; her maiden name Townsend, the daughter of Walter Frost and Sarah Oakley (Williams) Townsend, of Huntington, L. I. He was a farmer and merchant of Kinsman, Ohio, and died Feb. 4, 1864. The following obituary notice was published at the time: —

"In Kinsman, Ohio, Feb. 4, 1864, of congestion of the lungs, John Kinsman, Esq., in his seventy-first year.

"The deceased, being identified with the early settlement of the Western Reserve from his youth, and possessed of much energy and capacity as a business man, soon became connected with many of the public and benevolent enterprises of the day, and devoted much of his time and means to the development of the resources of the country, administering largely by advice and means to the wants of those around him.

"In his extensive business, large credits were freely given to relieve the wants of the early settlers, at a time when such credits were deemed almost indispensable to their success. His position in society has been one of much prominence and usefulness, and his loss will be deeply felt by his numerous and devoted friends."

His widow is living in Kinsman, O.

THEIR CHILDREN:

1. Rebecca Perkins, b. Feb. 5, 1847.
2. John Townsend, b. Jan. 21, 1849.
3. Jane Augusta, b. Aug. 24, 1851.

---

86. JOSEPH KINSMAN, son of John and Rebecca (p. 90), born in Lisbon, Ct., March 8, 1795; was a young man of promise; prepared at Colchester, Ct., and entered Yale College. Through too close application to his studies, his constitution became enfeebled, and he was advised to leave for his health. He at once shipped to spend the winter at St. Thomas and St. Croix; returned to New York, quite reduced; was removed from there to Norwich, Ct., where he died of consumption.

The following inscription is there found on the tablet to his grave in the old town burial-ground: —

"Memory of Joseph Kinsman, son of John and Rebecca Kinsman, of the town of Kinsman, Ohio, and member of the Senior Class in Yale College, who died June 17, 1819, aged 24 years."

87. OLIVE DOUGLAS KINSMAN, daughter of John and Rebecca (p. 90), born in Lisbon, Ct., Oct. 4, 1800; married GEORGE SWIFT, Aug. 7, 1821, the son of Hon. Z. Swift,[1] of Windham, Ct.

He was an Attorney of good repute; resided in Kinsman, Trumbull County, Ohio, and represented that County in the State Legislature. She died June 24, 1835. He died March 14, 1845.

THEIR CHILDREN:

1. JULIA REBECCA, b. Aug. 28, 1825: m. Dr. Julius Harmon, July 30, 1857; resided in Warren, Ohio; d. Feb. 13, 1868.
2. GEORGE KINSMAN, b. Aug. 28, 1827: d. July 16, 1865.
3. MARIA PERKINS, b Feb. 20, 1829: m. Cook Fitch Kirtland, of Poland, Ohio, May 14, 1851. He was elected in October, 1871, State Representative from Mahoning County, Ohio. She d. Aug. 13, 1874.

---

88. THOMAS KINSMAN, son of John and Rebecca (p. 90), born in Kinsman, Ohio, Aug. 20, 1804; married SOPHIA BURNHAM, Dec. 29, 1847. She was born March 10, 1825, the daughter of Jedediah and Sophia (Bidwell) Burnham, of Kinsman.

He was one of the most extensive farmers in Northern Ohio. His lands, comprising about two thousand acres, were located in the townships of Kinsman and Gustavus. The fine quality of its soil, well-watered by springs and spring-brooks, its good timber, and well-arranged farm-buildings, made his farm one of the most attractive in the State. It was mostly under fine cultivation; a part being devoted to dairy purposes, the number of cows ranging from sixty to eighty each year; the balance to promiscuous

[1] Author of Swift's Digest.

farming. His large and well-bred Durham herd constituted at all times a prominent and attractive feature of his business. He died April 26, 1875. His widow survives him.

The following is from an obituary written at the time: —

"Died, of paralysis, in Kinsman, Ohio, April 26, 1875, Mr. THOMAS KINSMAN, in the 71st year of his age.

"Judge Kinsman, his father, was the original proprietor of the township that bears his name, to which place he removed from Lisbon, Connecticut, with his family, in 1804. The deceased was the first of the family born in Ohio. His life, as a citizen of the town, numbers more years than any one that has preceded him, and at his death he was the oldest *native* inhabitant. His life, from childhood to old age, has been peculiarly marked by kindly relations with all with whom he had to do. Buoyant in spirits, with a strong mind abounding in wit and humor, he drew around him a circle of friends; while his marked integrity, consistent Christian character, and a modesty that withheld him from any aspirations for fame or official position, rendered him prominent as a counsellor and adviser with his neighbors and friends, and in every work of progress or benevolence. He was eminently social and hospitable, easily approached, while his genial presence cheered every one who came under its influence. He was an affectionate and faithful husband and father, loving and devoted as few husbands and fathers are; alike true to his Christian professions and the church of which he was a devoted member and constant attendant."

THEIR CHILDREN:

1.	SOPHIA BURNHAM,	b. May 28, 1850.
2.	CORNELIA PEASE,	b. March 2, 1852.
3.	ELLEN D.,	b. April 27, 1854: d. Nov. 26, 1861.
4.	THOMAS,	b. May 21, 1857.
5.	ALFRED,	b. Oct. 22, 1858.
6.	MARY B.,	b. Nov. 17, 1862.

89. FREDERICK KINSMAN, son of John and Rebecca (p. 90), born in Kinsman, Ohio, March 4, 1807; married OLIVE DOUGLAS PERKINS, Feb. 1, 1832. She was born in Warren, Ohio, Jan. 31, 1809, the daughter of Gen. Simon and Nancy Anna (Bishop) Perkins, and died Sept. 13, 1838. He married, second, CORNELIA GRANGER PEASE,[1] March 25, 1840. She was born in Warren, Ohio, May 11, 1820, the daughter of Hon. Calvin and Laura Grant (Risley) Pease, and died Feb. 18, 1873.

Obituary notices of her life and character were published at the time in several of the papers. The following, dated Feb. 20, 1873, and copied from the "Cleveland Herald," expresses the universal sentiment, and is a just and truthful tribute to her memory: —

"'Death loves a shining mark.' Never was the truth of this saying more fully exemplified than in the death of Mrs. Cornelia Pease Kinsman, wife of Judge Frederick Kinsman, of Warren, who died very suddenly of apoplexy, on Tuesday morning, 18th inst. . . .

Mrs. Kinsman was the youngest daughter of the late Judge Calvin Pease, of Warren. . . .

"In all the relations of life, public as well as private, the deceased may be regarded as a woman of inestimable worth. She was a devoted wife, a loving, faithful mother, a steadfast friend, a warm-hearted, earnest Christian, a leader in the best society, of a cultivated and intelligent mind, great refinement of taste, always exerting her wide-spread influence in behalf of all that was true, beautiful, and good.

"For many years Mrs. Kinsman has been a communicant and leading member of Christ Church, Episcopal, of Warren, and in her death the church has been sadly bereft of

---

[1] See N. E. Hist Gen. Register, Vol. 3, p. 392, for her ancestry.

one of its brightest jewels. Whether as chief officer of the Church Aid Society, as teacher in the Sunday School, or in the discharge of any other of the multifarious Christian duties she assumed, she was ever at her post, earnest, faithful, never discouraged, self-denying, proving her faith by her good works, and setting an example well worthy of imitation. Truly may her sisters in Christ say, in the language of their beautiful service for the dead, 'We do give thee thanks, Almighty God, for the good example of this thy servant, who, having finished her course in faith, doth now rest from her labors.'

"But not within church circles alone were this estimable lady's good works confined. Her charity was as broad as community itself. Standing as it were at the head of Warren society, her influence was felt in every direction, and always for good. Possessed of wealth, it was freely devoted to offices of charity, and in the majority of cases she was her own almoner, being indefatigable in her efforts to search out and by personal visitation alleviate the wants of the poor and the needy. Every charitable and worthy project found in her a warm supporter.

"Especially during the present inclement winter, have her sympathies been enlisted in behalf of suffering humanity. The continued severity of the weather had made more needy than usual that unfortunate class of persons who always, more or less, depend upon charity. This fact seemed to arouse more keenly than ever the sympathies of this benevolent lady, so that, being to a great extent confined to her home by poor health, she converted that charming home into society work-rooms, and gathering there her lady friends, day after day was spent in making up bedding and all kinds of garments for the needy poor. The humbler classes of Warren have lost in this lady a generous friend, and if there was ever one in our midst whom they may 'rise up and call blessed,' surely it was she. That one so full of goodness, one whose daily life was so fragrant with the incense of unselfish deeds of love, should be stricken down in the full tide of usefulness, is one of those inscrutable providences which prove indeed that

"'God moves in a mysterious way,
His wonders to perform.'

"The funeral services, very sad and solemn, were conducted by the Rev. Samuel Maxwell, of St. John's Church, Youngstown; the Warren rector, Rev. Mr. Taylor, being absent from home. The interment took place in the beautiful family mound, at Oakwood Cemetery, on Thursday afternoon."

Residence, Warren, Trumbull County, Ohio.

HIS CHILDREN BY OLIVE D. PERKINS:

1. NANCY PERKINS, b. Nov. 14, 1832: d. Jan. 7, 1833.
2. THOMAS, b. Jan. 11, 1835: d. April 25, 1836.
3. OLIVE PERKINS, b. Sept. 10, 1837: d. July 20, 1838.

HIS CHILDREN BY CORNELIA G. PEASE:

4. FREDERICK, b. Aug. 26, 1841: m. Mary Louisa Marvin. **175**
5. JOHN, b. April 2, 1843: m. Mary Van Gorder. **176**
6. THOMAS, b. March 4, 1846.
7. CHARLES PEASE, b. Dec. 17, 1847.
8. HENRY PERKINS, b. Oct. 25, 1850.

---

90. SARAH KINSMAN, daughter of Jeremiah and Sarah (p. 90), born in Plainfield, Ct., Feb. 17, 1785; married Capt. ROSWELL ADAMS, Feb. 7, 1810.

He was a farmer of Lisbon, Ct., and was elected a Representative to the State Legislature in 1828. She died May 18, 1842. He died April 29, 1859.

THEIR CHILDREN:

1. SIBIL MARIA, b. June 20, 1811: m. Edw'd Spalding, of Brooklyn, Ct., May 4, 1841. She died Feb. 9, 1854. Their children: Maria Elizabeth, b. March 12, 1846; Henry Adams, b. Sept. 1, 1850.
2. THOMAS KINSMAN, b. July 8, 1813: m. Sarah F. Swift, of Mansfield, Ct., April 28, 1846. Residence, Detroit, Mich. Their children: Isabel Ripley, b. Dec. 13, 1847; William and Laura, b. July 8, 1849; Henry Kinsman, b. October, 1851; Sarah Swift, b. Sept. 25, 1853; Frederic Swift, b. September, 1856; Edward Thomas, b. July, 1860.
3. SUSANNAH, b. July 5, 1815: m. James Johnson, of Jewett City, Ct., Feb. 7, 1837.
4. WILLIAM, b. Sept. 5, 1817: d. Jan. 5, 1822.
5. EDWARD, b. Sept. 16, 1819: d. May 7, 1842.
6. SARAH DOUGLAS, b. Jan. 22, 1822: d. May 26, 1863.
7. MARY KINSMAN, b. Oct. 12, 1824: m. Henry A. Lathrop, of Griswold, Ct., Dec. 22, 1860. Their children: Edward Adams, b. Sept. 25, 1861; Sarah Greenleaf, b. Nov. 12, 1862; Lydia Campbell, b. Nov. 10, 1864.
8. JEREMIAH KINSMAN, b. Sept. 26, 1826: m. Eliza Angell, of Scituate, R. I., Sept. 12, 1852. Their children: Edward Adams, b March 17, 1854, d. October, 1862; Andrew Angell, b. March 27, 1857; Elizabeth, b. July, 1859; Caroline, b. October, 1862; Alice Rudd, b. January, 1864.

---

91. JOANNA KINSMAN, daughter of Jeremiah and Sarah (p. 90), born in Lisbon, Ct., Oct. 21, 1790; married BENJAMIN BACON, October, 1824. He was born May 11, 1798; was a farmer of Plainfield, Ct., and Representative to the State Legislature in 1837. She died Jan. 23, 1859. He died March 28, 1864.

THEIR CHILDREN:

1. SARAH DOUGLAS, b. Jan. 12, 1826: d. Oct. 17, 1848.
2. MARY JOANNA, b. Nov. 12, 1829: m. Marvin H. Sanger, of Canterbury, Ct., Nov. 14, 1855. Their children: Olive Douglas, b. Dec. 14, 1861; Harriet Bacon, b. May 21, 1866.
3. HARRIET, b. May 24, 1830: d. Oct. 22, 1867.
4. OLIVE D., b Aug. 14, 1831: d. March 4, 1837.
5. BENJAMIN, b. July 13, 1833: d. June 22, 1839.

SEVENTH GENERATION.

92. SAMUEL KINSMAN, son of William and Esther (p. 91), born in Ipswich, Oct. 22, 1785; married RACHEL CARTER, daughter of Obed Carter. Resided in Manchester, Mass., where he died May 3, 1845. His widow was living Nov. 8, 1858.

THEIR CHILDREN:

1. RACHEL C., b. June 16, 1811: m. Daniel Kelham. Residence, Manchester.
2. MARY, b. May 8, 1813: m. Abiel Eastman, of Concord, N. H. Resided in Lockport, Niagara Co., N. Y.
3. SAMUEL, b. April 12, 1815: m. Elizabeth R. Gifford. **177**
4. OBED CARTER, b. May 25, 1817: m. Lydia Danforth. She died Sept. 8, 1841, aged 29. He married, second, Evoline Bennett, of Manchester, who died Oct. 23, 1844, aged 29. He married, third, Mary Choate, of Essex. He died in Manchester, Aug. 12, 1850, leaving no issue. His widow married in Ipswich, John C. Wells, Sept. 30, 1851; resided in Manchester, 1861.
5. EBENEZER, b. Oct. 4, 1819: d. unmarried.
6. ELIZA A., b. April 21, 1825: m. John C. Wells. Residence, Amesbury.
7. GEORGE FRANKLIN, b. April 19, 1828: m. Elizabeth H. Haskell. Residence, Manchester.

---

93. MARY KINSMAN, daughter of William and Esther (p. 91), born in Ipswich, Oct. 2, 1787; married Deacon EPHRAIM ANNABLE, Dec. 27, 1808. He was born in Ipswich, March 23, 1786, the son of Robert and Sarah (Whipple) Annable. They resided in Hamilton. She died Oct. 13, 1868. He died Oct. 27, 1871.

THEIR CHILDREN:

1. WILLIAM, b. April 13, 1809: m. Betsey Malone, Apr. 1834. Resided in Boston, and died April 6, 1846.
2. EPHRAIM, b. July 12, 1811: m. Sarah Veal, June, 1833. Resided in Salem, and died Dec. 3, 1850.

3. Sarah, b. Feb. 5, 1814: d. Aug. 16, 1816.
4. Mary, b. July 9, 1816: m. James Patch, May 10, 1838. Residence, Lynn.
5. Abigail Brown, b. Dec. 17, 1818: d. unm. March 2, 1858.
6. Rufus Anderson, b. Sept. 15, 1821.
7. Ezra, b. Dec. 6, 1823: d. Jan. 4, 1824.
8. Esther Knowlton, b. Nov. 15, 1824: m. George Appleton, May 9, 1852. Residence, Haverhill.
9. Charles, b. Aug. 30, 1826: d. Jan. 3, 1827.
10. Charles, b. Oct. 26, 1827: m. Rebecca Adams, July 18, 1852. Residence, Salem.
11. Sarah, b. July 17, 1830: d. Dec. 25, 1832.

---

94. THOMAS KINSMAN, son of William and Esther (p. 91), born in Ipswich, June 22, 1789; married in Salem, Sally Patch, Sept. 17, 1815. They resided in Beverly. She died Sept. 12, 1850, aged 60 years 7 months. He died May 30, 1858.

THEIR CHILDREN:

1. Sarah, b. March, 1817: d. Feb. 28, 1842.
2. Ebenezer, b. Jan. 1819: d. May 17, 1824.
3. Joseph, b. Nov. 28, 1820: m. Sarah A. Pike; D. S. Steadman. **178**

---

95. WILLIAM KINSMAN, son of William and Esther (p. 91), born in Ipswich, Dec. 13, 1791; married in Salem, Hannah Shatswell, July 2, 1818. He resided for a time in Salem; removed to Watertown, and from thence to Boston, where he died Sept. 1, 1829. His widow married Daniel Rust, of Hamilton, Oct. 14, 1832, and died in Hamilton, Sept. 2, 1842.

THE CHILDREN OF WILLIAM AND HANNAH:

1. Susan Parsons, b. Jan. 26, 1819: m. John F. Harris. **179**
2. Mary Esther, b. Novem. 1821: d. Oct. 3, 1822.
3. William Henry, b. Oct. 2, 1824: m. Mehitable Miller. **180**

96. ESTHER KINSMAN, daughter of William and Esther (p. 91), born in Hamilton, July 1, 1793; married MOSES SANBORN, April 20, 1815. He was born in Kensington, N. H., Aug. 25, 1791; resided in Salem, Mass., Newark, O., and last in Cleveland, O., where he died May 17, 1870.

THEIR CHILDREN:

1. ESTHER, b. April 20, 1816: d. Dec. 22, 1816.
2. WILLIAM, b. Oct. 9, 1817: d. Oct. 10, 1817.
3. WILLIAM M., b. Jan. 15, 1819: m. Hannah S. Prime, Aug. 20, 1843; residence, Cleveland, O.
4. ESTHER A., b. Dec. 10, 1820: d. May 10, 1868.
5. HENRY, b. Nov. 10, 1822: d. Dec. 4, 1825.
6. CHARLES, b. Dec. 1, 1824: d. Dec. 4, 1825.
7. HENRY, b. Sept. 15, 1826: m. Louisa Downie; res. Chicago, Ill.
8. CHARLES, b. April 7, 1828: m. Lizzie Roland, May 31, 1867.
9. MARY J., b. Dec. 6, 1829: m. George H. Smith, Feb. 7, 1849; residence, Newark, O.
10. GEORGE L., b. Nov. 16, 1832: m. Marian Holstein, April 2, 1863; residence, Living Springs, near Denver, Colorado.
11. CARRIE A., b. Dec. 13, 1834: m. John C. Hale, Dec. 27, 1859; residence, Elyria, O.
12. HATTIE M., b. Nov. 18, 1837.
13. EVA, b. Nov. 22, 1839: m. Edwin C. Jewett, Dec. 16, 1863; residence, Elizabeth, N. J.

---

97. ELMINA KINSMAN, daughter of William and Esther (p. 91), born in Hamilton, Dec. 29, 1804; married in Salem, EZEKIEL ROBERTS, Oct. 14, 1824. He was born in Rochester, N. H., April 9, 1796, the son of Moses and Alice (Tebbets) Roberts. Resided in Salem. She died Aug. 2, 1866. He died Aug. 26, 1866.

THEIR CHILDREN:

1. ADALINE, b. April 11, 1825: residence, Salem.
2. MATILDA, b. Dec. 12, 1828: m. Thomas A. Owen, March 16, 1865; residence, Highland, Washington Co., Iowa.
3. EZEKIEL, b. Dec. 3, 1831: d. March 9, 1832.
4. ELMINA KINSMAN, b. July 4, 1833: residence, Salem.
5. WILLIAM KINSMAN, b. March 4, 1836: residence, Salem.
6. ALICE, b. June 23, 1844: d. Aug. 28, 1844.

98. LYDIA KINSMAN, daughter of Stephen and Elizabeth (p. 92), born in Hopkinton, Sept. 16, 1763; married in Springfield, N. H., JOHN MORRILL, Dec. 22, 1796. Settled in Springfield, N. H., where he died April 30, 1862.

THEIR CHILDREN:

1. STEPHEN, b. May 22, 1798: m. Susan Dean, Nov. 11, 1819.
2. LYDIA, b. Dec. 30, 1803.
3. HANNAH, b. Jan. 29, 1808.
4. JOHN, b. Dec. 7, 1810: residence, Springfield, N. H.
5. ENOS, b. Dec. 7, 1814: residence, Springfield, N. H.

---

99. AARON KINSMAN, son of Stephen and Elizabeth (p. 92), born in Hopkinton, June 27, 1765; married there POLLY MELLEN, Dec. 3, 1786. He is said to have resided in Batavia, and Silver Creek, Chautauque County, in New York State, and to have removed to Cleveland, Ohio.

THEIR CHILDREN:

1. NEWELL, b. Sept. 27, 1787: d. Nov. 28, 1787, in Hopkinton.
2. AARON, b. July 3, 1789: married, and settled May, 1836, in Norwalk, Huron Co., Ohio.
3. RHODA, b. Dec. 20, 1792.

---

100. BETSEY KINSMAN, daughter of Stephen and Elizabeth (p. 92), born in Hopkinton, May 27, 1767; married JASON WALKER, Feb. 25, 1790. He was born in Hopkinton, March 9, 1768. They resided in Hopkinton, where their children were born. He died Jan. 21, 1834. She died June 5, 1836.

THEIR CHILDREN:

1. BETSEY, b. Nov. 10, 1790: m. Ira Barney; resided in Danbury, N. H., where he died June 8, 1867, and she was living Dec. 1871.
2. JERUSHA, b. Jan. 9, 1793: m. Ira Pierce; residence, Lyman, N. H.

3. APPLETON, b. Sept. 13, 1795: d. unm. April 9, 1816.
4. WILLARD, b. March 17, 1798: m. Hannah Currier; resided Wilmot and Danbury, N. H. He d. March 15, 1861. She d. October, 1869.
5. ROXANA, b. Dec 7, 1800: m Bernard Currier; residence, Wilmot, N. H. He died Dec. 8, 1836. She died Nov. 29, 1846.
6. HARMONY, b. Feb. 7, 1803: m Hannah Palmer; res., Haverhill.
7. SABRINA, b. May 4, 1805: unm.; residence Grafton, N. H.
8. LENITY, b. Oct. 7, 1807: m. Robinson Dean; residence, Grafton, N. H.
9. ALANSON, b. July 12, 1811: m. Anna Williams; residence, Grafton, N. H.

---

101. ISAAC KINSMAN, son of Stephen and Elizabeth (p. 92), born in Hopkinton, June 12, 1769; married MARY MURRAY, January, 1800. She was born in Bangor, Me., May 15, 1777, the daughter of James and Elizabeth (Durum) Murray. She removed to New Chester (now Hill), N. H., where they were married. They resided in Wilmot, N. H., where most of their children were born, and where he died Oct. 6, 1827. His widow died in Andover, N. H., May 15, 1855.

THEIR CHILDREN:

1. BETSEY, b. Feb. 1, 1801: m. John Moody. **181**
2. CARYL, b. Novem. 1802: d. September, 1805.
3. MARY, b. Oct. 25, 1804: m. Rev. Nathan Howard. March 19, 1844, then pastor of the Congregational Church in Andover, N. H. He was born in Grantham, N. H; graduated at Gilmanton Theological Seminary; settled in Andover, N. H., 1842. In the winter of 1855 he had a severe attack of bronchitis, and was obliged to leave the ministry. In October of the same year, hoping to benefit his health, he visited Mechanicsburg, Champaign County, Ohio, and has remained there to the present time. Mrs. Howard has the family record of her grandfather, Stephen Kinsman, in his own handwriting.
4. ISAAC, b. Sept. 12, 1812: graduated at Dartmouth College 1837; was preceptor of an academy at Pembroke, N. H., where he died unmarried, Oct. 28, 1843. As a tribute to his memory, the students erected a monument over his grave.
5. EMILY JANE, b. July 19, 1825: m. Frederick W. Greenough. **182**

102. ASA KINSMAN, son of Stephen and Elizabeth (p. 92), born in Hopkinton, Nov. 18, 1771; married SUSAN MURRAY. She was born in Derry, N. H., April 29, 1773, the daughter of William and Jane (Talford) Murray. They resided in Springfield, N. H., and New Chester (now Hill), N. H., where both died; she died Feb. 11, 1853.

THEIR CHILDREN:

1. LUCY, b. Jan. 9, 1798: m. Otis Barney. **183**
2. JANE T., b. March 2, 1800: m. Samuel E. Wyman. **184**
3. STEPHEN, b. June 11, 1802: m. Sophia Dundee. **185**
4. LYDIA M., b. Jan 22, 1805: m. Samuel P. Flanders. **186**
5. SUSAN, b. Nov. 27, 1807: m. Austin Lovering. **187**

---

103. JOHN KINSMAN, son of Stephen and Elizabeth (p. 92), born in Hopkinton, March 8, 1774; married SUSAN LUMBARD, in 1801. He was an under-graduate of Dartmouth College; practised medicine in Grafton, Lebanon, Orange, and Wilmot, N. H. Removed to Portsmouth, N. H., in 1840.

He died in Malden, Oct. 21, 1856. His widow died in Campton, N. H., Jan. 8, 1867, aged 85 years 8 months 14 days.

THEIR CHILDREN:

1. EZOA, b. July 25, 1803: m. John Barsantee. **188**
2. ORREN, b. 1805: d. October, 1807.
3. ELIZABETH, b. Feb. 8, 1807: m. Daniel B. Knox. **189**
4. JOHN JACKSON, b. 1809: m. Elizabeth Brown, of Hampton. He died April, 1836.
5. ADALINE, b. 1811: m , 1st, Nelson Barney; m., 2d, Aaron Douglass. Four children: Loring, Orren, Alanson, and Artemisia, by Nelson Barney. One child: Aaron, by Aaron Douglass.
6. ARTEMISIA R., b. Nov. 26, 1812: m. Elijah Rollins. **190**
7. STEPHEN DECATUR, b. 1816: m. Belinda Rowe; residence, Campton, N. H.
8. MOSES G., b. 1818: d. Nov. 12, 1829.
9. JAMES W., b. 1822: d. Oct. 7, 1827.

104. MOSES KINSMAN, son of Stephen and Elizabeth (p. 92), born in Hopkinton, March 6, 1784; married ABIGAIL WOOD, of Grafton, N. H., Jan. 1, 1805. She was born in Weare, N. H., July 5, 1782.

They resided in Springfield, and Wilmot, N. H., and lastly in Magog, Canada East, where she died May 24, 1867, and he died Oct. 4, 1870.

THEIR CHILDREN:

1. SOLON, b. July 5, 1806: m. L. Cook; L. F. Fletcher. **191**
2. DURA, b. July 5, 1808: m. M. Town; Z. Jones. **192**
3. CARYL, b. June 9, 1810: m. Lydia Carr. **193**
4. ERASTUS, b. May 2, 1812: d. unm. Sept. 18, 1837.
5. ELMINA, b. Aug. 18, 1814: m Caleb Carr. **194**
6. SARAH ANN, b. Oct. 3, 1816: m. Joshua Whitney. **195**
7. MALCOLM G, b. April 22, 1819: married; died on ship from Fortress Monroe, Jan. 8, 1863. His widow resided West Rochester, Vt.
8. MARY FREELOVE, b. April 17, 1823: m. William L. Bacon. **196**
9. GEORGE WASHINGTON, b. Feb. 6, 1825: m Abby P. Coolidge. **197**

---

105. STEPHEN KINSMAN, son of Nathan and Elizabeth (p. 93), born in Concord, N. H., Aug. 14, 1773; married RUTH F. OSGOOD, Nov. 25, 1802. She was born June 8, 1788, the daughter of John and Rachel (Lindsay) Osgood, of Pelham, N. H., and died Jan. 31, 1854. Resided in Landaff, N. H., and Clifton, Sherbrooke, Canada East, where he died Sept. 30, 1866.

THEIR CHILDREN:

1. ELIZABETH S., b. Jan. 29, 1806: m. Amasa T. Martin. **198**
2. EVELINA, b. June 1, 1808: m. William Little. **199**
3. HIRAM, b. March 29, 1810: m. A. E. Gilman; J. Skinner. **200**
4. PHILONAS, b. July 7, 1812: m. Adaline Shurtleff. **201**
5. MARY S., b. April 30, 1815: lives in Cambridgeport.
6. HARRIET, b. April 18, 1817: m. John Colby; C. Taplin. **202**
7. DAVID OSGOOD, b. July 22, 1819: m. R. A. Gilbert; E. Cheever. **203**
8. MARTHA R., b. Jan. 20, 1822: d. unm. Jan. 13, 1847.

9. Timothy, b. Sept. 21, 1824: d. Feb. 16, 1832.
10. John Osgood, b. Jan. 1, 1827: m. M. H. Magill; O. C Potter. **204**
11. Stephen, b. May 3, 1828: d. Feb. 23, 1832.
12. Lydia B., b. March 9, 1831: d. May 14, 1832.

---

106. NATHAN KINSMAN, son of Nathan and Elizabeth (p. 93), born in Concord, N. H., Nov. 14, 1777; married in Portland, Me., Eliza Dafforne, Sept. 26, 1802. She was born in Boston, Feb. 14, 1781, the daughter of John and Betsey (Ingersoll) Dafforne, and died in Portland, Me., June 28, 1841.

"Nathan Kinsman graduated at Dartmouth College in 1799, and studied law in the office of the late Chief-Justice Parker. He was admitted to the bar in Cumberland County, Maine, in 1803, and opened an office in Portland, where he continued until his lamented death, Feb. 26, 1829. Mr. Kinsman had a very extensive practice for many years, and more particularly in 1807, and subsequently in what were commonly called Embargo cases, in which he was more employed than all the other lawyers in Maine." [Amer. Quart. Reg., Vol. 12, page 282.] He was elected, in 1819, to represent Portland in the State Legislature.

THEIR CHILDREN:

1. John Dafforne, b. Oct. 13, 1805: m. Angela R. Cutter. **205**
2. Elizabeth Dafforne, b. Jan. 28, 1807: d. unm. in Portland, Me., June 8, 1831.
3. Martha, b. May 18, 1809: d. unm. June 28, 1841.
4. Elinor, b. July 12, 1812: residence, Danville, Me.

Son and four daughters born and died in infancy.

---

107. PETER KINSMAN, son of Nathan and Elizabeth (p. 93), born in Concord, N. H., Nov. 23, 1779; married

Mary Raymond, of Concord, N. H. She was born June 16, 1789, the daughter of William and Lydia Raymond.

He was a farmer, and settled on the place of his father in Landaff, N. H., where he died Dec. 24, 1838. His widow survived him, 1872.

THEIR CHILDREN:

1. Nathan, b. October, 1806: d. Aug. 11, 1809.
2. Eliza, b. Feb. 25, 1811: m. Bemsley Edwards. **206**

---

108. MARTHA KINSMAN, daughter of Nathan and Elizabeth (p. 93), born in Concord, N. H., Oct. 9, 1781; married Nathan Robbins, Feb. 14, 1810. He was born May 5, 1785, the son of Ephraim and Hannah Robbins. She died Aug. 27, 1831. (He married, second, Widow Abigail Culver, Feb. 14, 1833, and resides in Bridgewater.)

THEIR CHILDREN:

1. Eliza Kinsman, b. Aug. 14, 1812: m. George W. Holmes, of Bridgewater, May 12, 1857.
2. Huldah, b. Feb. 7, 1815: d. June 14, 1852.
3. Nathan Kinsman, b. Aug. 22, 1819: m. Fidelia C. Foster, Feb. 14, 1849. She died April 11, 1850, aged 26.

---

109. TIMOTHY KINSMAN, son of Nathan and Elizabeth (p. 93), born in Landaff, N. H., Aug. 17, 1783; married Lucy Stearns Abbott, of Bedford, Mass., March 17, 1808. She was born Feb. 11, 1792, the daughter of Moses and Alice Abbott. He died in Bedford, Feb. 26, 1826. His widow died in Boston, May 15, 1868.

THEIR CHILDREN:

1. George Shattuck, b. Aug. 5, 1809: m. Nancy S. Holden. **207**
2. Lucy Angelina, b. Sept. 8, 1811: m. Alfred Mudge. **208**
3. Alice Eliza, b. July 24, 1813: m. Benjamin Bradley. **209**
4. Martha Maria, b. April 20, 1815: m. Benjamin Bradley. **210**
5. Moses Abbott, b. March 5, 1817: d. Oct. 24, 1842.

110. AARON KINSMAN, son of Aaron and Rose (p. 93), born in Ipswich; baptized there Oct. 12, 1766; married HANNAH CRANE, of Hanover, N. H.; published in Concord, N. H., Jan. 23, 1790. She deceased, and he married, second, ANN WILLIS, June 11, 1802. She was born in Haverhill, Mass., Aug. 4, 1778, the daughter of Benjamin and Mary (Ball) Willis. Her Will dated at Groton, Middlesex Co., Mass., April 28, 1837; proved April, 1844; recorded Essex Probate, 130 : 141.

He graduated at Dartmouth College, in 1787. While there he procured from Harvard and Yale the charter of Alpha Chapter, New Hampshire, of the Phi Beta Kappa Society, for Dartmouth, and was its first President.

He studied medicine, and began practice in Portland, Me., where he attained a high place in the profession. He died in Portland, May 11, 1808.

HIS CHILDREN BY ANN WILLIS:

1. HENRY WILLIS, b. March 6, 1803: m. E. Willis; M. F. Titcomb. **211**
2. BENJAMIN WILLIS, b. : d. unm. May 15, 1833. Administration on the estate of "Benjamin W. Kinsman, late an Officer in the army of the United States of America, who died at Cantonment Gibson, a Military Post without the jurisdiction of any of the States in the Union," was granted to his brother Henry W. Kinsman, of Boston, June 10, 1833. [Suffolk Probate Files.]
3. ANN, b. 1808: m. Rev. D. Phelps, 1832. **212**

---

111. MARY KINSMAN, daughter of Aaron and Rose (p. 93), married THOMAS STEARNS SPARHAWK, May, 1797, when she was residing in Hanover, N. H. He was born in Templeton, Mass., in 1769, son of Rev. Ebenezer Sparhawk.

He received a part of his education at Dartmouth, and obtained the degree of Bachelor of Arts, 1791. Studied law, and was admitted to practise in the Judicial Courts in Massachusetts in 1796. Resided in Bucksport, Me., and died in 1807. She was living in Boston, April 28, 1837.

THEIR CHILDREN:

1. WILLIAM, b. : lost at sea.
2. EDWARD VERNON, b. : resided for a time in Montreal; afterwards became editor of a paper in Richmond, Va.
3. GEORGE, b. : editor of the "Oakland Whig," in Pontiac, Mich., 1863.
4. MARIA LOUISA, b. : m. Charles Fox, of Boston; she was the author of several works.
5. LUCIA K., b. : unmarried.

111½. JOHN KINSMAN, son of Rev. Ebenezer P. (bapt. Feb. 19, 1758: see p. 76)[1] and Susannah (Frost) Kinsman, born in Limerick, Me., Oct. 11, 1800; married, in Skowhegan, Me., SARAH B. CHANDLER, of Raymond, N. H., Sept. 30, 1830. She was born June, 1813, and died Oct. 18, 1864.

THEIR CHILDREN:

1. CHANDLER, b. July 21, 1831: d. March, 1866.
2. FRANK W., b. Jan. 5, 1833: m. Octavia A. Greely. 212½

---

112. MARY KINSMAN, daughter of Ephraim and Mary (p. 94), born in Hanover, N. H., Oct. 22, 1777; married MOSES REED, March 4, 1800. He was born in Lexington, Mass., Aug. 10, 1773, the son of Moses and Sarah (Whittemore) Reed, and removed with his father to Grafton, N. H. After their marriage, they settled in Williamstown, Vt., and in 1815 removed to Chester, Meigs Co., Ohio, where he died Aug. 29, 1824. She also died there Oct. 16, 1839.

---

[1] The other children of Rev. Ebenezer P. Kinsman were, Thomas F. and Calvin, deceased; Eliza, Susan, Ebenezer, Mary, and Hannah, living.

THEIR CHILDREN:

1. Alpha, b. Dec. 8, 1800: d. unm. in Virginia, 1837.
2. Laurilla, b July 2, 1803: m. Marcus Bosworth, Dec. 11, 1825; residence, College Hill, Hamilton Co., Ohio.
3. Samantha, b. April 12, 1806: m. John McDonald, Aug. 14, 1832; residence, Galena, Ill.
4. Emily, b. Feb. 4, 1809: m. Joseph Higley, April 13, 1831. He died in Indiana in 1840. She married, second, Phineas Robinson, March 28, 1848; residence, Chester, Ohio.
5. Mary, b. April 25, 1811: m. Harold Wells, Dec. 15, 1836; residence, Chester, Ohio.
6. John L., b. March 31, 1813: m. Sarah Lambert, 1845; residence, Davenport, Iowa.
7. Lucena, b. May 16, 1816: m. Myron Wells, March 4, 1838; residence, Chester, Ohio.
8. George M., b. Oct. 1, 1818: m. Indie Lodge, June 1, 1854; died in Madison, Indiana, Sept. 28, 1857.

---

113. SARAH KINSMAN, daughter of Ephraim and Mary (p. 94), born in Springfield, N. H., June 23, 1781; married Moses Dickerson. He was born in Rowley, Mass., June 12, 1774, the son of Moses Dickerson. They resided in Hill, N. H.

She died Feb. 8, 1842. He died July 12, 1852.

THEIR CHILDREN:

1. Sewell, b. Oct. 7, 1799: m. Hannah Dickerson; residence, Hill, N. H.
2. Watson, b. Feb. 5, 1801: m. Sarah Emery, May 17, 1829. She died Sept. 9, 1868. He m., 2d, Deborah Daniels, Nov. 13, 1869. Residence, East Andover, N. H.
3. John, b. Aug. 11, 1803: m. Adaline Taylor; d. Sept. 21, 1867.
4. Ariel, b. Aug. 20, 1805: m. ——; residence, Bristol.
5. Polly, b. Oct. 13, 1807: m. Nason Martin; d. Oct. 2, 1848.
6. Amos, b. April 3, 1811: d. Nov. 15, 1811.
7. Amos, b. March 7, 1815: m. Huldah Bartlett; d. Jan. 23, 1864.
8. Sabra, b. Oct. 25, 1817: m. John Clement.
9. Sally K., b. Jan. 4, 1820: m. Julius A. Kinsman, son of Ephraim (117) and Rebecca (Dow) Kinsman; residence, Sacramento, Cal.

114. ISAAC KINSMAN, son of Ephraim and Mary (p. 94), born in Springfield, N. H., May 18, 1783; married MATILDA KNAPP, July 9, 1806. She was born March 17, 1787. Resided in Northfield, Washington Co., Vermont. She died April 14, 1855. He died Jan. 22, 1867.

THEIR CHILDREN:

1. NELSON, b. March 9, 1808: m. Lydia Edwards. **213**
2. PHILURA, b. July 25, 1813: m. Roswell Carpenter. **214**
3. ZILPHA, b. Oct. 7, 1815: m. William D. Balch. **215**
4. MARY, b. March 15, 1818.
5. LUCY A., b. May 25, 1820: m. John H. Davis. **216**
6. DIANTHA, b. June 14, 1824: m. Nathan F. Sargeant. **217**

---

115. JAMES HALL KINSMAN, son of Ephraim and Mary (p. 94), born in Springfield, N. H., March 11, 1786; married in Williamstown, Vt., SARAH ROBINSON, in 1812. She was born in Putney, Vt., Jan. 14, 1784, the daughter of Solomon and Abigail Robinson. Resided in Williamstown, Vt., where all the children were born. He died in Princeton, Bureau Co., Ill., in February, 1853. His widow died in Sheffield, Bureau Co., Ill., June 28, 1866.

THEIR CHILDREN:

1. JAMES WATSON, b. Nov. 3, 1814: m. Rocina C. Martin. **218**
2. EMILY WHEELOCK, b. July 13, 1816: m. Egbert E. Colton. **219**
3. DENISON, b. July 6, 1818: m. Mary Martin; L. Burnham. **220**
4. AARON BOADWIN, b. Jan. 16, 1820: m. Louisa S. Hatch. **221**
5. MARSHALL CROYDON, b. Sept. 7, 1822: m. Ellen C. Luce; Sarah J. Snow. **222**
6. MARY LOUISA, b. March 22, 1824: m. Robert Tonkinson. **223**
7. NEWELL, b. Dec. 30, 1825: m. Ellen F. Cobb. **224**
8. MARTHA ANN, b. Nov. 30, 1827: d. Feb. 23, 1862, in Princeton, Ill.
9. LUCIUS, b. March 19, 1830.

116. AARON BODON KINSMAN, son of Ephraim and Mary (p. 94), born in Springfield, N. H., Dec. 25, 1789; married OLIVE MARTIN, March 13, 1811. She died Sept. 27, 1866. He married, second, JULIA GERTRUDE WEBSTER, Dec. 25, 1866. "He was ordained as an Evangelist, a travelling preacher; preached to all denominations of Christians over nearly one half of the States."

Residence, Williamstown, Vt.

HIS CHILD BY JULIA G. WEBSTER:

1. GEORGE AARON, b. July 15, 1868.

---

117. EPHRAIM KINSMAN, son of Ephraim and Mary (p. 94), born in Springfield, N. H., May 2, 1792; married in Plainfield, N. H., REBECCA DOW, Feb. 2, 1817. She was born in Plainfield, N. H., Aug. 17, 1793, the daughter of Gideon and Sarah Dow. She died July 4, 1855. He married, second, SARAH (WOODWARD) DANIELS, Sept. 3, 1857, the widow of John Daniels.

Residence, West Lebanon, N. H.

HIS CHILDREN BY REBECCA DOW:

1. WILLIAM M., b. Nov. 17, 1817: m. Maria Dean. **225**
2. FRANCIS S., b. March 2, 1820: m Susan K. Miller. **226**
3. JULIUS A., b. Jan. 8, 1822: m. Sally K. Dickerson, daughter of Moses and Sarah (Kinsman) Dickerson (113); res., Sacramento, Cal.
4. GIDEON D., b. March 23, 1824: unm.; residence, W. Lebanon, N. H.
5. MINERVA, b. March 21, 1826: m. Oliver M. Harding, Nov. 27, 1851; residence, Lowell, Mass.
6. LEWIS D., b. March 15, 1828: d. Dec. 11, 1859.
7. CHARLES A., b. April 5, 1830: d. Oct. 8, 1863
8. MARY S., } Twins, { d Sept. 29, 1865.
9. MARTHA P., } b. July 24, 1833: { m. Otis H. Chellis, Nov. 27, 1851; died without issue, Dec. 8, 1855.

118. NEWELL KINSMAN, son of Ephraim and Mary (p. 94), born in Springfield, N. H., June 21, 1795; married in Barre, Vt., LEONORA LAMB, Sept. 10, 1828. She was born in Hancock, Vt., March 8, 1810, the daughter of Reuben Lamb. They resided in Barre, Vt., where all their children were born. She died in Cleveland, Ohio, June 15, 1856. He died in Montpelier, Vt., Dec. 25, 1858. All of the family who have died are buried in "Green Mount Cemetery," Montpelier.

THEIR CHILDREN:

1. GEORGE LAMB, b. July 18, 1829: m. Ann E. Hubbard; Mary J. Moses. **227**
2. EDWARD CENTER, b. Aug. 11, 1831: graduated at Dartmouth College in 1852; d. in Cincinnati, O., Jan. 25, 1871.
3. ELLEN ALANTHA, b. Dec. 16, 1833: d. in Barre, Vt., May 26, 1852.

---

119. WILLIS KINSMAN, son of Ephraim and Mary (p. 94), born in Springfield, N. H., July 17, 1798; married in Hanover, N. H., FANNIE WARREN, March 3, 1824. She was born in Walpole, N. H., April 10, 1794, the daughter of Winslow and Sarah (Webber) Warren. Soon after their marriage they removed to Royalton, Vt., and remained there ten years; then removed to Hartford, Ct., where they now reside.

THEIR CHILDREN:

1. HENRY WILLIS, b. Jan. 30, 1825: m. Eliza W. Teafe; have no children; residence, Charleston, S. C.
2. SUMNER, b. Jan. 23, 1826: d. in California, June 3, 1851.
3. NORMAN WEBBER, b. Nov. 21, 1828: m. Fannie Sharrott; have no children; residence, Charleston, S. C.
4. WARREN, b. July 3, 1830: m. M. Ryan; Annie Ryan. **228**
5. SARAH, b. July 6, 1832: unm.; residence, Hartford, Ct.
6. FRANCES, b. Nov. 26, 1834: m. Monroe E. Merrill. **229**

120. SAMUEL KINSMAN, son of Daniel and Abigail (p. 95), born in Barre, Mass., March 1, 1769; married KEZIA NEWTON, Jan. 18, 1793. She was born in Southborough, Mass., Aug. 8, 1773.

He removed from Hubbardston, his father's residence, to Heath, Mass., about 1798, where his wife died March 22, 1829, and he died Sept. 4, 1839.

THEIR CHILDREN:

1. SUSANNA, b. April 18, 1795: d. Oct. 28, 1797.
2. LUCY, b. Aug. 14, 1797: m. Hiram Buck; d. in N. Y. State.
3. DAVID, b April 3, 1800: m. Sally Elliott; res., Greene, N.Y.
4. TITUS, b. June 25, 1802: m. Annise Elliott, of Leyden, Mass. She d. Sept. 9, 1871. He resides Diana, N. Y.
5. BLISS, b. May 1, 1804: m. Betsey Temple. **230**
6. CLARISSA, b. April 28, 1806: m. Nathan Elliott. He has deceased, and she resides with her son Nathan, in Natick.
7. SAMUEL AUSTIN, b. Jan. 24, 1808: m C. Barr; B H. Rice. **231**
8. KEZIA, b. Jan. 2, 1810: m. Eliphalet Howe. **232**
9. MERCY, b. Nov. 26, 1811: m Joseph H. Scott, of Coventry, N. Y. She d. in Oakland, Indiana.
10. ROXANA, b. Dec. 17, 1814: m. Miletus Henry. **233**

---

121. DAVID KINSMAN, son of Daniel and Abigail (p. 95), born in Hubbardston, Mass.; married ABIGAIL PUTNAM, of Shelburne, Mass. Settled in Heath, Mass., where he died before 1839.

THEIR CHILDREN:

1. ELIZA, 2. PHEBE, 3. HANNAH, 4. MARY, 5. ABIGAIL, } Living, 1832.

6. ADDISON, 7. SAMUEL, 8. DAVID, 9. CALVIN, 10. WILLIAM, } Living, 1832.

11. EASTMAN; living, 1837.

122. JOSEPH KINSMAN, son of Daniel and Abigail (p. 95), born in Hubbardston, Mass., Aug. 14, 1782; married KEZIA BANGS, April 29, 1804. She was born in Warwick, Mass., July 22, 1777, the daughter of Isaiah and Leah (Vining) Bangs, and died Nov. 4, 1860.

He settled in Heath, Mass., where he remained until March, 1826; then removed to Shrewsbury, Rutland Co., Vt., where he died Nov. 24, 1863.

THEIR CHILDREN:

1.	ADNAH BANGS,	b. May 9, 1805:	m. Asenath M. Chandler.	**234**
2.	DIANA,	b. Oct. 16, 1807:	m. Gardner Bullard.	**235**
3.	ELVIRA,	b. Oct. 15, 1809:	m. Joseph Kinsman (238).	
4.	JOHN,	b. July 22, 1811:	m. Lucy A. Greeley.	**236**
5.	SARAH,	b. May 26, 1815:	d. May 23, 1816.	
6.	JAMES A.,	b. March 28, 1817:	m. Hannah M. Holden.	**237**
7.	NANCY B.,	b. July 1, 1821:	m. John M. Kinsman (240).	

---

123. JOHN KINSMAN, son of Daniel and Abigail (p. 95), born in Hubbardston, Mass., Aug. 14, 1782; married in Templeton, Mass., EUNICE MERRITT, May, 1807. She was born in Templeton in 1774, and died in Shrewsbury, Vt., Feb. 15, 1832. He married, second, in Sudbury, Vt., ANNA MERRITT, March 8, 1833. She was born in Sudbury, January, 1791, the daughter of Noadiah Merritt. Residence, Potsdam, N. Y., where she died Feb. 7, 1871. He adopted a son, naming him Erbon Kinsman, who settled in Clarendon, Vt., and whose descendants are numerous.

HIS CHILDREN BY EUNICE MERRITT:

1.	JOSEPH,	b. Nov. 9, 1809:	m. Elvira Kinsman.	**238**
2.	PARKER,	b. Jan. 26, 1811:	m. H. E. Holden; M. A. Fairbank.	**239**
3.	JOHN M.,	b. June 9, 1816:	m. N. B. Kinsman; D. A. Foote.	**240**
4.	EUNICE A.,	b. Sept. 20, 1819:	unm.; residence, Potsdam, N. Y.	

124. JAMES KINSMAN, son of Daniel and Abigail (p. 95), born in Hubbardston, Mass., July 7, 1783; married NANCY MILLER, 1805. She was born in Hubbardston, Jan. 17, 1783. They resided for a time in Hubbardston, and removed from there to Shrewsbury, Vt., where they lived until 1812; then settled in Darien, Genesee Co., N. Y. She died there July 23, 1825. He married, second, —— LINCOLN. In February, 1837, he removed to Milford, Oakland Co., Mich., where he died July 19, 1846. His widow died August, 1871, aged 90 years.

HIS CHILDREN BY NANCY MILLER:

1. LUCY, b. May 18, 1806: m. Eli Rich; residence, Napierville, Du Page Co., Ill.
2. MARY ANN, b. Jan. 29, 1809: m. Daniel W. Jefferson. **241**
3. ELISHA, b. Jan. 17, 1812: m. L. Hoyle; A.E. Benjamin. **242**
4. HARRIET, b. Aug. 27, 1813: m. —— Kimball, who has deceased. She resides Watseka, Ill.
5. NANCY, b. Jan. 4, 1816: d. July 23, 1823.
6. SOPHRONIA, b. Feb. 20, 1818: married, and is a widow; resides Corunna, Shiawassee Co., Michigan.
7. WILLIAM MILLER, b June 20, 1820: m. Sarah J. Munn. **243**
8. SAUL, b. Dec. 24, 1822: m. Mary A. Voorheis. **244**
9. JOHN CLINTON, b. Jan. 11, 1825: m., in Farmington, Oakland Co, Mich, Elsie M. Reed. She was born in Goshen, Orange Co., N. Y., Jan. 14, 1825, the daughter of William and Elizabeth Reed. They reside at the homestead in Milford; have adopted two sons.

---

125. LYDIA KINSMAN, daughter of Jeremiah and Martha (p. 95), born in Ipswich, July 7, 1772; married EPHRAIM GIBSON, Aug. 29, 1795. He was born Nov. 10, 1767. Resided in Fitchburg, Mass. He died Sept. 7, 1844. She died Sept. 3, 1863.

THEIR CHILDREN:

1. LYDIA, b. March 18, 1799: d. Nov. 29, 1819.
2. EUNICE, b. April 6, 1801: m. Abram Bennett; Fitchburg.
3. ARINGTON, b. April 3, 1803: m. Susan Weston; Fitchburg.

4. Ephraim, b. April 17, 1806: m. Mary Brown; Ashby.
5. Lucy, b. June 26, 1808: m. C. Stephens; Townsend.
6. Mary Ann, b. Aug. 18, 1812: m. Isaac D. Wiswell, of Fitchburg, Dec. 19, 1848.
7. Jeremiah Kinsman, b. July 4, 1815: m. Loenza C. Gibson; Ashby.

---

126. JEREMIAH KINSMAN, son of Jeremiah and Martha (p. 95), born in Ipswich, Aug. 19, 1775; married Olive Messinger, Aug. 31, 1798. She was born June 26, 1778, the daughter of Thomas and Olive Messinger, of Fitchburg. Resided in Fitchburg, where he died July 14, 1857, and she died Nov. 5, 1857.

THEIR CHILDREN:

1. Susan, b. Jan. 3, 1800: m. Stephen Lowe. **245**
2. Maria, b. Oct. 23, 1801: m. Leonard Farnsworth. **246**
3. Olive, b. April 2, 1804: m. Amos Pierce. **247**
4. Jeremiah, b. March 8, 1806: m. Abigail F. Hutchinson. **248**
5. Timothy W., b. June 21, 1808: m. Joanna Downe. **249**
6. Horace Preston, b. Aug. 12, 1811: d. March 27, 1832.
7. Mahala, b. June 13, 1813: m. Elisha Pierce. **250**
8. William L., b. April 13, 1816: m. Eliza Blanchard. **251**
9. Mary L., b. April 9, 1819: m. William H. Atherton. **252**

---

127. DANIEL KINSMAN, son of Jeremiah and Martha (p. 95), born in Ipswich, March 30, 1778; married Lucy Monroe, of Ashburnham, Mass. He married, second, Hannah Carr, May 16, 1834, the daughter of John and Dorcas Carr, of Sudbury, Mass. Resided in Ashburnham, and afterward in Fitchburg, where he died Sept. 15, 1867.

HIS CHILDREN BY LUCY MONROE:

1. Louisa, b. May 20, 1803: m. Flint Sheldon, of Fitchburg.
2. Lucy M., b. Sept. 4, 1804: m. Francis Hinds. **253**

3. CHARLES, b. Sept. 3, 1807: m. Hannah Ross Smith, Dec. 6, 1832. She was born in Rutland, Aug. 3, 1812, and died May 1, 1861.
4. CYRUS, b. May 2, 1810: m. M. F. Allen; H. D. Allen. **254**
5. MARTHA A., b. Oct. 20, 1814: m. William Perkins; E. J. Boardman. **255**
6. MIRANDA R., b. Sept. 10, 1815: m. Charles R. Foster; have two children, Charles and Louisa. Residence, Bloomfield, Wis.
7. DANIEL ALFRED, b. Dec. 5, 1820: m. M.C. Houghton; S. Briant. **256**
8. MONROE E., b. Jan. 13, 1826: m. Lucy A. Brown. **257**

---

128. LUCY KINSMAN, daughter of Jeremiah and Martha (p. 95), born in Ipswich, Aug. 15, 1783; married SILAS LAWRENCE, of New Ipswich, N. H., Dec. 28, 1815. She died Nov. 9, 1861.

THEIR CHILDREN:

1. HARRIET, b. : m. —— Shattuck.
2. CHARLES, b. :

---

129. JOHN KINSMAN, son of Jeremiah and Martha (p. 95), born in Fitchburg, April 24, 1786; married NANCY SHERWIN, Jan. 1, 1816, the daughter of Zimri and Polly Sherwin, of Townsend, Mass. Resided in Fitchburg, where he died Sept. 30, 1834. His wife survives him.

THEIR CHILDREN:

1. WILLIAM HARVEY, b. Nov. 23, 1816: m. Phebe M. Bowman, Nov. 9, 1840. She died July 4, 1865, aged 47. He married, second, Alcey Lyon, of Fitzwilliam, N. H.
2. CHARLOTTE S., b. Nov. 2, 1818: m. F. Phillips, Oct. 8, 1839.
3. JOHN SUMNER, b. July 27, 1820: m. Sarah A. Derby. **258**

---

130. ASA KINSMAN, son of Jeremiah and Martha (p. 95), born in Fitchburg, March 30, 1793; married

Martha Stone, April 16, 1816. She died Sept. 3, 1823. He married, second, Hannah Burnap, Dec. 15, 1825, who died before her husband. He died Aug. 21, 1873.

HIS CHILDREN BY MARTHA STONE:

1. Zulima Lawrence, b. Sept. 21, 1817: m. James W. Joy. **259**
2. Lorenzo, b. Nov. 20, 1819: m. Lydia Blood. **260**

HIS CHILD BY HANNAH BURNAP:

3. George Washington, b. Oct. 4, 1831: m. Sybil B. Daby. **261**

---

131. ANNA KINSMAN, daughter of William and Anna (p. 96), born in Ipswich, May 27, 1773; married Benjamin Potter, April 8, 1794. He was born in Hamilton, May 6, 1771, and died Sept. 22, 1827. She died in Danversport, Dec. 28, 1869, aged 96.

THEIR CHILDREN:

1. Benjamin, b. Nov. 29, 1794: m. Anna Bailey, of Rowley.
2. William K., b. April 9, 1796: d. Dec. 19, 1798.
3. Henry, b. Aug. 27, 1797: m. Mary Baker, of Wenham; he died at sea in 1821.
4. William K., b. May 9, 1800: d. in 1819.
5. Dudley, b. Dec. 25, 1802: d. unm. Oct. 22, 1828.
6. Mary Ann, b. Dec. 5, 1804: m. Allen Gould.
7. Louisa B., b. Oct. 7, 1807: m. John Hines, of Danvers; she died Feb. 5, 1844.
8. Elizabeth S., b. Aug. 6, 1809: m. William Smith, of Danvers; m., 2d, Abraham Towle, of Salem. She died Jan. 19, 1871.
9. Rachel M., b. Dec. 20, 1811: m. James B. Sawyer, April 3, 1834. He died Aug. 25, 1847. Residence, Danversport.

---

132. WILLIAM KINSMAN, son of William and Anna (p. 96), born in Ipswich, Sept. 4, 1776; married Sarah Brown, Sept. 4, 1802. She was born Sept. 16, 1782, the daughter of Stephen and Elizabeth (Dodge) Brown, and died March 11, 1860. He died Nov. 12, 1866.

The following obituary was published at the time: —

"Died at Ipswich, Nov. 12, Mr. WILLIAM KINSMAN, aged ninety years and two months. Mr. K. died in the same house in which he was born, having spent most of his days in his native place. He belonged to a lineage of remarkable longevity: his parents died at the age of ninety-one years; his grandfather, on the paternal side, died at the age of ninety-three years; his only sister survives him, aged nearly ninety-four years. He was a kind husband, an affectionate father, and beloved by all who knew him."

THEIR CHILDREN:

1.	BETSEY BROWN,	b. June 24, 1803:	d. May 23, 1841.	
2.	LOUISA,	b. Feb. 12, 1805:	m. Henry S. Holmes.	**262**
3.	SIMON BROWN,	b. Jan. 26, 1807:	m. Elizabeth B. Stone.	**263**
4.	NANCY,	b. April 1, 1809:	m. S. Blatchford.	**264**
5.	JACOB,	b. March 29, 1811:	m. Abbie Staniford.	**265**
6.	SUSAN,	b. April 17, 1813:	d. Aug. 3, 1831.	
7.	SARAH,	b. July 5, 1815:	m. Oliver M. Whipple.	**266**
8.	WILLIAM HENRY,	b. Feb. 1, 1818:	m. Frances J. Lamson.	**267**
9.	MARIA,	b. April 15, 1820:	m. Lewis Emerson.	**268**
10.	WILLARD BENAIAH,	b. Feb. 3, 1822:	m. Harriet Manning.	**269**
11.	CHARLOTTE AUGUSTA,	b. April 18, 1824:	m. Andrew Burnham.	**270**
12.	GEORGE,	b. Jan. 26, 1826:	m. Elzina A. Tilton.	**271**
13.	DANIEL FITZ,	b. Jan. 10, 1828:	m. Mattie A. Wood.	**272**

---

133. JACOB B. KINSMAN, son of William and Anna (p. 96), born in Ipswich, April 9, 1779; married BETHIAH DODGE, the daughter of Michael Dodge, of Hamilton; published April 10, 1802.

He was a ship-master, and died in Hispaniola, Jan. 27, 1811. (His widow married Nicholas Woodberry, of Hamilton, May 24, 1831, and died Jan. 24, 1861, aged 79.)

THEIR CHILDREN:

1.	CHARLOTTE,	b. Sept. 24, 1803:	m. Isaac W. Roberts.	**273**
2.	OLIVER DODGE,	b. Sept. 26, 1805:	m. Ruth Thompson.	**274**
3.	JACOB,	b. Jan. 20, 1808:	d. Oct. 8, 1810.	
4.	WILLIAM,	b. Oct. 18, 1809:	m. Nancy D. Greene.	**275**

134. JOSEPH CHARLES THIOT KINSMAN, son of Joseph and Eliza (p. 98), born in Cornville, Me., Feb. 7, 1821; married CATHERINE E. DOW, Aug. 3, 1855. She was born in Athens, Me., Oct. 6, 1824, the daughter of Joseph and Margaret (Weston) Dow. He has been Brigadier-General of the State of Maine. Residence, Cornville, Me.

THEIR CHILDREN:

1. JOSEPH CHARLES, b. May 8, 1856: d. Sept. 2, 1867.
2. MARGARET ELIZA, b. Oct. 22, 1857.
3. CASSIUS C., b. June 5, 1860.
4. FRANCIS BURNHAM, b. Dec. 4, 1861: d. Sept. 6, 1867.
5. MARY ELIZABETH, b. Dec. 29, 1863: d. Oct. 16, 1864.
6. EDWARD EVERETT, b. Aug. 23, 1865: d. Sept. 8, 1867.

---

135. JOSIAH BURNHAM KINSMAN, son of Joseph and Eliza (p. 98), born in Cornville, Somerset Co., Me., April 29, 1824. He was educated to the law, and after a preparatory course at the North Yarmouth Classical Institute, went to Cambridge, and received his degree at Harvard University in 1854. Entered B. F. Butler's office in Boston, and was admitted to the bar, but remained several years at Cambridge, engaged in editing law works, besides publishing one of his own on "Municipal Law and the Rights and Duties of Municipal Officers"; went into a successful practice in Boston, and continued it until the breaking out of the Rebellion. He entered the service as a volunteer Aide-de-Camp on the staff of General Butler, without commission or pay; and served in that capacity at Fortress Monroe, Ship Island, and New Orleans, as First Lieutenant, but without pay or rank, until, for meritorious services at the taking of Forts Jackson and St. Philip, President Lincoln, unsolicited, commissioned him a Lieut.-Colonel in the Regular Army. For his successful expedition and capture of the city of Thibodeauxville, in southwestern Louisiana, and the rescue of its Union citizens; his expedition from New Orleans to Mississippi, and capture of the noted Rebel steamer "Gray Cloud," afterward renamed the "Kinsman"; also for his discovery and capture of $800,000 in silver from the enemy, he was promoted to be Colonel, Brigadier-General, and Major-General of Volunteers. Was Provost Judge at New Orleans, and also filled the laborious and responsible position of Commissioner of Sequestration of Rebel estates and property.[1] After leaving New Orleans he was actively engaged in other service, and since the War has been employed by Government in different capacities at home and abroad. Is unmarried.

---

136. JONATHAN BURNHAM KINSMAN, son of Jonathan and Abigail (p. 98), born in Athens, Me., May 22, 1807; married Elizabeth Bodwell, of Athens. He was a medical graduate of Dartmouth College, Hanover, N. H., in 1832, and has been a successful practitioner of medicine in Somerset Co., Me., for many years; served as Contract Surgeon in the United States Hospitals at Hampton, Va., during one year of the late war. Residence, Solon, Me. He has no children.

---

137. RHODA KINSMAN, daughter of Joseph and Rhoda (p. 100), born in Gloucester, Mass., Dec. 20, 1814; married Capt. Henry Thurston, of Portland, Me., Sept. 9, 1834. She died May 11, 1845. He died in Portland, March 18, 1858.

---

[1] For details of these and other services, see Parton's History of "General Butler in New Orleans."

THEIR CHILDREN:

1. HENRIETTA MARIA, b. Aug. 28, 1836: d. Sept. 28, 1849.
2. GEORGE HENRY, b. July 25, 1838: residence, Boston.
3. WILLIAM EDWARD, b. March 29, 1840: was lost overboard from the schooner "El Dorado," on the passage from New York to Wilmington, N. C., Feb. 20, 1858.
4. CHARLES AUGUSTUS, b. March 15, 1842: residence, Boston.

---

138. JOSEPH KINSMAN, son of Joseph and Rhoda (p. 100), born in Gloucester, Mass., Jan. 7, 1819; married LUCINDA JORDON, Sept. 29, 1849, the daughter of Rufus Jordon, of Cape Elizabeth, Me. He died in 1862. She died Dec. 12, 1864, aged 37.

THEIR CHILDREN:

1. JOSEPH HENRY, b. Jan. 30, 1856: residence, Cape Elizabeth.
2. RUFUS ALBERT, b. Sept. 12, 1857: residence, Cape Elizabeth.

---

139. WILLIAM HALES KINSMAN, son of Joseph and Rhoda (p. 100), born in Gloucester, Mass., Jan. 14, 1821; married ELIZABETH ANN HOSACK, Aug. 1, 1847. She was born July 25, 1823, the daughter of Charles and Betsey (Dorsett) Hosack, of Portland, Me. She died April 22, 1862. He married, second, REBECCA GREEN VARNEY, March 1, 1864. She was born June 24, 1827, the daughter of Ezekiel and Eliza (Collins) Varney, of Windham, Me. He resided in Portland, Me., until 1857; since then has been in business in Boston, his residence being Winchester.

HIS CHILDREN BY ELIZABETH A. HOSACK:

1. WILLIAM CLARENCE, b. July 21, 1849.
2. LIZZIE EDNA, b. April 6, 1853: d. Sept. 19, 1854.
3. FRANK EDGAR, b. April 12, 1855: d. Oct. 3, 1855.
4. ANNA ELIZABETH, b. July 28, 1858.
5. EDGAR AUGUSTUS, b. Feb. 28, 1861: d. July 27, 1862.

HIS CHILDREN BY REBECCA G. VARNEY:

6. Edith Webber, b. Oct. 12, 1866.
7. Edward Hales, b. Oct. 10, 1869.

---

140. JOHN KINSMAN, son of Joseph and Rhoda (p. 100), born in Gloucester, Sept. 25, 1828; married Regina Hedman, March 12, 1851, the daughter of Charles Hedman. She died July 21, 1858. He married, second, Clara Walker, Oct. 11, 1860, the daughter of Rev. Charles Walker, of Portland, Me. Residence, Portland.

HIS CHILDREN BY REGINA HEDMAN:

1. Chares H, b. May 2, 1853.
2. Mary Ellen, b. Sept. 15, 1857: d. Feb. 18, 1859.

HIS CHILDREN BY CLARA WALKER:

3. Ellen W., b. Oct. 30, 1862.
4. Alice W., b. Dec. 20, 1866.

---

141. GEORGE KINSMAN, son of Joseph and Rhoda (p. 100), born in Gloucester, Aug. 18, 1830; married Sarah Soule Trowbridge, July 10, 1853. She was born Feb. 20, 1830, the daughter of Nathan and Judith (Alden) Trowbridge, of Portland, Me. He resided in Portland until 1864; then removed to Boston, where he now lives.

THEIR CHILDREN:

1. George Henry, b. June 30, 1854.
2. Frederick Leon Talbot, b. Aug. 15, 1861.

---

142. NATHANIEL KINSMAN, son of Nathaniel and Deborah (p. 100), born in Salem, Feb. 6, 1798; married there, REBECCA CHASE, June 9, 1835. She was born in Salem, April 23, 1810, the daughter of Abijah and Mary (Abbot) Chase.

He was a ship-master and merchant of Salem, and died at Macao, in China, April 30, 1847.

The "Salem Gazette" of Aug. 3, 1847, contained the following obituary notice: —

"Died at Macao, about May 1, 1847, Nathaniel Kinsman, of this city. Mr. Kinsman, as a ship-master, was distinguished for his nautical skill; as a merchant, for his shrewdness, honor, and mercantile talents. These qualifications marked him out as eminently qualified to take the lead of a mercantile house in a foreign country, and the house of Wetmore & Co., of Canton, invited him to become their partner. For a limited term he consented to leave his country and engage in this partnership. But the disease with which he had previously been visited, again attacked him, and proved fatal. Like his brother, he has died in a foreign clime, and quickly followed his interesting little daughter, who died on her passage home. In his death, our city has sustained the loss of one of her most honorable, honest, and amiable citizens, and his family an irreparable calamity."

His widow married Joseph Grinnell, of New Bedford, Sept. 19, 1865.

THE CHILDREN OF NATHANIEL AND REBECCA:

1. WILLIAM LOW, b. March 10, 1836: m. S. Augusta Nichols. **276**
2. REBECCA REED, b. April 27, 1839: d. at sea, Aug. 16, 1846, on board the bark "Douglas," on the passage from China; buried in Salem, Sept. 2, 1846.
3. NATHANIEL, b. Feb. 23, 1841: m. Lucy E. Winchester. **277**
4. ABBOT, b. Oct. 6, 1844, in Macao, China, and came to Salem on the return of his family in 1847. In 1863 he visited China, the place of his birth and of his father's death; and a business situation offering, he located at Manila and afterward at Legaspi, on the island of Luzon. He died at Iloilo, another port of the Philippine Islands, July 4, 1864, in his twentieth year.

143. JOSHUA KINSMAN, son of Nathaniel and Deborah (p. 100), born in Salem, Aug. 12, 1801; married Mary Brown, Oct. 21, 1830. She was born in Salem, May 13, 1804, the daughter of Nathaniel and Mary Brown.

He was a ship-master of Salem, and died at sea, on board the "Eliza Ann," Aug. 3, 1841. He was much esteemed for his uprightness and the uniform kindness of his disposition; his associates and friends erected a granite monument to his memory in Harmony Grove Cemetery, Salem.

It is stated in Felt's "Annals of Salem," under date of March 15, 1833, that "The Royal Humane Society of London date their thanks, inscribed on vellum, to Capt. Joshua Kinsman, of the brig 'Gazelle,' for rescuing from the wreck of the British schooner 'William and Elizabeth,' October, 1831, her distressed company, and generously providing for their wants."

His widow died in Salem, Feb. 7, 1868.

THEIR CHILDREN:

1. Nathaniel Joshua, b. Sept. 14, 1831: m. Mary F. Shatswell. **278**
2. Mary Ellen, b. Nov. 18, 1833: d. Jan. 25, 1844.
3. Annie Elizabeth, b. June 29, 1838: m. Manuel F. C. Fenollosa. **279**
4. Infant Son, b. May 13, 1841: d. the same day.

---

144. ELIZABETH KINSMAN, daughter of Nathaniel and Deborah (p. 100), born in Salem, Dec. 14, 1804; married there, John Allen Southwick, Oct. 17, 1826. He was born in Salem, Oct. 25, 1802, the son of John and Rebecca (Alley) Southwick, and died in Salem, Aug. 19, 1831. She died there Nov. 30, 1831.

THEIR CHILDREN:

1. Mary Ann, b March 24, 1828: m. George Cabot Ward, Jan. 22, 1852; residence, New York City.
2. Eliza Kinsman, b. Sept. 30, 1829: m. Nathaniel Brown, Aug. 18, 1852; residence, Salem.

145. JOHN KINSMAN, son of John C. and Anna (p. 101), born in Ipswich, Sept. 3, 1810; married NANCY BICKFORD FOGG, Aug. 8, 1833. She was born in Salem, Jan. 23, 1811, the daughter of Joseph and Lydia (Proctor) Fogg, and died in Springfield, Ohio, April 25, 1862. He married, second, MARTHA LORD, Jan. 15, 1863. She was born in Salem, Feb. 23, 1817, the daughter of David and Lucy (Harris) Lord.

He removed to Salem in 1825; learned the carpenter's trade, and was extensively engaged in building for several years; was Superintendent of the Eastern Railroad from 1842 to 1855, when he removed to Ohio, and took charge of the Mad River and Lake Erie Railroad, and afterwards of the Cincinnati and Marietta Railroad; purchased and still owns the Gas-works in Springfield, O., where he resided till 1864; then returned to Salem, where he now lives.

HIS CHILDREN BY NANCY B. FOGG:

1. JOHN HENRY, b. Aug. 1, 1836: a medical graduate of Harvard University, in 1858; now and for several years a surgeon in the regular army.
2. SARAH ELLEN, b. Oct. 25, 1840: m. Henry Appleton Hale, Sept. 29, 1869. He was b. in Salem, July 15, 1840, son of Henry and Sarah Winn (Appleton) Hale; residence, Salem.
3. GEORGIANA PROCTOR, b. July 4, 1845.
4. ALBERT SYLVESTER, b Jan. 26, 1848.
5. CHARLES AUGUSTUS, b. Feb. 28, 1850.
6. GRACE LANCASTER, b. April 1, 1855: d. in Springfield, O., July 28, 1857.

---

146. NATHANIEL KINSMAN, son of John C. and Anna (p. 101), born in Ipswich, June 6, 1819; married CLARISSA ROGERS HODGKINS, April 24, 1843. She was born in Salem, March 30, 1820, the daughter of John and Lucy Mary (Rogers) Hodgkins, and died Dec. 1, 1844. He married, second, MARY KIMBALL, Oct. 27, 1847.

She was born in Salem, March 12, 1821, the daughter of Jonathan Choate and Mary (Lord) Kimball, and died in Springfield, Ohio, Dec. 22, 1858. He married, third, PHEBE SUSAN PARKER, Aug. 15, 1859. She was born in Bluehill, Me., Jan. 4, 1818, the daughter of Marble and Hannah (Lovejoy) Parker.

He removed to Salem in 1833, and from there to Springfield, Ohio, in 1855; is Superintendent of the Gas-works in the latter place.

HIS CHILD BY CLARISSA R. HODGKINS:

1. CLARA ELLEN, b. Jan. 10, 1844; m. Samuel Knoop Statler. **280**

---

147. JOSEPH KINSMAN, son of Joseph and Eunice (p. 102), born in Ipswich, June 24, 1811; married MARY E. BROWN, Sept. 20, 1842, the daughter of Joseph and Rebecca (Appleton) Brown. She died Feb. 20, 1861. He married, second, HANNAH S. PERT, Jan. 24, 1863, the daughter of Samuel and Abigail Pert, of Manchester. Residence, Ipswich.

HIS CHILDREN BY MARY E. BROWN:

1. JOSEPH FARLEY, b. April 27, 1844: m. Carrie Brown, Oct. 1, 1873.
2. GUSTAVUS, b. Aug. 19, 1850.

---

148. ABIGAIL KINSMAN, daughter of Nathaniel and Joanna (p. 102), born in Ipswich, Oct. 9, 1831; married JOSEPH MARSHALL, May 30, 1860. He was born in Marblehead, April 24, 1830, the son of William and Lucy (Butler) Marshall. Residence, Ipswich.

THEIR CHILD:

1. HELEN ABBY, b. May 28, 1869.

149. DANSON KINSMAN, son of Benjamin A. and Mary (p. 104), born in Cornwallis, Kings Co., N. S., April 23, 1813; married ELIZABETH A. DOUGLAS, Sept. 19, 1839. She was born in Liverpool, N. S., Sept. 9, 1820, the daughter of John and Abigail Douglas. Residence, Fonthill, Welland Co., Ontario, C. W.

THEIR CHILDREN:

1. JOHN DOUGLAS, b. June 21, 1840: m. Anna P. Westerfield. **281**
2. AVERY, b. Jan. 27, 1843: m. Lettie Lamb. **282**
3. HATTIE E., b. March 21, 1848: residence, Fonthill, C. W.
4. JAMES, b. July 22, 1850: residence, Woodstock, C. W.
5. ANSON, b. May 29, 1852: residence, St. Catherines, C. W.
6. FRED, b. Oct. 14, 1862: residence, Fonthill, C. W.

---

150. MARY L. KINSMAN, daughter of Benjamin A. and Mary (p. 104), born in Cornwallis, N. S., Feb. 23, 1815; married there JOHN P. CROWE, Sept. 10, 1835. He was born in Horton, N. S., July 31, 1815, the son of William B. and Margaret (Murray) Crowe. Residence, Sharon, Mass.

THEIR CHILDREN:

1. WILLIAM HENRY, b. Aug. 11, 1836: m. Eliza Caldwell, Mar. 31, 1858; residence, Chelsea.
2. JAMES, b. Aug. 16, 1838: d. unm., May 26, 1859.
3. ELIZABETH, b. Sept. 16, 1840: residence, Sharon.
4. JOHN WILSON, b. Feb. 15, 1843: m. Ruth A. Weaver, Nov. 7, 1865; residence, Chelsea.
5. GEORGE ALBERT, b May 26, 1845: m. Cynthia Patterson, Dec. 31, 1865; residence, Cornwallis, N. S.
6. RACHEL AMELIA, b. Nov. 2, 1847: m. Philip B. Weaver, Dec. 1863; residence, Cornwallis, N S.
7. RICHARD ROBERT, b. Jan. 8, 1850: m. Emeline Caldwell, Nov. 25, 1871; residence, Chelsea.
8. SIDNEY RUPERT, b. Dec. 9, 1852: unm.; residence, Chelsea.
9. BENJAMIN AVERY, b. June 8, 1855: d. Nov. 8, 1862.

151. AVERY BENJAMIN KINSMAN, son of Benjamin A. and Mary (p. 104), born in Horton, Kings Co., N. S., Feb. 12, 1824; married ANN MARIA WHITMAN, Aug. 22, 1849. She was born Aug. 4, 1824, the daughter of Isaac and Deborah (Barss) Whitman. Residence, Fonthill, Welland Co., Ontario, C. W.

THEIR CHILDREN:

1. ALBERT WHITMAN, b. Aug. 26, 1850: residence, Toronto, C. W.
2. ADA MARIA, b. Nov. 19, 1851.
3. FRANK BUDD, b. Aug. 10, 1863.
4. FLORA JANE, b. Sept. 3, 1864.

---

152. WILLIAM GRANDISON KINSMAN, son of Benjamin A. and Mary (p. 104), born in Cornwallis, N. S., March 15, 1826; married SARAH ABIGAIL PORTER, April 24 (1848?). Has resided in Paradise, Annapolis Co., N. S.; Westborough, Mass.; New York State; and 1872 in Boston, Mass.

THEIR CHILDREN:

1. HARRIET THERESA, b. June 13, 1849: m. Charles Lewis Alley, Jan. 17, 1871; residence, Lynn, Mass.
2. SOPHIA LAVINIA, b. Sept. 23, 1855: residence, Swampscott, Ma
3. WILLIAM IRVING, b March 23, 1861: residence, Swampscott, M .

---

153. LEE ENGLISH KINSMAN, son of Benjamin A. and Mary (p. 104), born in Cornwallis, N. S., May 5, 1828; married SARAH NEWCOMB. Residence, Canning (Cornwallis), N. S.

THEIR CHILDREN:

1. RUPERT, b.
2. ARCHIBALD, b.
3. ANNA BELL, b.
4. FREDERICK, b.

154. JOSEPH CHARLES KINSMAN, son of Amos and Abigail (p. 104), born in Cornwallis, N. S., Jan. 10, 1803; married SARAH MARTIN. Residence, Cornwallis.

THEIR CHILDREN:

1. MARIA CONTENT, b. Jan. 30, 1834: m. Stanley Masters, Dec. 12, 1860.
2. ELIZABETH CAROLINE, b. Jan. 31, 1836: m. William Rockwell, July 27, 1857.
3. WILLIAM MARTIN, b. April 2, 1838: m. Augusta Burgess; residence, Somerville, Mass.
4. AMOS HENRY, b. Sept. 2, 1841.
5. ANNIE ALINA, b. Sept. 26, 1846: m. Watson Porter, M. D., Nov. 5, 1867; lives in Florida.
6. ROBERT WHITFIELD, b. Feb. 28, 1848.
7. JOHN CALDWELL, b. Aug. 18, 1850.

---

155. ESTHER KINSMAN, daughter of Amos and Abigail (p. 104), born in Cornwallis, N. S., Jan. 4, 1807; married BENJAMIN BURGESS. Residence, Cornwallis.

THEIR CHILDREN:

1. GEORGE STRUTHERS, b. Oct. 31, 1836: d. March 17, 1843.
2. JOSHUA, b. April 8, 1840: d. Oct. 22, 1841.
3. HANNAH, b. July 16, 1842: d. March 18, (1843?).
4. ELLEN MARIA, b. March 7, 1844.
5. GEORGE ALMON, b. Feb. 2, 1846.

---

156. MARY JANE KINSMAN, daughter of Amos and Abigail (p. 104), born in Cornwallis, N. S., Nov. 18, 1808; married JOHNSTON PATTERSON. Residence, Cornwallis.

THEIR CHILDREN:

1. Amos Kinsman, b. March 11, 1839.
2. James, b. Jan. 25, 1841.
3. Robert Dorsan, b. May 11, 1842.
4. Rebecca, b. April 19, 1844.
5. Abigail, b. March 9, 1846.
6. Elizabeth, b. Sept. 7, 1847.
7. Jessie, b. March 19, 1850.

---

157. OLIVIA ANN KINSMAN, daughter of Amos and Abigail (p. 104), born in Cornwallis, N. S., March 12, 1811; married Isaac Hiram Newcomb, March 2, 1833. He was born in Cornwallis, June 24, 1808, the son of Eddy and Mary (West) Newcomb. Residence, Cornwallis.

THEIR CHILDREN:

1. Letitia Adelia, b. Dec. 11, 1833: m. Henry Condon, Sept. 26, 1854.
2. Amos Kinsman, b. July 31, 1836: m. Clara Illsley, June 29, 1869.
3. Mary, b. Jan. 31, 1841: m. Andrew Chipman, Jan. 27, 1862.
4. Robert, b. May 11, 1845: m. Pauline Gilliatt, July 6, 1870.
5. Abbie, b. July 15, 1851: d. March 3, 1855.

---

158. HANNAH KINSMAN, daughter of Amos and Abigail (p. 104), born in Cornwallis, N. S., March 14, 1813; married Elias Calkins, July 2, (1833?). Residence, Cornwallis.

THEIR CHILDREN:

1. Edmund, b. April 25, 1836: married; lives in Indiana.
2. Mary, b. Jan. 4, 1838: d. young.
3. William, b. Oct. 5, 1839.
4. Joseph, b. Nov., 1840: lost at sea, Oct. 4, 1868.
5. Jane, b. March 4, 1848.

159. JOSHUA KINSMAN, son of Amos and Abigail (p. 104), born in Cornwallis, N. S., Aug. 11, 1819; married MARY A. CALDWELL, March 7, 1849. Residence, West Cornwallis.

THEIR CHILDREN:

1. JOSEPH A., b. Jan. 16, 1850.
2. ANNABELL, b. April 18, 1852.
3. AMOS CLARE, b. Dec. 15, 1854: d. Oct. 4, 1867.
4. JOHN THOMAS, b. Sept. 4, 1857: d. Nov. 27, 1867.
5. ETHEL JANE, b. March 28, 1860.
6. ALMA DILL, b. Oct. 28, 1862.

---

160. BENJAMIN KINSMAN, son of Amos and Abigail (p. 104), born in Cornwallis, N. S., June 5, 1821; married MARY A. BURGESS, Nov. 5, 1850. She died Feb. 14, 1861. Residence, Cornwallis.

THEIR CHILDREN:

1. CLARA SIGOURNEY, b. April 27, 1853.
2. MARY JANE, b. April 27, 1855: d. March 1, 1859.
3. FRED, b. Jan. 7, 1857.
4. FORRESTER, b. Oct. 20, 1858.

---

161. JETHRO KINSMAN, son of James and Dorothy (p. 105), born in Cornwallis, N. S., June 2, 1805; married there, REBECCA TUPPER, Dec. 3, 1827. She was born in Cornwallis, Feb. 21, 1809, the daughter of James Tupper. She died March 7, 1866, and he died Oct. 16, 1866, in Cornwallis.

THEIR CHILDREN:

1. WILLIAM, b. Oct. 16, 1828: m. H. Armstrong; Lucy Keating. **283**
2. JAMES, b. Oct. 5, 1829: m. Deborah Norton. **284**
3. JULIA, b. Sept. 15, 1834: m. George E Cox, May 10, 1859; residence, Horton, N. S.
4. MAHALA, b June 6, 1837: m. Bishop I. Fuller, Jan. 26, 1859. He d. Aug. 18, 1862. She m., 2d, Benjamin Woodworth, Mar. 24, 1870.

162. REBECCA KINSMAN, daughter of James and Dorothy (p. 105), born in Cornwallis, N. S., Oct. 10, 1808; married there, WILLIAM FOOTE, Feb. 25, 1829. He was born in Cornwallis, March 31, 1805, the son of Robert Foote. Residence, Cornwallis, where she died Sept. 10, 1870.

THEIR CHILDREN:

1. LYDIA, b. 1830: m. Preston Illsley, 1850.
2. ESTHER, b. Nov. 12, 1833: m. Enoch Arnold, April 24, 1854.
3. NANCY, b. March 31, 1835: m. Jeremiah Foote April 18, 1854.
4. ROBERT H. C., b. July 31, 1837: m. Susan Clarke, July 28, 1869.
5. JELINA, b. Feb. 26, 1841: m. Guy Lyons, Oct 20, 1858.
6. POPE, b. Oct. 15, 1843: m. Margaret Morton, Jan. 1, 1867.
7. SYLVANUS W., b. Aug. 17, 1845: m. Sarah A. Clarke, Feb. 5, 1872.
8. MARY A., b. Nov. 12, 1850.
9. AUGUSTA, b. April 14, 1852.

---

163. EPHRAIM KINSMAN, son of James and Dorothy (p. 105), born in Cornwallis, N. S., Sept. 21, 1812; married there, EUNICE BORDEN, April 3, 1839. She was born in Cornwallis, Aug. 7, 1815, the daughter of Edward Borden. Residence, Cornwallis.

THEIR CHILDREN:

1. JAMES E., b. Jan. 12, 1840: m. Calena J. Sheffield. **285**
2. ARABELLA L., b. March 3, 1842.
3. ALBERT, b. Oct. 22, 1844.
4. ANNIE M., b. Oct. 8, 1846.
5. MARTHA T., b. June 7, 1851.
6. H. RICHMOND, b. Nov. 27, 1853.
7. ARTHUR, b. March 9, 1858.

---

164. ESTHER KINSMAN, daughter of James and Dorothy (p. 105), born in Cornwallis, N. S., Aug. 31, 1815; married there, NELSON PATTERSON, Jan. 31, 1844. He was born in Cornwallis, Sept. 1, 1802, the son of Alexander Patterson. They resided in Aylesford, where she died Dec. 16, 1855.

THEIR CHILDREN:

1. JERUSHA, b. Feb. 4, 1847: m. Kirk P. Wallace, in 1871; residence, Aylesford.
2. ANNIE, b. Sept. 26, 1850.

---

165. THEODORUS KINSMAN, son of James and Dorothy (p. 105), born in Cornwallis, N. S., Nov. 18, 1817; married there, ROXANA BORDEN, May 2, 1846. She was born in Cornwallis, July 14, 1821, the daughter of Edward Borden. Residence, Cornwallis.

THEIR CHILDREN:

1. ALTHEA M., b. Oct. 14, 1849.
2. F. SMALLWOOD, b. Aug. 29, 1852.
3. JAMES E., b. Jan. 20, 1855.
4. CLARENCE E., b. April 14, 1862.

---

166. JERUSHA KINSMAN, daughter of James and Dorothy (p. 105), born in Cornwallis, N. S., Sept. 9, 1825; married there, HUGH PATTERSON, March 20, 1855. He was born in Cornwallis, May 11, 1822, the son of James Patterson. Residence, Cornwallis.

THEIR CHILDREN:

1. EMMA, b March 5, 1857.
2. JAMES, b. Feb 24, 1861.

---

167. OLIVIA ANN KINSMAN, daughter of Theodorus and Esther (p. 106), born in Cornwallis, N. S.,

March 4, 1830; married JOHN RAND. Residence, Berwick (Cornwallis), N. S.

THEIR CHILDREN:

1. MARY FULLER, b. Nov., 1852.
2. ARTHUR W., b. June, 1856.
3. JOHN THEODORUS, b. Jan., 1861.

---

168. ROBERT N. KINSMAN, son of Theodorus and Esther (p. 106), born in West Cornwallis, N. S., Dec. 11, 1834; married in Boston, Mass., ELIZA ANN ROBINSON, Feb. 10, 1855. She was born in Cornwallis, N. S., Oct. 9, 1834, the daughter of Samuel and Elizabeth Robinson. Residence, South Boston.

THEIR CHILDREN:

1. ANNIE BELL, b Oct. 20, 1857.
2. MARY OLIVIA, b. Feb. 15, 1860.
3. WINFIELD SCOTT, b. Aug. 28, 1861.
4. OMAR GRANT, b. March 9, 1864.
5. ALICE MARIA, b. June 12, 1868.
6. WALTER EMERSON, b. Oct. 4, 1870.

---

169. EZEKIEL N. KINSMAN, son of Theodorus and Esther (p. 106), born in West Cornwallis, N. S., Dec. 11, 1834; married there, ELIZABETH SCRIBNER, April 21, 1861. She was born in St. Stephen's, N. B., Oct. 20, 1836, the daughter of James and Elizabeth (Trafton) Scribner. Residence, South Boston.

THEIR CHILDREN:

1. FRED CHASE, b. Dec. 19, 1864.
2. ELLEN MAUD, b. July 16, 1868.
3. LIZZIE GERTRUDE, b. June 16, 1870.

170. HANNAH ELIZABETH KINSMAN, daughter of Theodorus and Esther (p. 106), born in West Cornwallis, N. S., Nov. 14, 1836; married HENRY PINEO, Nov. 25, 1857. He was born in West Cornwallis, May 19, 1823, the son of William and Harriet (Shaw) Pineo. Residence, Waterville (Cornwallis), N. S.

THEIR CHILDREN:

1. WILLIAM WELSFORD, b. Sept. 22, 1858.
2. CHARLOTTE MARIA, b. Oct. 27, 1860.
3. HORACE HASTINGS, b. April 12, 1864.
4. ALICE MAUD, b. Aug. 27, 1865.

---

171. CHARLOTTE KINSMAN, daughter of Theodorus and Esther (p. 106), born in West Cornwallis, N. S., Sept. 4, 1839; married DAVID BURGESS. Residence, Cornwallis.

THEIR CHILDREN:

1. ALICE CHASE, b. Nov., 1868.
2. BERNARD BARNES, b. Nov., 1871.

---

172. CALEB KINSMAN, son of John and Sarah (p. 107), born in Orford, N. H.; married ELIZA BENSON, of Stratford, Vt. Both died before 1872.

THEIR CHILDREN:

1. HENRY, b. : m., and lived in Springfield.
2. OSCAR, b. : m., and lived in Providence, R. I.
3. MARY ANN, b.

4 and 5. Two daughters.

173. JOHN KINSMAN, son of John and Sarah (p. 107), born in Orford, N. H.; married JULIA A. ——. Residence, Thetford, Vt.

THEIR CHILDREN:

1. ONSLOW GEORGE, b. Aug. 13, 1851.
2. CHARLES CARROLL, b. July 30, 1853.
3. ISABEL, b. Jan. 3, 1855: d. Sept. 10, 1867.
4. SARAH HOLTON, b. March 16, 1856.
5. ANNETTE HEATH, b July 20, 1859.
6. JOHN, b. Dec. 1, 1866.
7. MINNIE ISABEL, b. Jan. 23, 1869.

---

174. ADOLPHUS KINSMAN, son of Ebenezer and Mary (p. 108), born in Cornwallis, N. S., in 1811; married in Milton, Mass., REBECCA WHITING, Sept. 1, 1842. Residence, Hyde Park.

THEIR CHILDREN:

1. WILLIAM HENRY STEVENS, b. Aug. 19, 1843: drowned June 26, 1855.
2. EBENEZER, b. 1847: m. Cornelia S. Preston, of Beverly, Sept. 27, 1871.

---

175. FREDERICK KINSMAN, son of Frederick and Cornelia (p. 114), born in Warren, Ohio, Aug. 26, 1841; married MARY LOUISA MARVIN, Sept. 18, 1867. She was born in Bazetta, Ohio, April 22, 1846, the daughter of Joseph and Lucy Temple (Dana) Marvin.

He served during the late war in Company D, 84th Regiment, O. V. I., Col. Lawrence commander; was stationed at Cumberland, Maryland. Nothing of note attended this service of one hundred days. He also enlisted in Company A, 171st Regiment, O. N. G., Col. Asper commander; was elected Lieutenant of his company, and stationed at Johnson's Island to guard prisoners. On an alarm given in June, 1864, that Morgan and his forces were preparing for a raid on Cincinnati, the regiment, under Col. Asper, was ordered to Cynthiana, Ky., where Morgan, aware of their approach, lay in wait for them. An engagement ensued (Gen. Hobson commanding), in which most of the regiment, including Lieut. Kinsman, were taken prisoners. The General and Colonel being left behind, to be disposed of otherwise, the rest were hastily marched from the ground, and after a severe tramp of about forty miles, were all paroled by Morgan, and left by him to find their way to the Ohio River, where they procured a boat and finally reached Cincinnati.

Residence, Warren, Trumbull Co., Ohio.

THEIR CHILDREN:

1. Frederick Joseph, b. Sept. 27, 1868.
2. Cornelia Pease, b. Oct. 25, 1872.

---

176. JOHN KINSMAN, son of Frederick and Cornelia (p. 114), born in Warren, Ohio, April 2, 1843; married Mary Van Gorder, Oct. 17, 1866. She was born in Warren, O., Aug. 8, 1845, the daughter of Cyrus Jackson and Jane Williamson (Seely) Van Gorder.

He was one of the "Squirrel Hunters" who were called to meet an expected raid by Kirby Smith (who failed, however, to put in an appearance), as is shown by the following discharge: —

"THE SQUIRREL HUNTERS' DISCHARGE. Cincinnati was menaced by the enemies of our Union. David Tod, Governor of Ohio, called on the Minute Men of the State, and the 'Squirrel Hunters' came by thousands to the rescue. You, John Kinsman, were one of them, and this is your Honorable Discharge.

CHAS. W. HILL,
SEPT. 1, 1862. *Adjt.-Gen'l of Ohio.*

Approved by
DAVID TOD, *Governor.*
MALCOM McDONELL, *Major & A. D. C.*"

He was in the unfortunate engagement at Cynthiana, Ky., with his brother; was wounded on the field of battle, and, with his dead and wounded companions, abandoned by the enemy. The wounded were gathered up and taken to our hospitals at Covington, Ky. His wounds (a gunshot through the fleshy part of the leg above the knee, and the loss of a thumb, the end of which was shot off) were not so serious as to prevent his leaving the hospital, after about four weeks' confinement, to join his regiment again at Johnson's Island. [See Greeley's "American Conflict," Vol. 2, page 623.]

Residence, Warren, Trumbull Co., Ohio.

THEIR CHILD:

1. MARY CORNELIA, b. June 24, 1873.

EIGHTH GENERATION.

177. SAMUEL KINSMAN, son of Samuel and Rachel (p. 116), born April 12, 1815; married ELIZABETH R. GIFFORD, of Salem. Residence, Salem.

THEIR CHILDREN:

1. SAMUEL AUGUSTUS, b. Aug. 7, 1840: m. Sarah E. Hardy. **286**
2. JAMES GIFFORD, b. Nov. 22, 1855: d. Nov. 27, 1859.

---

178. JOSEPH KINSMAN, son of Thomas and Sally (p. 117), born in Salem, Nov. 28, 1820; married SARAH A. PIKE, Dec. 7, 1843. She died Feb. 29, 1852, aged 27 years 3 months 13 days. He married, second, DIARDAMA SHAFFNER STEADMAN, of Granville, N. S., July 27, 1852. She died in Salem, Nov. 30, 1873, aged 57 years 28 days. He lives in Salem.

HIS CHILDREN BY SARAH A. PIKE:

1. MARY ABBY, b. Jan. 27, 1845.
2. JOSEPH NORRIS, b. Nov. 22, 1846: was a member of Co. A, 23d Regt. Mass. Vols., and d. at Newbern, N. C., Oct. 16, 1864.
3. BENJAMIN HENRY, b. Nov. 28, 1848: m. Ida W. Tufts, April 15, 1874; residence, Salem.
4. SARAH ANN, b. Jan. 25, 1852: d. July 8, 1852.

HIS CHILDREN BY DIARDAMA S. STEADMAN:

5. WILLIAM KENNEDY, b. March 20, 1853: d. June 7, 1853.
6. EDWARD SHAFFNER, b. May 1, 1857: d. Nov. 22, 1857.

---

179. SUSAN PARSONS KINSMAN, daughter of William and Hannah (p. 117), born in Salem, Jan. 26, 1819; married JOHN FRIEND HARRIS, Aug. 25, 1837. He was born Aug. 18, 1815. Residence, Manchester, Mass.

THEIR CHILDREN:

1. JOHN HENRY, } Twins, { d. June 5, 1867.
2. WILLIAM EDWARD, } b. Feb. 5, 1839: { d. March 6, 1839.
3. SUSAN HANNAH, b. Dec. 20, 1840: m. William H. Bell, May 25, 1859.
4. WILLIAM, b. Nov. 22, 1842: d. same day.
5. ELIZABETH JANE, b. Jan. 12, 1844.
6. CAROLINE MATILDA, b. Jan. 3, 1846: m. John H. Dennis.
7. RUTH ANNA, b. March 27, 1848: m. Tristram Appleton.
8. RACHEL, b. May 21, 1850: m. Putnam Emerson, Oct. 11, 1871; residence, Salem.
9. NANCY ALLEN, b. May 12, 1852: d. Jan. 24, 1855.
10. CHARLES OBED, b. March 22, 1854.
11. FRANK BURNSIDE, b. May 31, 1862.

---

180. WILLIAM HENRY KINSMAN, son of William and Hannah (p. 117), born in Watertown, Oct. 2, 1824; married MEHITABLE MILLER. Residence, Gloucester.

THEIR CHILDREN:

1. CAROLINE, b. Sept. 7, 1848: d. Nov. 4, 1861.
2. WILLIAM HENRY, b. Sept. 11, 1850: m. Susan A. Lufkin, Dec. 19, 1872.
3. BENJAMIN, b. Nov. 29, 1852.
4. MARY ESTHER, b. Oct. 19, 1854.
5. CHARLES HOVEY, b. Aug. 17, 1856.
6. FREDERICK ADAMS, b. Nov. 28, 1858.
7. JOHN ELMER, b. July 21, 1861: d. June 2, 1864.
8. GRACE LOUISA, b. Feb. 16, 1870.

---

181. BETSEY KINSMAN, daughter of Isaac and Mary (p. 120), born in Springfield, N. H., Feb. 1, 1801; married there, JOHN MOODY, February, 1818. Resided in Wilmot, N. H.; removed in May, 1838, to Union, Champaign Co., Ohio, where he died Oct. 15, 1857.

THEIR CHILDREN:

1. Moses Uran, b. June 7, 1819: m. Maria Guy, of Canada, Nov., 1841; residence, Union, O.
2. James Murray, b. June 21, 1821: m. Judith Elkins, of Andover, N. H., March, 1847; residence, Des Moines, Iowa.
3. William Kinsman, b. July 7, 1823: d. Dec., 1825.
4. Eliza Jane, b. March 18, 1827: m. John M. Smith, of Concord, N. H., Feb., 1866; residence, Union, O.
5. Albert K., b. Dec. 26, 1829: m. Mary J. Goves, of Goshen, O., Jan., 1853; residence, Union, O.
6. Oren Tracy, b. Sept. 15, 1832: m. and lives in Kansas.
7. Nancy Maria, b. April 1, 1837: m. Joseph Allen Bullard, April, 1863, son of Gardner and Diana (Kinsman) Bullard (235).

---

182. EMILY JANE KINSMAN, daughter of Isaac and Mary (p. 120), born in Wilmot, N. H., July 19, 1825; married in Andover, N. H., Frederick William Greenough, Nov. 19, 1848. He was a merchant in Boscawen, N. H.; removed, in 1850, to New York City, where they remained until 1855; and removed to Mechanicsburg, Champaign Co., Ohio, where they now reside.

THEIR CHILDREN:

1. John Kinsman, b. Nov. 19, 1849.
2. Willie Isaac, b. April 27, 1851.
3. Harry Howard, b. Aug. 4, 1853: d. Dec. 29, 1860.
4. Mary Emily Grace, b. March 23, 1856.
5. Edward Frederick, b. Sept. 12, 1859.
6. Ellen Jane, b. Sept. 9, 1862.

---

183. LUCY KINSMAN, daughter of Asa and Susan (p. 121), born in Springfield, N. H., Jan. 9, 1798; married Otis Barney. He was born in Grafton, N. H., May 7, 1800, the son of Otis and Rhuhamah (Walker) Barney. Residence, Andover, N. H.

THEIR CHILDREN:

1. MARY WOODMAN, b. Feb. 13, 1824: m. Charles W. Kendall; residence, Andover, N. H.
2. STEPHEN, b. Dec. 5, 1829: died young.
3. HORACE, b. April 2, 1832: m. Mary J. Bartlett; residence, Haverhill, Mass.
4. SUSAN RHUHAMAH, b. July 11, 1835: m. Elisha Knowles Morrill, June 2, 1858. He was b. July 5, 1825, the son of Stephen and Susan (Dean) Morrill, and grandson of John and Lydia (Kinsman) Morrill. Residence, Charles City, Floyd Co., Iowa.

---

184. JANE T. KINSMAN, daughter of Asa and Susan (p. 121), born in Springfield, N. H., March 2, 1800; married SAMUEL E. WYMAN, Nov. 20, 1829. He was born in Woburn, Mass., Feb. 17, 1778, the son of Samuel E. and Anna Wyman. Residence, Woburn, where he died June 10, 1860.

THEIR CHILDREN:

1. JANE KINSMAN, b. Dec. 27, 1830: m. Josiah F. Starkweather, Sept. 20, 1852; residence, Boston.
2. SAMUEL E., b. Nov. 6, 1835: m. Allie Hall, Dec. 18, 1867; residence, Woburn.
3. HARRY, b. Feb. 20, 1837: d. March 10, 1837.
4. HENRY, b. March 5, 1838: unm.; residence, Boston.

---

185. STEPHEN KINSMAN, son of Asa and Susan (p. 121), born in New Chester (now Hill), N. H., June 11, 1802; married SOPHIA DUNDEE, and settled in Alabama about 1822. He was living, in 1840, in Greenfield, Ala.

THEIR CHILDREN:

1. WILLIAM FRANKLIN.
2. JANE ELIZA.
3. SUSAN SOPHIA.
4. LUCY EMILY.

186. LYDIA M. KINSMAN, daughter of Asa and Susan (p. 121), born in New Chester (now Hill), N. H., Jan. 22, 1805; married SAMUEL P. FLANDERS, Sept. 19, 1824. He was born in Danbury, N. H., Jan. 8, 1804, the son of Levi Flanders. Resided in Danbury. He died Sept. 27, 1827. She married, second, LUTHER C. ELLIOTT, Oct. 18, 1828. He was born in Rowley (Byfield), Mass., Sept. 1, 1801. They removed to Topsham, Vt., then to Canterbury, N. H., and lastly to Concord, N. H., where he died May 11, 1842. She now lives in Alexandria, N. H.

HER CHILD BY SAMUEL P. FLANDERS:

1. NANCY STICKNEY, b. Aug. 31, 1826: m. Lowell R. Roby, Jan. 29, 1848. Residence, Alexandria, N. H.

HER CHILDREN BY LUTHER C. ELLIOTT:

2. LUTHER PLUMMER, b. Feb. 19, 1831: m. Lethe Riddle; residence, Minneapolis, Minn.
3. FIDELIA JANE, b. Dec. 3, 1832: d. Feb. 21, 1848.
4. SARAH ANN, b. June 31, 1835: m. Erastus E. Rand; residence, South Amesbury.
5. CAROLINE GIBSON, b. Feb. 28, 1838: m. John H. Carter; residence, Newburyport.
6. EMELINE BAKER, b. Sept. 1, 1839: m. Nason M. Cass; residence, Grinnell, Iowa.

---

187. SUSAN KINSMAN, daughter of Asa and Susan (p. 121), born in New Chester (now Hill), N. H., Nov. 27, 1807; married AUSTIN LOVERING, the son of Jonathan Lovering, of Springfield, N. H. They deceased in Springfield, N. H.

THEIR CHILDREN:

1. ELIJAH WYMAN, b. Nov., 1835: m.; resides Vt.
2. GILBERT, b. : unm.; resides Vt.

188. EZOA KINSMAN, daughter of John and Susan (p. 121), born in Portsmouth, N. H., July 25, 1803; married there, JOHN BARSANTEE, Sept. 5, 1820. He was born in Portsmouth, N. H., Feb. 24, 1797, the son of John and Mary Anna (Bartlett) Barsantee, and died Sept. 1, 1875. She is living in Medford.

THEIR CHILDREN:

1. EMILY, b. April 3, 1821: m. Nathan Robbins; Seabrook, N. H.
2. ELIZA JANE, b. March 30, 1823: m. John Pitts; East Somerville.
3. JOHN HENRY, b. April 3, 1825: m. Louisa A. Strew; d. in Texas, Nov. 2, 1859.
4. ANDREW JACKSON, b. March 16, 1827: m. Hannah Hayes; Madison, Wis.
5. JAMES WILLIAM, b. July 25, 1829: m Anna Cole; East Somerville.
6. GEORGE WASHINGTON, b. Jan. 15, 1831: d. March 25, 1831.
7. ONSLOW, } Twins, b. June 4, 1832: m. Asenath A. Aldrich; Providence, R. I.
8. ALFONSO, } Twins, b. June 4, 1832: d. Boston, June 11, 1866.
9. GEORGE EDWIN, b. March 7, 1835: m. Sarah A. Preston; Dover, N. H.
10. ANNA AUGUSTA, b. Sept. 26, 1838: m. John T. Gray; Charlestown.
11. SARAH ELLEN, b. May 15, 1839: residence, Epping, N. H.
12. CARRIE, b. July 6, 1846: m. Geo. P. Chaplin; East Somerville.

---

189. ELIZABETH KINSMAN, daughter of John and Susan (p. 121), born in Portsmouth, N. H., Feb. 8, 1807; married, in Boston, DANIEL B. KNOX, March 24, 1844. He was born in Ossipee, N. H., 1816, the son of Edward and Sarah (Burrows) Knox. He was for many years engaged in business in Boston. Residence, Medford.

THEIR CHILDREN:

1. ADELIA WADSWORTH, b. Oct. 31, 1846: d Sept. 15, 1848.
2. MARY ELIZABETH, b. Nov. 8, 1850.

190. ARTEMISIA R. KINSMAN, daughter of John and Susan (p. 121), born in Portsmouth, N. H., Nov. 26, 1812; married ELIJAH ROLLINS, Nov. 13, 1836. He was born Dec. 2, 1812, the son of Ebenezer and Betsey (Rollins) Rollins. Resided in Manchester, N. H., where he died Sept. 5, 1872. She is living in Milford, N. H.

THEIR CHILDREN:

1. SUSAN AUGUSTA, b. May 22, 1847: m. John B. Johnson, of New Haven, Ct., Dec. 13, 1866.
2. JOHN BURNS WESTON, b. May 25, 1851: d. Jan. 21, 1863.

---

191. SOLON KINSMAN, son of Moses and Abigail (p. 122), born in Grafton, N. H., July 5, 1806; married LYDIA COOK, of Clarendon, Vt., Jan. 12, 1832. She was born in Westford, Vt., June 1, 1805, and died July 3, 1846. He married, second, in Franklin, Vt., LOPRUCIA F. FLETCHER, Sept. 8, 1847. She was born June 25, 1823, the daughter of Isaac and Dorinda (Day) Fletcher. Resided in Franklin, Vt., until after 1858, then removed to Magog, Canada East.

HIS CHILDREN BY LYDIA COOK:

1.	BETSEY JANE,	b. Nov. 1, 1834:	m. Charles Bryant.	**287**
2.	ERASTUS FRANCIS,	b. March 28, 1837:	d. Dec. 29, 1863.	
3.	HELEN MARIAN,	b. Jan. 26, 1840:	m. Alfr'd Beauregard.	**288**
4.	WILLIAM PEARSON,	b. Dec. 7, 1844.		

HIS CHILDREN BY LOPRUCIA F. FLETCHER:

5.	FLETCHER ISAAC,	b. Sept. 11, 1848.
6.	MARY LODOUSKY,	b. June 18, 18[illegible]0.
7.	GEORGE WASHINGTON,	b. June 18, 1852.
8.	JULIA ELIZA,	b. Sept. 12, 1854.
9.	CHARLES FREMONT,	b. Nov. 21, 1856.
10.	FLORA ANN,	b. Dec. 21, 1858.
11.	MALCOLM GRÆME,	b. Sept. 30, 1862.
12.	IDA ERMINA,	b. April 25, 1866.

192. DURA KINSMAN, son of Moses and Abigail (p. 122), born in Springfield, N. H., July 5, 1808; married MARY TOWN, Dec. 8, 1831. She was born in Temple, N. H., Aug. 12, 1812, the daughter of Joseph and Mary Averill Town, and died in Rochester, Vt., Jan. 25, 1838. He married, second, ZILPHA JONES, Dec. 5, 1839. She was born in Hancock, Vt., Dec. 9, 1805, the daughter of Daniel and Sally (Baker) Jones. Residence, West Rochester, Vt.

HIS CHILDREN BY MARY TOWN:

1. LAURA MARIA, b. Feb 22, 1833: m. Edward Epeneter. **289**
2. MARY ELIZABETH, b. Aug 6, 1834: d. April 28, 1853.
3. ROXA ARVILLA, b. Feb. 6, 1836: m. William P. Whitney. **290**
4. SARAH ALMEDA, b. Jan. 1, 1838: m. Royal I. Laird; Milton T. Crossman. **291**

HIS CHILDREN BY ZILPHA JONES:

5. ELLEN I., b. Feb. 26, 1841.
6. EMMA J., b. March 27, 1843: m. Martin L. Dutton, May 2, 1870; residence, Goshen, Vt.
7. HENRY M., b. March 6, 1845.
8. JULIA A., b. July 1, 1847: d. July 15, 1853.

He adopted Adolph E. Epeneter, orphan son of his eldest daughter, about November, 1864.

---

193. CARYL KINSMAN, son of Moses and Abigail (p. 122), born in Wilmot, N. H., June 9, 1810; married in Goshen, Vt., LYDIA CARR, April 24, 1834. She was born in Clarendon, Vt., March 26, 1816, the daughter of William and Elizabeth (Pierce) Carr. Residence, Brandon, Vt.

THEIR CHILDREN:

1. ELVIRA DEAN, b. Aug. 18, 1835: m. Alonzo E. Lord. **292**
2. HENRY, b. Oct. 10, 1837, in Brandon, Vt.; m. there, Ellen Janette Hendry, Oct. 10, 1865. She was b. in Brandon, April 17, 1843, the daughter of William and Janette (Brown) Hendry. He resides in Brandon, and has rendered valuable assistance in the collection of his family record.
3. CHARLES CARYL, b. April 28, 1840: m. Abby M. Ross. **293**

194. ELMINA KINSMAN, daughter of Moses and Abigail (p. 122), born in Wilmot, N. H., Aug. 18, 1814; married in Rochester, Vt., CALEB CARR, Feb. 21, 1833. He was born in Clarendon, Vt., Nov. 14, 1813, the son of William and Elizabeth (Pierce) Carr. He died in Brandon, Vt., May 5, 1868. She resides in Brandon.

THEIR CHILDREN:

1. WARNER CORY, b. June 10, 1835: d. Oct. 28, 1835.
2. EDWIN GEORGE, b. Oct. 9, 1836: m. Melva A. Jones, Nov. 23, 1858.
3. CARLOS WELLINGTON, b. July 13, 1838: m. Sarah A. Goodenough, March 26, 1860.
4. SUSAN GREENMAN, b. July 6, 1840: m. Jason K. Campbell, April 5, 1864.
5. RIAL FAYETTE, b. Nov. 3, 1845: d. in Winchester, Va., Nov. 13, 1864.
6. WARNER CHARLES, b. Nov. 19, 1851.

---

195. SARAH ANN KINSMAN, daughter of Moses and Abigail (p. 122), born in Fitzwilliam, N. H., Oct. 3, 1816; married JOSHUA WHITNEY, Nov. 25, 1837. He was born in Goshen, Vt., Feb. 25, 1813, the son of Oliver and Rebecca (Nichols) Whitney. Residence, West Rochester, Vt.

THEIR CHILDREN:

1. ERASTUS A., b. July 21, 1839: d. March 23, 1841.
2. ROBERT B., b. Aug. 15, 1841: d. New Orleans, June 13, 1862.
3. JOHN O., b. Aug. 14, 1844.
4. IDA J., b. Dec. 18, 1846.
5. SIDNEY C., b. March 9, 1849.
6. ANNA C., b. March 26, 1854.
7. MARY E., b. Aug. 22, 1857.

196. MARY FREELOVE KINSMAN, daughter of Moses and Abigail (p. 122), born in Clarendon, Vt., April 17, 1823; married WILLIAM L. BACON, Dec. 27, 1843. He was born in Brandon, Vt., July 30, 1819, the son of Levi and Sybil (Bemis) Bacon, and died in Brandon, April 7, 1859. She died in Brooklyn, N. Y., Jan. 5, 1872.

THEIR CHILDREN:

1. HARVEY L., b. April 8, 1845.
2. GEORGE W., b. Jan. 27, 1848: d. Jan. 12, 1872.
3. FORDYCE W., b. Dec. 24, 1850.
4. HATTIE E. A., b. Jan. 23, 1854.
5. JESSIE S., b. April 27, 1856.
6. WILLIE L., b. July 27, 1858: d. Sept. 26, 1859.

---

197. GEORGE WASHINGTON KINSMAN, son of Moses and Abigail (p. 122), born in Clarendon, Vt., Feb. 6, 1825; married ABBY P. COOLIDGE, Dec. 8, 1853. She was born in Plymouth, Vt., Sept. 10, 1834, the daughter of Luther and Betsey (Taylor) Coolidge. Residence, Brandon, Vt.

He adopted Nov. 12, 1864, Frankie Maria, orphan daughter of Edward and Laura Maria (Kinsman) Epeneter (289).

---

198. ELIZABETH S. KINSMAN, daughter of Stephen and Ruth (p. 122), born in Landaff, N. H., Jan. 29, 1806; married AMASA T. MARTIN, Feb. 6, 1833. He was born March 30, 1803, the son of Abram and Candace Martin. Residence, Clifton, Canada East.

THEIR CHILDREN:

1. ALONZO G., b. Feb. 15, 1834: m. Jennette Skinner, Dec. 28, 1864.
2. MARY E., b. Feb. 10, 1836: m. Frederick F. Bowen, March 31, 1862.
3. MELINDA M., b. Oct. 17, 1837.
4. AMASA, b. Jan. 29, 1839: m. Elinor Tarbox.
5. EMILY M., b. June 17, 1841: m. George Davidson, July 2, 1868.
6. ABRAM F., b. Dec. 31, 1845.
7. CHAPEN A., b. Feb. 15, 1849: m. Elinor Manning.

---

199. EVELINA KINSMAN, daughter of Stephen and Ruth (p. 122), born in Landaff, N. H., June 1, 1808; married WILLIAM LITTLE. They resided in Sutton, N. H. She died in Cambridge, Sept. 1, 1866.

THEIR CHILDREN:

1. HIRAM KINSMAN, b. : m.; d. at Petersburgh, July 4, 1864.
2. CYRUS B., b. : deceased.
3. WILLIAM, b.
4. THOMAS, b.

---

200. HIRAM KINSMAN, son of Stephen and Ruth (p. 122), born in Landaff, N. H., March 29, 1810; married AUGUSTA E. GILMAN, Feb. 6, 1844, the daughter of Ebenezer and Elizabeth Gilman. She died March 18, 1865. He married, second, JULIA SKINNER, June 20, 1866, the daughter of Nathan and Sally Skinner. Residence, Clifton, Canada East.

HIS CHILDREN BY AUGUSTA E. GILMAN:

1. LYDIA B., b. July 17, 1846: m. M. C. Bedell, Jan. 25, 1871.
2. MARTHA E., b. May 31, 1848: d. aged 14.
3. GEORGE W., b. Oct. 3, 1851.
4. ALICE M., b. June 21, 1854: d July 25, 1854.
5. ALICE M., b. May 22, 1859.
6. MARTHA AUGUSTA, b. Aug. 4, 1862.

HIS CHILDREN BY JULIA SKINNER:

7.	Hiram Elmer,	b. Nov. 8, 1867.
8.	Maria Estelle,	b. Jan. 25, 1870.
9.	Charles,	b. 1872.

---

201. PHILONAS KINSMAN, son of Stephen and Ruth (p. 122), born in Landaff, N. H., July 7, 1812; married Adaline Shurtleff. She was born in Hatley, Canada East, April 18, 1809. He was a farmer. Enlisted for the War of the Rebellion, at Beloit, Wis., in 1861; died July 26, 1863, at Gettysburg, Penn., of wounds received in battle, July 1, at that place. She died Nov. 25, 1874, at Philadelphia, Penn.

THEIR CHILDREN:

1.	Henry Harrison,	b. Sept. 16, 1840:	m. Lydia M. Levering.	**294**
2.	Amanda,	b.	in Canada East: d. in infancy.	
3.	Sarah Ada,	b. Aug. 4, 1845:	m. Edward A. Wanless.	**295**
4.	Waldo Scott,	b.	in Tewksbury: d. in infancy.	
5.	Rosina Alma,	b. July 29, 1848,	in Harvard, Mass.	
6.	Daughter,	b.	lived only a few days.	

---

202. HARRIET KINSMAN, daughter of Stephen and Ruth (p. 122), born in Landaff, N. H., April 18, 1817; married John Colby, Feb. 11, 1836. He died June 22, 1844. She married, second, Caleb Taplin, Feb. 28, 1847. She died Jan. 9, 1869.

HER CHILDREN BY JOHN COLBY:

1. Eveline R., b. Nov. 19, 1836: m. George Taplin, Jan. 25, 1858.
2. Clark T., b. Aug. 27, 1838: d. Dec. 26, 1863.
3. Stephen K., b. April 27, 1841: d. Aug. 26, 1842.

203. DAVID OSGOOD KINSMAN, son of Stephen and Ruth (p. 122), born in Landaff, N. H., July 22, 1819; married RUTH ANN GILBERT, Dec. 20, 1843. She was born Feb. 21, 1816, the daughter of Nathan and Elizabeth Gilbert, and died July 4, 1868. He married, second, ELIZABETH CHEEVER. Residence, St. Johnsbury, Vt.

HIS CHILDREN BY RUTH ANN GILBERT:

1. ALICE JANE, b. Nov. 8, 1848: d. Nov. 12, 1865.
2. JULIA F., b. May 11, 1853.

HIS CHILD BY ELIZABETH CHEEVER:

3. AMMON, b. Aug. 31, 1874.

---

204. JOHN OSGOOD KINSMAN, son of Stephen and Ruth (p. 123), born in Landaff, N. H., Jan. 1, 1827; married MARGARET H. MAGILL, Jan. 1, 1850, the daughter of James and Thankful Magill. She died Feb. 20, 1866. He married, second, OLIVE C. POTTER, Nov. 26, 1866, the daughter of David and Ada Potter. Residence, Cambridgeport.

HIS CHILDREN BY MARGARET H. MAGILL:

1. IDA M., b. Sept. 19, 1851: d. Nov. 18, 1868.
2. EDGAR OSGOOD, b. April 6, 1856.
3. ALBERT HERBERT, b. April 21, 1860: d. Sept. 19, 1860.

HIS CHILD BY OLIVE C. POTTER:

4. ADA RUTH, b. Dec. 28, 1867.

---

205. JOHN DAFFORNE KINSMAN, son of Nathan and Eliza (p. 123), born in Portland, Me., Oct. 13, 1805; married ANGELA RICHMOND CUTTER, March 9, 1830. She was born in Portland, Feb. 16, 1803, the daughter of William and Margaret (Dicks) Cutter.

He graduated at Bowdoin College, in 1825; was a distinguished and brilliant scholar and orator; a lawyer in Portland, and United States Marshal for District of Maine, appointed under President Harrison; afterwards practised law in Wisconsin. He died in Belfast, Me., May 27, 1850. His widow resides in Clinton, Iowa.

THEIR CHILDREN:

1. JOHN DAFFORNE, b. Dec. 4, 1830: d. March 16, 1842.
2. OLIVER DORRANCE, b. Feb. 18, 1835: m. Emma M. L. Richardson, Washington, Oct. 19, 1871. He served in the army during the late war; has the rank of Colonel. Is in the War Department, Washington, D. C.

3 and 4. Two sons, b. : d. in infancy.

---

206. ELIZA KINSMAN, daughter of Peter and Mary (p. 124), born in Landaff, N. H., Feb. 25, 1811; married BEMSLEY EDWARDS.

THEIR CHILDREN:

1. ELIZA JANE, b. May 3, 1829: d. March 3, 1832.
2. GEORGE KINSMAN, b. Jan. 3, 1831.

---

207. GEORGE SHATTUCK KINSMAN, son of Timothy and Lucy (p. 124), born in Bedford, Mass., Aug. 5, 1809; married NANCY S. HOLDEN, March 15, 1832. She was born Oct. 20, 1813, the daughter of Thomas and Sophia Holden. He commanded a steamboat running between Mobile and Montgomery, Ala., and died in Galveston, Texas, Feb. 10, 1843.

THEIR CHILDREN:

1. GEORGIANNA,
2. GEORGE GRANVILLE,
3. THOMAS,
4. HANNEY,

} Died in infancy.

208. LUCY ANGELINA KINSMAN, daughter of Timothy and Lucy (p. 124), born in South Reading, Mass., Sept. 8, 1811; married ALFRED MUDGE, Dec. 22, 1831. He was born in Portsmouth, N. H., April 25, 1809, the son of Capt. Samuel and Anna (Breed) Mudge. He is the author of the "Genealogy of the Mudge Family," and senior partner of the firm of Alfred Mudge & Son, No. 34 School Street, Boston, one of the largest Book and Job Printing houses in New England. They are the publishers of this Genealogy.

Residence, Boston.

THEIR CHILDREN:

1. LUCY ANNA ANGELINA, b. Oct. 13, 1832: m. William Parker Jones, Jan. 1, 1856; residence, Boston. Their child: Frederic Kinsman Mudge, b. Nov. 11, 1856.
2. ALFRED AUGUSTUS, b. Nov. 10, 1833: m. Abbie Clinton King, March 25, 1856. Associated with his father in the firm of Alfred Mudge & Son. Residence, Boston. Their children: Carrie King, b June 4, 1857; Frank Herbert, b. Feb. 10, 1859; Clarence Bradford, b. Dec. 30, 1863; Angelina Kinsman, b. May 25, 1868; Alfred, b. May 3, 1870.

---

209. ALICE ELIZA KINSMAN, daughter of Timothy and Lucy (p. 124), born in Bedford, Mass., July 24, 1813; married BENJAMIN BRADLEY, of Boston, Nov., 1832. She died in Boston, April 7, 1843.

THEIR CHILDREN:

1. ELIZA ABBOTT, b. July 27, 1833: m. George Ansley Mudge, of Brookline, Oct 17, 1855. She d. Nov. 28, 1873. Their children: George Bradley, b. Aug. 9, 1859; Florence Eliza, b. June 4, 1864.
2. BENJAMIN KINSMAN, b. Dec., 1837: d. April 24, 1840.

210. MARTHA MARIA KINSMAN, daughter of Timothy and Lucy (p. 124), born in Bedford, Mass., April 20, 1815; married BENJAMIN BRADLEY, Nov. 15, 1844. He was born Jan. 20, 1802, and had previously married her sister. He died Jan. 16, 1862.

THEIR CHILDREN:

1. ANGELINA MARIA, b. April 6, 1848: d March 13, 1850.
2. ALICE MARIA, b. Dec. 18, 1854.
3. BENJAMIN ABBOTT, b. Dec 21, 1856.

---

211. HENRY WILLIS KINSMAN, son of Aaron and Ann (p. 125), born in Portland, Me., March 6, 1803; married ELIZABETH WILLIS, Oct. 1, 1828. She was born Oct. 25, 1807, the daughter of Benjamin Willis, of Boston, and died May 3, 1856. He married, second, MARTHA FROTHINGHAM TITCOMB, Oct. 5, 1858, the daughter of Joseph Moody and Sarah Elizabeth (Willis) Titcomb, of Newburyport.

He graduated at Dartmouth College, in 1822, and read law with Daniel Webster, with whom he was a partner in 1826. Represented Boston in the State Legislature, in 1833, 1834, and 1835; delivered the Fourth of July Oration before the city authorities of Boston, July 4, 1836. Removed his office to Newburyport in 1836; was a Representative from that place also, in 1839, 1849, and 1854, and State Senator from Essex County for one year. Collector of Customs at Newburyport from 1841 to 1845, also from 1849 to 1853.

He died Dec. 4, 1859. (His widow married Francis Lyman Winship, Oct. 2, 1867, and resides in Allston.)

HIS CHILDREN BY ELIZABETH WILLIS:

1. HENRY WILLIS, b. July 29, 1829: d. July 9, 1847.
2. ELIZABETH ANN, b. Jan. 20, 1831: d. Dec. 11, 1844.

3. BENJAMIN WILLIS, b. Jan. 8, 1833: a medical graduate of Brown University in 1852; d. Nov., 1855, at Paris, France, where he was perfecting himself in his medical studies.
4. GEORGE EDWARD, b. Jan. 27, 1835: died in infancy, and was buried under Park Street Church.
5. CLARA CROWNINSHIELD, b. Nov. 24, 1837: m. Gam. Bradford. **296**
6. MARY MCKINSTRY, b. March 10, 1839: m. Wm. G. Howe. **297**
7. GEORGE EDWARD, b. April 12, 1841: d. Sept. 4, 1841.
8. ANNA, b. Feb. 26, 1843: d. Jan. 23, 1846.
9. EDWIN, b. Feb. 12, 1845: d. May 1, 1845.
10. ROBERT D., b. July 20, 1846: d. May 1, 1856, and was buried the same day with his mother.
11. LOUISA HAMILTON, b. Nov. 12, 1849: d. in Haverhill, Sept. 10, 1870.

---

212. ANN KINSMAN, daughter of Aaron and Ann (p. 125), born in Portland, Me., about 1808; married Rev. DUDLEY PHELPS. He was born in Hebron, Ct., Jan. 24, 1799, the son of Obadiah Phelps. Resided in Groton, Mass. She died in 1834. He died Sept. 24, 1849.

THEIR CHILD:

1. BENJAMIN KINSMAN, b. Sept. 16, 1832, in Haverhill: graduated at Yale College, 1853; studied law, and has practised in New York City for many years. He m. Hannah Maria Cutler, Oct. 21, 1857, the daughter of Julius and Mary Cutler, of Hartford, Ct., and has three children: Mary Cutler, b. Oct. 11, 1858; Dudley, b. Oct. 7, 1861; Ann Kinsman, b. March 9, 1865.

212½. FRANK W. KINSMAN, son of John and Sarah (p. 126), born in Augusta, Me., Jan. 5, 1833; married in Providence, R. I., July 8, 1851, OCTAVIA A. GREELY, of Palermo, Me. She was born Dec. 7, 1831. He is a druggist; residence, Augusta, Me.

THEIR CHILDREN:

1. Ralph B., b. Feb. 26, 1852: d. July 29, 1874.
2. Sarah Lottie, b Feb. 27, 1854: d. Sept. 12, 1856.
3. Hattie Lee, b. Sept. 19, 1856.
4. Frank W., b. Aug. 19, 1858.
5. Fred G., b. Aug. 10, 1862.

---

213. NELSON KINSMAN, son of Isaac and Matilda (p. 128), born in Northfield, Vt., March 9, 1808; married Lydia Edwards, 1827. He died Dec. 7, 1837.

THEIR CHILDREN:

1. Isaac,
2. Lydia,
3. Christopher,
4. Cyrenus,
5. Matilda,

} Live in West Wisconsin.

---

214. PHILURA KINSMAN, daughter of Isaac and Matilda (p. 128), born in Northfield, Vt., July 25, 1813; married Roswell Carpenter, January, 1835. Residence, Northfield.

THEIR CHILDREN:

1. Carrie M., b. Oct. 9, 1835: m. William S. Smith, April 4, 1852.
2. Sophia M., b. Aug. 24, 1837: m. C. B. George, Jan. 1, 1868.
3. Darwin E., b. Aug. 31, 1840: m. Hattie Morse, July, 1867.
4. George C., b. Nov. 24, 1842: m. Mary Davenport, January, 1865.
5. Julia, b. Dec. 28, 1850.
6. Frank, b. Dec. 19, 1858.

---

215. ZILPHA KINSMAN, daughter of Isaac and Matilda (p. 128), born in Northfield, Vt., Oct. 7, 1815; married William D. Balch, Dec. 4, 1834. Residence, Northfield.

THEIR CHILDREN:

1. Mattie S., b. Sept. 26, 1835: m. N. B. Stevens, Bradford, Vt., May 9, 1871.
2. Minnie C., b. March 15, 1840: m. George Crane, Moretown, June, 1856.
3. Mary E., b. April 2, 1842: m. George Simmons, Manchester, N. H., May, 1862.
4. Henry C., b. May 7, 1844: residence, Michigan.
5. Lucy A., b. Dec. 3, 1846: m. Charles French, Franklin, N. H.
6. Sarah, b. Dec. 11, 1848: m. H. H. Priest, Burlington, Vt., July 15, 1867.
7. Lizzie D., b. May 24, 1852.
8. Jessie F., b. May 27, 1855.
9. Ida M., b. Feb. 11, 1861.

---

216. LUCY A. KINSMAN, daughter of Isaac and Matilda (p. 128), born in Northfield, Vt., May 25, 1820; married John H. Davis, of Cincinnati, O., 1840.

THEIR CHILDREN:

1. Susan, b. 1843: m. M. J. Turrell, of N. Y., 1866.
2. Lizzie, b. 1848: m. Hon. Benjamin Eggleston, D. C., 1867. He was a member of the State Senate, of Ohio, in 1862, 1863, 1864, and 1865; was elected to the Thirty-ninth Congress; re-elected to the Fortieth Congress. Residence, Cincinnati, O.
3. Charles, b. 1849: residence, Cincinnati, O.
4. Harry, b. 1854: residence, Cincinnati, O.

---

217. DIANTHA KINSMAN, daughter of Isaac and Matilda (p. 128), born in Northfield, Vt., June 14, 1824; married Nathan F. Sargeant, 1839. Residence, Northfield.

THEIR CHILDREN:

1. Rosette, b. 1848: d. 1870, in Leavenworth, Kansas.
2. Aroline, b. 1850: residence, Leavenworth, Kansas.
3. Ellen, b. : residence, Manchester, N. H.

218. JAMES WATSON KINSMAN, son of James H. and Sarah (p. 128), born in Williamstown, Vt., Nov. 3, 1814; married there ROCINA C. MARTIN, May 3, 1838. She was born in Williamstown, April 13, 1813, the daughter of Daniel and Betsey Martin. He died in Williamstown, Feb. 25, 1842. His widow resides in Chelsea, Vt.

THEIR CHILDREN:

1. ELIZABETH, b. April 17, 1839: d. March 12, 1842.
2. GERTRUDE M., b. July 16, 1841.

---

219. EMILY WHEELOCK KINSMAN, daughter of James H. and Sarah (p. 128), born in Williamstown, Vt., July 13, 1816; married in Princeton, Ill., EGBERT E. COLTON, Dec. 2, 1842. He was born in Gouverneur, N. Y., Dec. 2, 1815, the son of Jonathan and Betsey Colton, and died 1855. She resides in Princeton, Ill.

THEIR CHILD:

1. LUCIA M., b. March 14, 1847: m. Charles P. Bascom, Dec. 11, 1867. Residence, Princeton, Ill.

---

220. DENISON KINSMAN, son of James H. and Sarah (p. 128), born in Williamstown, Vt., July 6, 1818; married there, MARY MARTIN, Nov. 24, 1839. She was born in Williamstown, March 11, 1818, the daughter of Gurdon and Sarah Martin, and died in Princeton, Ill., Dec. 12, 1865. He married, second, LORA BURNHAM, March 21, 1867. She was born Dec. 26, 1825, the daughter of David and Betsey Burnham. Residence, Winterset, Madison Co., Iowa.

23

HIS CHILDREN BY MARY MARTIN:

1. Rosannah Mary, b. Nov. 28, 1840: residence, Larkspur, Cal.
2. Jason Martin, } Twins, { d. Dec. 10, 1856, in Princet'n, Ill.
3. James Watson, } b. Aug. 19, 1842: { residence, Columbus.
4. Herman Artaman, b. March 25, 1844: m. Nancy Sophia Ward, March 10, 1869; residence, Winterset, Iowa.
5. Sarah Wise, b. Aug. 26, 1845.

---

221. AARON BOADWIN KINSMAN, son of James H. and Sarah (p. 128), born in Williamstown, Vt., Jan. 16, 1820; married there, Louisa Sophia Hatch, May 25, 1843. She was born in Williamstown, March 11, 1824, the daughter of Sanford and Sophia Hatch. Residence, Sheffield, Bureau Co., Ill.

THEIR CHILDREN:

1. Martha Elizabeth, b. April 10, 1844: d. April 21, 1844.
2. Lizzie Sarah, b. May 20, 1845: m. Joseph A. Mercer, Oct. 24, 1867; residence, Sheffield, Ill.
3. George Sanford Hatch, b. March 21, 1847.
4. Barna Lewis, b. Jan. 6, 1856.
5. Ann Emily, b. Dec. 20, 1860: d. April 19, 1863.
6. Henry Clay, b. Oct. 26, 1863.
7. Hattie Louisa, b. March 11, 1869.

---

222. MARSHALL CROYDON KINSMAN, son of James H. and Sarah (p. 128), born in Williamstown, Vt., Sept. 7, 1822; married there, Ellen Calista Luce, Sept. 1850. She was born in Williamstown, Feb. 26, 1826, the daughter of Ephraim and Mary Luce, and died in Princeton, Ill., April 20, 1851. He married, second, Sarah Jane Snow, in Provo City, Utah, and died there Feb. 5, 1863.

HIS CHILDREN:

1. George, b.
2. Sarah Louisa, b.
3. Emily Wheelock, b.

223. MARY LOUISA KINSMAN, daughter of James H. and Sarah (p. 128), born in Williamstown, Vt., March 22, 1824; married in Princeton, Ill., ROBERT TONKINSON, December, 1856. He was born in Wolverhampton, Staffordshire, England, April 16, 1824, the son of John and Sarah Tonkinson. Residence, Princeton, Ill.

THEIR CHILDREN:

1. HENRY, b. Sept. 27, 1858.
2. CLARIABELL, b. Sept. 7, 1860.
3. ELLEN, b. July 9, 1863.
4. FRANK, b. Sept. 28, 1865.

---

224. NEWELL KINSMAN, son of James H. and Sarah (p. 128), born in Williamstown, Vt., Dec. 30, 1825; married in Wyanet, Ill., ELLEN FRANCES COBB, June 5, 1866. She was born in Sutton, Mass., Aug. 20, 1840, the daughter of Lewis T. and Jane Cobb. Residence, Fontanella, Adair Co., Iowa.

THEIR CHILDREN:

1. WILLARD, b. March 8, 1867.
2. MINNIE, b. Oct. 2, 1869.

---

225. WILLIAM M. KINSMAN, son of Ephraim and Rebecca (p. 129), born in Plainfield, N. H., Nov. 17, 1817; married Mrs. MARIA DEAN, March 14, 1846, the widow of Benjamin Dean. She was born in Claremont, N. H., Feb. 26, 1820, the daughter of William Frederick and Ruth (Bond) Munger. Residence, Cornish Flat, N. H.

THEIR CHILD:

1. DARWIN BRYANT, b. in Plainfield, N. H., Feb. 21, 1847: m. Adaline Estella Chase, Jan. 17, 1871, dau. of Moses and Fidelia (Alden) Chase, of Cornish, N. H.; residence, Cornish.

226. FRANCIS S. KINSMAN, son of Ephraim and Rebecca (p. 129), born March 2, 1820; married, in Barrington, R. I., SUSAN K. MILLER, Jan. 6, 1850. She was born in Swanzey, Mass., March 12, 1832, the daughter of Jonas H. and Wealthy W. Miller. Residence, Aurora, Ohio.

THEIR CHILDREN:

1. EMMA F., b. Feb. 4, 1852, Barrington, R. I.
2. ELIZABETH A., b. Nov. 24, 1857, Aurora, O.
3. FRANK D., b. June 24, 1860, Streetsboro', O.

---

227. GEORGE LAMB KINSMAN, son of Newell and Leonora (p. 130), born in Barre, Vt., July 18, 1829; married, in Montpelier, Vt., ANN ELIZA HUBBARD, May 31, 1853. She was born in Springfield, Mass., Nov. 1, 1828, the daughter of William B. and Eliza Ann Hubbard, of Montpelier, and died in Montpelier, Feb. 4, 1858. He married, second, in Milwaukee, Wis., Mrs. MARY J. MOSES, Jan. 4, 1869, the daughter of Howard and Elizabeth Bosworth. Residence, Milwaukee.

HIS CHILD BY ANN E. HUBBARD:

1. ELLEN MARIA, b. in Montpelier, Vt., Dec. 3, 1855, and has lived there with her grandparents since her mother's death.

---

228. WARREN KINSMAN, son of Willis and Fannie (p. 130), born in Royalton, Vt., July 3, 1830; married MARY RYAN, who died about a year afterward. He married, second, her sister, ANNIE RYAN, Sept. 13, 1860. Residence, Charleston, S. C.

HIS CHILDREN BY ANNIE RYAN:

1. WILLIS NORMAN, b. March 27, 1862.
2. SUMNER HENRY, b. Nov. 17, 1864.
3. FANNIE, b. Aug. 3, 1866: d. Oct. 17, 1870.
4. MARY ELIZABETH, b. Sept. 30, 1870.

229. FRANCES KINSMAN, daughter of Willis and Fannie (p. 130), born in Royalton, Vt., Nov. 26, 1834; married, in Hartford, Ct., Judge MONROE ERASMUS MERRILL, April 5, 1866, the son of Merlin and Clarissa (Newton) Merrill. Residence, Hartford.

THEIR CHILD:

1. WILLIAM EATON, b. July 8, 1870.

---

230. BLISS KINSMAN, son of Samuel and Kezia (p. 131), born in Heath, Mass., May 1, 1804; married BETSEY TEMPLE, Oct. 30, 1831. She was born June 25, 1811. Residence, Heath, where he died July 16, 1873.

THEIR CHILDREN:

1. DAVID N., b. May 3, 1834: m. Isabelle L. Stevens. **298**
2. HENRY B., b. July 10, 1836: studied law, and was admitted to the bar, in Ohio, Aug. 12, 1862. He enlisted in Co. A, 114th Regt., Ohio Vols., Aug. 13, 1862, and died at Young's Point, La., Jan. 25, 1863. His body was carried to Heath for interment.
3. HELEN M., b. April 18, 1838: d. Jan. 13, 1847.
4. CHRISTIANA B., b. Jan. 22, 1841: m. Gilford W. Lamb, January, 1869; residence, Heath.
5. MARIAN E., b. April 6, 1843: m. John A. Dwight. **299**
6. ALICE L., b. Sept. 3, 1846: d. Aug. 25, 1851.
7. WALTER E., b. July 12, 1847: m. Clara J. Bassett. **300**
8. KATE E., b. July 29, 1853: m. Oscar A. Sumner. **301**

---

231. SAMUEL AUSTIN KINSMAN, son of Samuel and Kezia (p. 131), born in Hubbardston, Mass., Jan. 24, 1808; married CHRISTIANA BARR, of New Braintree, Sept. 25, 1838. She was the daughter of Jonathan and Penelope Barr, and died Dec. 23, 1840, aged 25. He married, second, BETSEY H. RICE, Dec. 8, 1843, the widow of Freeman Rice, and daughter of Artemas and Polly Hapgood. Residence, Barre, Mass. Has no children.

232. KEZIA KINSMAN, daughter of Samuel and Kezia (p. 131), born in Heath, Mass., Jan. 2, 1810; married ELIPHALET HOWE. He was born in Barre, Mass., Feb. 22, 1804, the son of Eliphalet and Mary (Henry) Howe. Resided in Barre. He died in 1857. She resides in Westborough, Mass.

THEIR CHILDREN:

1. SAMUEL A., b. May 6, 1834: m. Lucy J. Warner, 1858; residence, Westborough.
2. MERCY ELLEN, b. Dec. 25, 1835: m. Franklin Babbitt, 1851; residence, Barre.
3. ELLIOTT A., b. Sept. 22, 1837: m. Nancy M. Wheelock, 1859.
4. MARIA, b. Nov. 22, 1839: m. Davis E. White, 1859; residence, Westborough.
5. CRESSIE B., b. May 4, 1841: m. Charles Wheeler, of Hardwick, 1865.
6. FRANCIS E., b. Jan. 22, 1852: residence, Westborough.

---

233. ROXANA KINSMAN, daughter of Samuel and Kezia (p. 131), born in Heath, Mass., Dec. 17, 1814; married MILETUS HENRY, May 21, 1835. He was born in Boston, Aug. 18, 1812, the son of John and Mary (Stearns) Henry, of Barre, Mass. She died Jan. 12, 1867. He resides in Westborough, Mass.

THEIR CHILDREN:

1. MARY STEARNS, b. May 21, 1836: m. Charles Robinson, May 21, 1860; residence, Barre.
2. MARTHA, b. June 20, 1838: m. Joseph H. Shepardson, of Royalston, Oct. 17, 1865. She d. April 29, 1869.
3. MARIA ELIZABETH, b. Oct. 6, 1840: m. Marcus M. Wadsworth, Oct. 6, 1859; residence, West Newton.
4. JOHN EDWIN, b. Dec. 17, 1845: m. Mary J. Dewey, Jan. 20, 1870; residence, Westborough.
5. BENJAMIN FRANKLIN, b. July 23, 1848: d. July 4, 1871.

234. ADNAH BANGS KINSMAN, son of Joseph and Kezia (p. 132), born in Heath, Mass., May 9, 1805; married, in Hinsdale, N. Y., ASENATH M. CHANDLER, of that place, April 19, 1835. Residence, Ellington, N. Y.

THEIR CHILDREN:

1. EMILY M., b. March 4, 1836: m. Robert P. Boodie, of Rochester, N. Y., Dec. 19, 1858; residence, Chesterfield, O.
2. JOHN A., b. Feb. 8, 1838: m. Cynthia J. Billings. **302**
3. JAMES M., b. July 1, 1840: d. Sept. 24, 1861.
4. JEANNIE E., b. Sept. 16, 1842: residence, Ellington, N. Y.
5. FRANC M., b. Sept. 7, 1844: " " "
6. ELLA M., b. Jan. 18, 1847: m. Chauncey Crumb. **303**
7. GEORGE CHANDLER, b. Aug. 22, 1850: m. Lora S. Christiancy. **304**
8. WILLIS CLAYTON, b. Sept. 6, 1853: residence, Ellington, N. Y.

---

235. DIANA KINSMAN, daughter of Joseph and Kezia (p. 132), born in Heath, Mass., Oct. 16, 1807; married, in Shrewsbury, Vt., GARDNER BULLARD, Aug. 11, 1830. He was born Sept. 27, 1805, the son of John and Lucy (Buxton) Bullard, of Shrewsbury. Residence, Hinsdale, N. Y.

THEIR CHILDREN:

1. DIANA K., b. July 5, 1832: m. Samuel P. Farwell, March 11, 1854.
2. JOSEPH ALLEN, b. Feb. 24, 1834: m. Nancy Maria Moody, April, 1863, dau. of John and Betsey (Kinsman) Moody (181); residence, Union, Champaign Co., O.
3. JANE ANN, b. Oct. 8, 1835: m. William H. Wing, Aug. 11, 1858; residence, Mechanicsburg, O.
4. EDWIN GARDNER, b. Nov. 29, 1837: m. Mary V. Billings, May 27, 1866.
5. JOHN ALMON, b. Sept. 11, 1847: d. April 13, 1861.
6. ELLEN FRANCES, b. Oct. 31, 1849: residence, Hinsdale, N. Y.

---

236. JOHN KINSMAN, son of Joseph and Kezia (p. 132), born in Heath, Mass., July 22, 1811; married, in Fitchburg, LUCY A. GREELEY, June 3, 1841. She was born

April 4, 1816, the daughter of Dustin and Sarah (Woodburn) Greeley. Resided in Shrewsbury, Vt., where he died Dec. 28, 1865. His widow resides in South Reading, Vt.

THEIR CHILDREN:

1. SARAH J., b. Jan. 17, 1844: m. Henry O. Waite. 305
2. HELEN N., b. March 26, 1848.
3. MARTHA K., b. April 23, 1849.
4. JAMES A., b. Jan. 13, 1852.
5. LIZZIE M., b. May 25, 1858.

---

237. JAMES A. KINSMAN, son of Joseph and Kezia (p. 132), born in Heath, Mass., March 28, 1817; married, in Shrewsbury, Vt., HANNAH MASON HOLDEN, Sept. 26, 1843. She was born in Shrewsbury, March 20, 1819, the daughter of Harry and Elizabeth Green (Spencer) Holden. Resided in Burlington, Vt. He died in Rutland, Vt., July 12, 1853.

THEIR CHILDREN:

1. MARCIA KEZIAH, } Twins, b. Jan. 21, 1846: m. Herbert W. Eaton; residence, Boston.
2. MARTHA ELIZABETH, } Twins, b. Jan. 21, 1846: d. July 12, 1846.

---

238. JOSEPH KINSMAN, son of John and Eunice (p. 132), born in Shrewsbury, Vt., Nov. 9, 1809; married there, ELVIRA KINSMAN, Oct. 21, 1838. She was born in Heath, Mass., Oct. 15, 1809, the daughter of Joseph (122) and Kezia (Bangs) Kinsman. Resided in Shrewsbury, Vt. He died in Ellington, N. Y., Sept. 11, 1861. His widow resides in Sinclairsville, N. Y.

THEIR CHILDREN:

1. NANCY JANE, b. April 30, 1840: m. Zoroaster Nichols, Aug. 10, 1862; residence, Charlotte, N. Y.
2. WILLIAM HARRISON, b. April 30, 1848: residence, Sinclairsville, N. Y.

239. PARKER KINSMAN, son of John and Eunice (p. 132), born in Shrewsbury, Vt., Jan. 26, 1811; married HARRIET E. HOLDEN, June 17, 1841. She was born in Shrewsbury, the daughter of Harry and Elizabeth Green (Spencer) Holden, and died May, 1850. He married, second, in Cavendish, Vt., MARY A. FAIRBANK, Jan. 27, 1853. She was born in Acton (now Townsend), Vt., July 17, 1817, the daughter of Ira and Hannah (Quaid) Fairbank. Residence, Shrewsbury, Vt., until 1857; since then South Reading, Vt.

HIS CHILD BY HARRIET E. HOLDEN:

1. INFANT SON, b. April, 1850: lived but eight days.

---

240. JOHN M. KINSMAN, son of John and Eunice (p. 132), born in Shrewsbury, Vt., June 9, 1816; married NANCY B. KINSMAN, Aug. 23, 1841. She was born in Heath, Mass., July 1, 1821, the daughter of Joseph (122) and Kezia (Bangs) Kinsman, and died in Potsdam, N. Y., Nov. 16, 1848. He married, second, DELANIA A. FOOTE, Aug. 23, 1849. She was born in Potsdam, N. Y., Jan. 23, 1830, the daughter of Orsemus L. and Mary A. Foote. Residence, Potsdam Junction, N. Y.

HIS CHILD BY NANCY B KINSMAN:

1. HELEN N., b. March 1, 1844: m. Henry D. Morgan. **306**

HIS CHILDREN BY DELANIA A. FOOTE:

2. HENRY M, b. Aug. 21, 1857.
3. GENNIE D., b. Jan. 5, 1859: d. June 11, 1867.
4. CARRIE L., b. Feb. 19, 1869: d. Aug. 21, 1869.

---

241. MARY ANN KINSMAN, daughter of James and Nancy (p. 133), born in Shrewsbury, Vt., Jan. 29,

1809; married DANIEL W. JEFFERSON, Jan. 29, 1829. He was born in Vermont, July 22, 1804. Residence, Darien, Genesee Co., N. Y.

THEIR CHILDREN:

1. WALLACE W., b Aug. 27, 1830: m. Libbie Artenburg, April 10, 1860.
2. EDWIN B., b. Nov. 19, 1831: m. Amanda Steadman, Sept. 4, 1848.
3. ZINA, b. May 24, 1833: d. July 18, 1837.
4. ADNAH K., b. June 28, 1835.
5. ELLIOTT I., b. June 16, 1837: m. Luelyn M. Barross, Nov. 12, 1868.
6. JAMES D., b. Aug. 6, 1844.
7. MARY ANN, b. Oct. 7, 1846: d. Dec. 18, 1849
8. LODEMA, b. April 12, 1848: d. Sept. 7, 1854.

---

242. ELISHA KINSMAN, son of James and Nancy (p. 133), born in Darien, Genesee Co., N. Y., Jan. 17, 1812; married there, LYDIA HOYLE, May 1, 1831. She was born in Darien, N. Y., June 20, 1814, the daughter of William and Catharine Hoyle, and died in Richfield, Genesee Co., Mich., Aug. 25, 1852. He married, second, in Richfield, Mich., ALVIRA E. BENJAMIN, May 15, 1853. She was born in Farmington, Mich., June 22, 1833, the daughter of Myron and Sarah Benjamin. He moved to Richfield in 1844, and from thence to Vernon, Shiawassee Co., Mich., in 1866.

HIS CHILDREN BY LYDIA HOYLE.

1. JOSEPH JEROME, b March 4, 1832: m. Martha E. Fuller. **307**
2. JOHN, b. Feb. 10, 1834, in Bennington, N. Y.; enlisted in the 8th Michigan Infantry, Aug. 15, 1861, and was killed on James Island, South Carolina, June 16, 1862.
3. JULIUS, b. Nov. 18, 1836: m. Maria Grove. **308**
4. WILLIAM E., b. July 1, 1844: m. Cassie Chapman. **309**

HIS CHILDREN BY ALVIRA E. BENJAMIN.

5. MANUEL E., b. Oct 13, 1854.
6. ARLEY MALVINA, b. March 28, 1857: d. July 21, 1865.
7. GRANT, } Twins,
8. SHERMAN, } b. Nov. 13, 1864.

243. WILLIAM MILLER KINSMAN, son of James and Nancy (p. 133), born in Pembroke, Genesee Co., N. Y., June 20, 1820; married, in Novi, Oakland Co., Mich., Sarah Jane Munn, April 4, 1844. She was born in New York State, Sept. 6, 1823, the daughter of William and Betsey Munn. Residence, Vernon, Shiawassee Co., Mich.

THEIR CHILDREN:

1. Harriet Adelia, b. Sept. 30, 1845: m. William M. Brown. **310**
2. Alma Maria, b. Nov. 14, 1848: m. Edward Neuman. **311**
3. Perry Green, b. July 11, 1851.
4. James William, b. Nov. 12, 1858.
5. Adelbert Elmor, b. June 3, 1864.

---

244. SAUL KINSMAN, son of James and Nancy (p. 133), born in Darien, Genesee Co., N. Y., Dec. 24, 1822; married in Ann Arbor, Mich., Mary A. Voorheis, March 23, 1843. She was born in Wheatland, Genesee Co., N. Y., March 8, 1823, the daughter of John and Roxana Voorheis. Residence, Tyrone, Livingston Co., Mich.

THEIR CHILDREN:

1. James, b. March 7, 1844: d. Nov. 11, 1865.
2. Mary, b. Aug. 29, 1846: m. Austin R. Gardner, Nov. 19, 1867.
3. Emma, b. Aug. 24, 1850: m. Romie Gardner, Nov. 21, 1871.
4. Helen, b. Aug. 26, 1852.
5. William Wallace, b. May 29, 1854.
6. Jennie Elsie, b. Jan. 1, 1857.
7. Floyd Ernest, b. Aug. 12, 1863.

---

245. SUSAN KINSMAN, daughter of Jeremiah and Olive (p. 134), born in Fitchburg, Mass., Jan. 3, 1800; married Stephen Lowe, April 26, 1821, the son of Joseph and Mary Lowe of Fitchburg. He died June 10, 1845, aged 46. She died Sept. 18, 1849.

THEIR CHILDREN:

1. JOSEPH HENRY, b. July 15, 1822: m. Frances C. Thurston, Dec. 11, 1845.
2. CHARLES H., b. July 28, 1824: m. Jane L. Sylvester, Dec. 22, 1847.
3. SAMUEL HAWES, b. Aug. 13, 1826: m. Harriet M. Mann. He d. April 19, 1852.
4. MARY HAWES, b. Oct. 14, 1828: m. Austin S. Childs, Nov. 7, 1849; residence, Fitchburg.
5. SUSAN MARIA, b. Nov. 26, 1830.
6. GEORGE PRESTON, b. June 12, 1834: m. Mary C. Underwood.
7. ELVIRA MAHALA, b July 19, 1836.
8. LUCY ANN, b. May 6, 1838: m. Marshall Putnam, Aug. 16, 1867.
9. ELIZABETH PHELPS, b. Oct. 9, 1841: m. George A. Hitchcock, Oct. 6, 1868.
10. ABBA LOUISE W., b. April 6, 1844: m. William Steele, March 18, 1868; residence, Dixon, Cal.

---

246. MARIA KINSMAN, daughter of Jeremiah and Olive (p. 134), born in Fitchburg, Oct. 23, 1801; married LEONARD FARNSWORTH, May 26, 1825, the son of Joseph and Hannah Farnsworth, of Fitchburg. She died Oct. 26, 1848.

THEIR CHILD:

1. ELLEN M., b. 1832: d. Oct. 15, 1848.

---

247. OLIVE KINSMAN, daughter of Jeremiah and Olive (p. 134), born in Fitchburg, April 2, 1804; married AMOS PIERCE, Oct. 28, 1830, the son of Elisha and Dorcas Pierce. Resided Westminster, Mass. She died Nov. 9, 1845. He died Aug. 17, 1873, aged 67 years.

THEIR CHILDREN:

1. Hannah Maria, b. Aug. 24, 1831: m. Charles F. Everett, of Walpole. She d. Feb. 7, 1866.
2. George William, b. Dec. 26, 1832.
3. Henry Orlando, b. July 14, 1844: enlisted in Co. D, 2d Mass Regt., May 4, 1861; served nearly two years, and died Feb. 2, 1863, one month after his return home.

---

248. JEREMIAH KINSMAN, son of Jeremiah and Olive (p. 134), born in Fitchburg, March 8, 1806; married Abigail Flagg Hutchinson, April 19, 1832. Residence, Fitchburg.

THEIR CHILDREN:

1. Henry, b. May 13, 1834: d. March 9, 1836.
2. Sarah Jane, b. April 2, 1837: d. Sept. 11, 1838.
3. Frederic Gibbs, b. April 22, 1839: enlisted in the Army, May 11, 1861; served as hospital steward to the 2d Regt. Mass. Infantry, from April 8, 1865; was honorably discharged July 27, 1865.
4. Abbie Maria, b. April 19, 1842: d. June 5, 1843.
5. Frank Eugene, b. July 12, 1844: m. Esther Maria Mullen, Nov. 1, 1871.
6. John Flagg, b. Dec. 11, 1847.
7. Alfred Jerome, b. Aug. 15, 1850.

---

249. TIMOTHY W. KINSMAN, son of Jeremiah and Olive (p. 134), born in Fitchburg, June 21, 1808; married Joanna Downe, Jan. 26, 1832, the daughter of Deacon Timothy and Polly Downe of Fitchburg. Residence, Fitchburg, where he died June 17, 1852.

THEIR CHILDREN:

1. Emily Eliza, b. May 14, 1833: d. June 5, 1838.
2. Warren Downe, b. Oct. 11, 1837: m. Addie L. Dowe. **312**
3. Thomas Stewart, b. Nov. 2, 1839: m. E. E Eaton; J. D. Slade. **313**
4. Hattie Freelove, b. Nov. 7, 1843: d. June 14, 1866.

250. MAHALA KINSMAN, daughter of Jeremiah and Olive (p. 134), born in Fitchburg, June 13, 1813; married ELISHA PIERCE, Dec. 7, 1865, the son of Elisha Pierce, of Westminster, Mass. He died March 2, 1868, aged 61. She resides in Fitchburg, and has rendered valuable aid in the preparation of this record.

---

251. WILLIAM L. KINSMAN, son of Jeremiah and Olive (p. 134), born in Fitchburg, April 13, 1816; married ELIZA BLANCHARD, Oct. 13, 1840, the daughter of Isaac and Hannah Blanchard, of Fitchburg. Residence, Fitchburg, where he died Aug. 15, 1869.

THEIR CHILDREN:

1. HANNAH ELIZABETH, b. July 14, 1841: m. Francis R. Billings. **314**
2. OLIVE AMANDA, b. April 9, 1844: m. Calvin A. Bigelow. **315**
3. CHARLES WILLIAM, b Nov. 26, 1846.
4. ADDISON, b. April 16, 1850.
5. MARIA LOVINA, b. Jan. 22, 1853: m. William H. Dow, Jan. 19, 1872.
6. ABBA LOUISE, b. Aug. 26, 1855.
7. FRANK EVERETT, b. June 27, 1857.

---

252. MARY L. KINSMAN, daughter of Jeremiah and Olive (p. 134), born in Fitchburg, April 9, 1819; married WILLIAM H. ATHERTON, of Boxford, April 6, 1847. She died July 18, 1850.

THEIR CHILD:

1. MARY L., b. July 18, 1850, in Fitchburg; residence, Boston Highlands.

---

253. LUCY M. KINSMAN, daughter of Daniel and Lucy (p. 134), born in Ashburnham, Mass., Sept. 4, 1804;

married in Fitchburg, Francis Hinds, May 27, 1826. He was born in New Salem, June 4, 1800. Residence, Ashburnham, where he died Sept. 29, 1861.

THEIR CHILDREN:

1. Louisa A., b. April 2, 1827: m. Joseph Clark, April 15, 1847.
2. Arvilla L., b. Sept. 9, 1829: m. George Duncan, July 4, 1850.
3. Francis, b. May 7, 1833: d. same day.
4. Sarah J., b. Aug. 1, 1834: m. Warren Pratt, May 1, 1856.
5. Addie P., b. April 5, 1839: m. Harvey Clark, Dec. 28, 1864.
6. Ellen R., b. Jan. 5, 1847: m. George F. Corey, June 24, 1869.
7. Emogene, b. Sept 18, 1849: m. Henry Russell, Nov. 16, 1869.

---

254. CYRUS KINSMAN, son of Daniel and Lucy (p. 135), born in Fitchburg, May 2, 1810; married Mary F. Allen, Oct. 22, 1833. She was born Sept. 19, 1811, the daughter of Capt. David and Sarah Allen, of Leominster, Mass. He married, second, her sister, Helen D. Allen, May 10, 1848. She was born July 30, 1815. Residence, Leominster.

HIS CHILDREN BY MARY F. ALLEN:

1. George Hamilton, b. Oct. 13, 1834: m. Mary Goodall. **316**
2. Mary Louisa A., b. March 7, 1840: m. Albert H. Lawrence, March 18, 1868.

HIS CHILDREN BY HELEN D. ALLEN:

3. Frank Eugene, b. Aug. 14, 1852.
4. Arthur Monroe, b. Nov. 19, 1854.

---

255. MARTHA A. KINSMAN, daughter of Daniel and Lucy (p. 135), born in Fitchburg, Oct. 20, 1814; married William Perkins, of Westminster, June 18, 1834. He was born Nov. 30, 1807, and died June 26, 1843. She married, second, E. J. Boardman Baker, Dec. 3, 1846. He was born Feb. 27, 1821. Residence, Ashburnham.

HER CHILDREN BY WILLIAM PERKINS:

1. Harriet Elmna, b. May 18, 1835.
2. Everett William, b. Aug. 26, 1837: m. Louise A. Knowlton, Dec. 6, 1869. She d. Dec. 8, 1870. He m., 2d, Etta C. Sawyer, Jan. 11, 1872.
3. Emily Maria, b. Jan. 27, 1840.
4. Francis Hinds, b. April 14, 1842: d. Jan. 3, 1871.

HER CHILD BY E. J. BOARDMAN BAKER:

5. Eva Elvira, b. July 28, 1854.

---

256. DANIEL ALFRED KINSMAN, son of Daniel and Lucy (p. 135), born in Fitchburg, Dec. 5, 1820; married Maria C. Houghton, of Bolton, Mass. She died, and he married, second, Susan Briant, of Clinton, Mass. Residence, Ashburnham.

HIS CHILD BY MARIA C. HOUGHTON:

1. Frank M , b. Feb. 17, 1854, in Clinton.

---

257. MONROE E. KINSMAN, son of Daniel and Lucy (p. 135), born in Fitchburg, Jan. 13, 1826; married Lucy A. Brown, June 3, 1855. Residence, Willet, Cortland Co., N. Y.

THEIR CHILDREN:

1. Velorous M., b. March 14, 1856.
2. Addie E., b March 31, 1858.
3. Evie L., b. Oct. 15, 1860.
4. Ida E., b. May 29, 1862.
5. Cyrus A., b. Jan. 29, 1866.
6. Francis E., b. June 15, 1869.

---

258. JOHN SUMNER KINSMAN, son of John and Nancy (p. 135), born in Fitchburg, July 27, 1820; married in Brattleboro', Vt., Sarah Arvilla Derby, April 17, 1841,

the daughter of Aaron and Sally Derby, of Fitchburg. Residence formerly, Ashburnham, Mass.; since, Keene, N. H.

THEIR CHILDREN:

1. Nancy Elizabeth, b. June 22, 1843: m. William A. Parmenter. **317**
2. George Herbert, b. April 21, 1845: m. Sarah A. Tolman. **318**
3. Sarah Amanda, b. June 15, 1848: m. Francis M. Carter. **319**
4. Adeline, b. Feb. 27, 1850: m. Sidney E. Tolman. **320**

---

259. ZULIMA LAWRENCE KINSMAN, daughter of Asa and Martha (p. 136), born in Fitchburg, Sept. 21, 1817; married James W. Joy, of Fitchburg, Jan. 17, 1849.

THEIR CHILD:

1. Warren Elliott, b. Sept., 1850, in Sterling, Mass.

---

260. LORENZO KINSMAN, son of Asa and Martha (p. 136), born in Fitchburg, Nov. 20, 1819; married Lydia Blood, May 27, 1845. Residence, Fitchburg.

THEIR CHILDREN:

1. Cyrus, b. April 20, 1846: m. Angie A. Underwood. **321**
2. Martha A., b. July 25, 1849: m. Robert Taylor. **322**
3. John S., b. Nov. 20, 1851: m. Lydia Houghton, of Jay, N. Y.
4. Susan, b. Sept. 18, 1853: m. Harvey V. Reynolds, Oct. 2, 1869; residence, Fitchburg; has daughter Hattie, b. 1871.
5. Everett J., b. Oct. 3, 1856.
6. Anna Maria B., b. Oct. 5, 1859.
7. Lizzie C., b. Oct. 15, 1861.

---

261. GEORGE WASHINGTON KINSMAN, son of Asa and Hannah (p. 136), born in Fitchburg, Oct. 4, 1831; married Sybil B. Daby, of Jay, N. Y., Aug. 29, 1866. He served three years, eleven months, and twenty days in the late war, and was wounded in the leg at the battle of Cold Harbor.

THEIR CHILDREN:

1. JENNIE AMANDA, b. Nov. 27, 1867.
2. WALTER LORING, b. Jan. 1, 1872.

---

262. LOUISA KINSMAN, daughter of William and Sarah (p. 137), born in Ipswich, Feb. 12, 1805; bapt. May 4, 1806; married Capt. HENRY STORY HOLMES, May 17, 1825. He was born in Essex, Nov. 8, 1799, the son of William and Lydia (Story) Holmes; bapt. Nov. 5, 1836. Residence, Ipswich. On the 17th of May, 1875, the golden wedding of Mr. and Mrs. Holmes was celebrated in Ipswich, at the Kinsman homestead (which is one hundred years old), and in the same room where they were married, fifty years before. Of their seven children now living, six were present on the interesting occasion.

THEIR CHILDREN:

1. INFANT SON, d. July 21, 1826.
2. HENRY EDWARD, b. Feb. 13, 1827: bapt. Sept. 2, 1827; was an adventurous pioneer to California in 1849; residence, Sacramento, Cal.
3. WILLIAM RUFUS, b. May 16, 1829: bapt. Sept. 6, 1829; d. May 30, 1859.
4. WARREN GUILFORD, b. Sept. 21, 1831: bapt. Nov. 4, 1831; went to California in 1854; residence, Scott Bar, Scott River, Siskiyou Co., Cal.
5. SUSAN LOUISE, b. March 28, 1834: bapt. Nov. 3, 1834.
6. SARAH BROWN, b. April 4, 1837: bapt. July 15, 1837; m. Capt. Josiah Dudley, Jan. 3, 1860; residence, Ipswich.
7. OTIS SYLVESTER, b. Aug. 1, 1840: bapt. Nov. 6, 1840. He enlisted at Boston, in Co. A, 1st Batt. Heavy Artillery, Mass. Vols., under Capt. Cabot, for three years service, Feb. 24, 1862; sent to Fort Independence; transferred to Fort Warren, May 24, 1862; and to Champlain, N. Y, for frontier service, Dec. 20, 1864; discharged Feb. 24, 1865.
8. ALBERT BIGELOW, b. Aug. 6, 1844: bapt Nov. 1, 1844; residence, Salem.
9. ANNIE MARSHALL, b. Feb. 15, 1847: bapt. Nov. 7, 1847.

263. SIMON BROWN KINSMAN, son of William and Sarah (p. 137), born in Ipswich, Jan. 26, 1807; bapt. Sept. 13, 1807; married ELIZABETH B. STONE, the daughter of Azor and Lydia (McVoy) Stone. She was born in Salem, Feb. 10, 1810. Residence, Woburn.

THEIR CHILDREN:

1. MARY ELIZABETH, b. Jan. 21, 1830: bapt. Nov. 5, 1843; d. March 1, 1844.
2. RHODA ELVIRA, b. July 19, 1831: bapt. Nov. 5, 1843; d. Oct. 3, 1851.
3. LYDIA ANN, b. June 19, 1834: m. Charles A. Homans. **323**
4. MARTHA ELLEN, b. June 5, 1839: bapt. Aug. 25, 1845.
5. LIZZIE, b. Feb. 27, 1846: d. Jan. 16, 1873.

---

264. NANCY KINSMAN, daughter of William and Sarah (p. 137), born in Ipswich, April 1, 1809; bapt. Aug. 15, 1831; married STEPHEN BLATCHFORD, Aug. 14, 1834. He was born in Rockport, Oct. 13, 1806; bapt. Nov. 5, 1827. Residence, Hamilton.

THEIR CHILD:

1. ANN AUGUSTA, b. June 14, 1835: bapt. Nov. 3, 1835; m. Emerson A. Whipple, April 25, 1858; residence, Hamilton.

---

265. JACOB KINSMAN, son of William and Sarah (p. 137), born in Ipswich, March 29, 1811; bapt. Aug. 15, 1831; married ABBIE STANIFORD, Feb. 23, 1837. She was born in Ipswich, Aug. 10, 1807; bapt. April 10, 1808, the daughter of James and Abbie (Patch) Staniford. Residence, Topsfield.

THEIR CHILDREN:

1. ABBIE ELLEN, b. Nov. 26, 1838: m. Capt. David Augustus Roberts, Dec. 26, 1867; residence, Salem.
2. AUSTIN STANIFORD, b Sept. 17, 1841. Enlisted in Hamilton, Sept., 1862, under Capt. Langdon Ward, in Co. B, 50th Regt. Mass. Vols., and served at Baton Rouge, La.; returning home on a furlough, died at Memphis, Tenn., Aug. 4, 1863.
3. MARY ELIZABETH, b. July 23, 1844.
4. JAMES ALVIN, b. Oct. 13, 1848.

---

266. SARAH KINSMAN, daughter of William and Sarah (p. 137), born in Ipswich, July 5, 1815; bapt. Aug. 15, 1831; married OLIVER MAYHEW WHIPPLE, May 15, 1844. He was born in Weathersfield, Vt., May 4, 1794. Residence, Lowell. He died April 26, 1872.

THEIR CHILD:

1. FRANK MILTON, b. Dec. 9, 1844: d. Aug. 14, 1849.

---

267. WILLIAM HENRY KINSMAN, son of William and Sarah (p. 137), born in Ipswich, Feb. 1, 1818; bapt. Aug. 15, 1831; married FRANCES J. LAMSON, Jan. 1, 1857. She was born in Hamilton, May 11, 1826, the daughter of Obadiah and Fanny (Baker) Lamson. Residence, Ipswich.

THEIR CHILDREN:

1. MARY FRANCES, b. Nov. 28, 1857: bapt. Jan. 12, 1858; d. Jan. 14, 1858.
2. ALICE FRANCES, b. Dec. 12, 1858: bapt. Sept. 5, 1859; d. Oct. 6, 1859.
3. CHARLES HENRY, b. Feb. 18, 1860: bapt. Sept. 2, 1860; d. Mar. 24, 1872.
4. ALICE FRANCES, b. April 6, 1861: d. Oct. 3, 1861.
5. RHODA FRANCES, b. Sept. 30, 1862: bapt. April 21, 1868.
6. ALICE AUGUSTA, b. Sept. 23, 1864: bapt. April 21, 1868; d. May 18, 1869.
7. ARTHUR DANIEL, b. June 8, 1866: bapt. April 21, 1868.

268. MARIA KINSMAN, daughter of William and Sarah (p. 137), born in Ipswich, April 15, 1820; bapt. Aug. 15, 1831; married LEWIS EMERSON, Nov. 24, 1844. He was born in Waltham, July 24, 1818. Residence, Waltham.

THEIR CHILD:

1. ALICE LOUISE, b. May 4, 1847.

---

269. WILLARD BENAIAH KINSMAN, son of William and Sarah (p. 137), born in Ipswich, Feb. 3, 1822; bapt. Aug. 15, 1831; married HARRIET MANNING. She was born in Ipswich, May 19, 1822, the daughter of William and Mary (Parsons) Manning. Residence, Ipswich.

THEIR CHILDREN:

1. SARAH MARIA, b. July 3, 1844: m. Joseph A. Story. 324
2. ANNIE MANNING, } Twins, {
3. HATTIE MANNING, } b. Sept. 24, 1846: } m. Edward B. Wildes, May 26, 1870; residence, Ipswich.
4. MARY BROWN, b. March 9, 1848.
5. WILLARD FRANCIS, b. Nov. 29, 1849.
6. RHODA E., b. Sept. 6, 1854: d. Oct. 13, 1859.
7. LOUISE EMMA, b. May 27, 1861.

---

270. CHARLOTTE AUGUSTA KINSMAN, daughter of William and Sarah (p. 137), born in Ipswich, April 18, 1824; bapt. Aug. 15, 1831; married ANDREW BURNHAM, Nov. 21, 1844. He was born in Essex, Dec. 27, 1820. Residence, Essex.

THEIR CHILDREN:

1. ANDREW FRANK, b. Sept. 13, 1845. Enlisted in Capt. Babson's Company for Coast Defence, for one year; first two months at Fort Warren, Boston Harbor, and subsequently at Marblehead; was discharged at the close of the war.

2. Elbridge K., b. Nov. 1, 1846.
3. Sarah E., b. Aug. 27, 1849: m. Samuel P. Gilbert, Nov. 16, 1868. He d. June 15, 1869.
4. Mary A., b. June 27, 1853.
5. Allis K., b. Jan. 23, 1861: d. May 3, 1869.

---

271. GEORGE KINSMAN, son of William and Sarah (p. 137), born in Ipswich, Jan. 26, 1826; bapt. Aug. 15, 1831; married Elzina Amelia Tilton, Aug. 27, 1865. She was born in St. Albans, Vt., Oct. 5, 1837, the daughter of Odlin P. and Roxana A. (Bogue) Tilton, and died in Waterford, Ct., July 23, 1872. He resides in New London, Ct.

---

272. DANIEL FITZ KINSMAN, son of William and Sarah (p. 137), born in Ipswich, Jan. 10, 1828; bapt. Aug. 15, 1831; married Mattie A. Wood, June 13, 1855. She was born in Union, Ill., Dec. 31, 1838, the daughter of Clement and Nancy (Dobbins) Wood. Residence, Colorado City, Colorado.

THEIR CHILDREN:

1. Wilmer M., b. May 21, 1856, in Bentonsport, Iowa.
2. Clement W., b. May 28, 1859, in " "
3. Viola V., b. Jan. 1, 1864, in Colorado City, Col.
4. Clarence, b. March 1, 1869, in " " "

---

273. CHARLOTTE KINSMAN, daughter of Jacob B. and Bethiah (p. 137), born in Ipswich, Sept. 24, 1803; married Isaac W. Roberts, Jan. 15, 1824. He was born in Winchendon, Mass., April 21, 1803, the son of David and Elizabeth (Woodbury) Roberts. Residence, Wenham.

THEIR CHILDREN:

1. ELIZABETH WOODBURY, b. Aug. 17, 1824: m. Ansell Burnham, of Essex, Nov., 1844. Has deceased.
2. JACOB KINSMAN, b Dec. 19, 1826: m. Ann F. Porter, May 7, 1848; residence, Salem.
3. CHARLOTTE KINSMAN, b. June 11, 1829: m. Edward P. Potter, Dec. 8, 1849; residence, Lynn.
4. ISAAC NEWTON, b. Oct. 16, 1832: m. Asenath A. Sawyer. She d. in Danvers, Sept. 14, 1863. He d. in Newberne, N. C., Oct. 19, 1863.
5. SILAS, b. Oct. 16, 1834: d. Feb. 23, 1841.
6. HANNAH, b. Jan. 31, 1836: d. May 21, 1845.
7. OTIS, b. April 16, 1839: d Jan , 1840.
8. OTIS WARREN, b. Nov. 2, 1842: m. Sarah Standley, July 3, 1861; residence, Marblehead.

---

274. OLIVER DODGE KINSMAN, son of Jacob B. and Bethiah (p. 137), born in Manchester, Sept. 26, 1805; married RUTH THOMPSON, Sept. 20, 1827. She was born in Manchester, Jan. 8, 1806, the daughter of Benjamin and Ruth (Tewksbury) Thompson. Residence, Beverly.

THEIR CHILDREN:

1. JOSEPH MARSTERS, b Feb. 7, 1829: unm.; residence, Fresno Co., Cal.; engaged in mining.
2. OLIVER ALLAN, b. Feb. 20, 1831: unm.; is with his brother in California.
3. MARGARETTA PEIRCE, b. June 20, 1833: residence, Beverly.
4. WILLIAM HENRY, b. June 8, 1835: m. Catharine C. Jordan. **325**
5. JACOB, b. May 10, 1837: m. Lydia A. Smith; Sarah E. Thomas. **326**
6. BENJAMIN FRANKLIN, b. Dec. 13, 1839: A. B.; tutor in Tufts College, as "Walker Special Instructor in Mathematics," from 1865 to 1869. Is unmarried. Residence, Beverly.
7. ANNA BROWN, b. July 12, 1842: d. Feb. 1, 1845.
8. RUTH AUGUSTA, b. June 25, 1844: m. George F. Standley. **327**
9. CHARLES FOSTER, b. May 31, 1847: m. Hannah J. Mears. **328**

---

275. WILLIAM KINSMAN, son of Jacob B. and Bethiah (p. 137), born in Ipswich, Oct. 18, 1809; married NANCY D. GREENE, of Kensington, N. H. She was born May 5, 1806, the daughter of Nathan and Mary (Dow) Greene. Residence, Ipswich.

THEIR CHILDREN:

1. NICHOLAS W., b. April 15, 1838: m. in San Francisco, Cal., Maggie Miller, July 11, 1868.
2. BETHIAH D., b. Feb. 18, 1841: residence, Ipswich.

---

276. WILLIAM LOW KINSMAN, son of Nathaniel and Rebecca (p. 142), born in Salem, March 10, 1836; married there, SARAH AUGUSTA NICHOLS, Oct. 19, 1870. She was born in Salem, Aug. 25, 1844, the daughter of William Frye and Abigail (Buffington) Nichols. Residence, Salem.

THEIR CHILD:

1. REBECCA NICHOLS, b. Oct. 16, 1873.

---

277. NATHANIEL KINSMAN, son of Nathaniel and Rebecca (p. 142), born in Salem, Feb. 23, 1841; married, in Peabody, LUCY ELIZABETH WINCHESTER, Aug. 1, 1872. She was born in Salem, Nov. 3, 1844, the daughter of Jacob and Elizabeth (Lang) Winchester. Residence, Salem.

THEIR CHILDREN:

1. MARY ABBOT, b. Oct. 23, 1873.
2. NATHANIEL, b. Jan. 7, 1875.

---

278. NATHANIEL JOSHUA KINSMAN, son of Joshua and Mary (p. 143), born in Salem, Sept. 14, 1831; married there, MARY FLETCHER SHATSWELL, April 28, 1857.

She was born in Salem, June 23, 1830, the daughter of Joseph and Sarah (Pulsifer) Shatswell, and died June 17, 1861, without issue.

He was a ship-master from an early age, like his father and grandfather before him, and of marked ability in his calling. He met with an untimely end at the age of thirty-six, having been lost at sea by the probable foundering of the Spanish steamer "Malespina," by which he took passage from Hong Kong for Manila, in September, 1867; the vessel never being heard from afterward.

His death was the fifth that occurred away from home, out of seven, in the families of the brothers Nathaniel and Joshua: two, father and son, lie buried in the far East; two more, also father and son, found their graves in the ocean; and one, a little daughter, died at sea on the passage from China. Two only, mother and daughter, died at home.

---

279. ANNIE ELIZABETH KINSMAN, daughter of Joshua and Mary (p. 143), born in Salem, June 29, 1838; married there, MANUEL FRANCISCO CIRIACO FENOLLOSA, July 26, 1869. He was born in Malaga, Spain, Dec. 24, 1822, the son of Manuel and Isabel del Pino Fenollosa. Residence, Salem.

THEIR CHILDREN:

1. CLARENCE, b. Nov. 25, 1870.
2. SYDNEY KINSMAN, b. May 4, 1873.
3. MANUEL EMILIO, b. June 7, 1875.

---

280. CLARA ELLEN KINSMAN, daughter of Nathaniel and Clarissa (p. 145), born in Salem, Jan. 10, 1844; married SAMUEL KNOOP STATLER, Feb. 18, 1874. He was born March 18, 1844, the son of George and Elizabeth Statler. Residence, Piqua, Ohio.

THEIR CHILD:

1. ELIZABETH KINSMAN, b. Feb. 28, 1875.

---

281. JOHN DOUGLAS KINSMAN, son of Danson and Elizabeth (p. 146), born in Liverpool, N. S., June 21, 1840; married ANNA PAULINE WESTERFIELD, Sept. 14, 1870. Residence, New York City.

THEIR CHILDREN:

1. CARRIE PAULINE, b. Sept. 16, 1871: d. Dec. 16, 1872.
2. WILLIAM DANSON, b. May 15, 1874.

---

282. AVERY KINSMAN, son of Danson and Elizabeth (p. 146), born in Liverpool, N. S., Jan. 27, 1843; married LETTIE LAMB, May 29, 1867. Residence, Watertown, N. Y.

THEIR CHILD:

1. LORRANCE BERTON, b. Nov. 12, 1868.

---

283. WILLIAM KINSMAN, son of Jethro and Rebecca (p. 150), born in Cornwallis, Kings Co., N. S., Oct. 16, 1828; married there, HARRIETT ARMSTRONG, Aug. 9, 1859. She died Oct. 14, 1862. He married, second, LUCY KEATING, Jan. 12, 1869, the daughter of Joseph Keating. Residence, Cornwallis, N. S.

HIS CHILD BY HARRIETT ARMSTRONG:

1. HOMER A., b. June 28, 1860: d. Nov. 20, 1862.

HIS CHILD BY LUCY KEATING:

2. EMMA M., b. 1871.

284. JAMES KINSMAN, son of Jethro and Rebecca (p. 150), born in Cornwallis, N. S., Oct. 5, 1829; married there, DEBORAH NORTON, the daughter of Rev. Jacob Norton. Resided in Cornwallis, where he died Feb. 14, 1862.

THEIR CHILDREN:

1. MARIA E., b. May 25, 1855.
2. MARY R., b. Dec. 31, 1857.
3. JAMES JETHRO, b. July 9, 1859.

---

285. JAMES E. KINSMAN, son of Ephraim and Eunice (p. 151), born in Cornwallis, N. S., Jan. 12, 1840; married there, CALENA JANE SHEFFIELD, May 24, 1868. She was born May 15, 1836. Residence, Cornwallis.

THEIR CHILDREN:

1. FLORA, b. Aug. 7, 1869.
2. HARVEY, b. Dec. 5, 1871.

NINTH GENERATION.

286. SAMUEL AUGUSTUS KINSMAN, son of Samuel and Elizabeth (p. 158), born in Salem, Aug. 7, 1840; married SARAH E. HARDY. Residence, Salem.

THEIR CHILDREN:

1. MARY E., b. April 6, 1862.
2. HATTIE WEBB, b. Aug. 30, 1866.

---

287. BETSEY JANE KINSMAN, daughter of Solon and Lydia (p. 164), born in Franklin, Vt., Nov. 1, 1834;

married CHARLES BRYANT. He was born in Bolton, Canada West, June 12, 1824. Residence, Bolton, C. W.

THEIR CHILD:

1. LILLIS BELL, b. June 9, 1870.

---

288. HELEN MARIAN KINSMAN, daughter of Solon and Lydia (p. 164), born in Franklin, Vt., Jan. 26, 1840; married ALFRED BEAUREGARD. He was born in St. Charles, Canada East, Jan. 2, 1837. Residence, Magog, C. E.

THEIR CHILDREN:

1. CHARLES ALFRED, b. July 28, 1861.
2. WILLIAM ERASTUS, b. Jan. 19, 1864.
3. ERNEST SOLON, b. May 16, 1866.
4. GEORGE, b. June 8, 1868.
5. FRANK EDSON, b. April 9, 1871.

---

289. LAURA MARIA KINSMAN, daughter of Dura and Mary (p. 165), born in Rochester, Vt., Feb. 22, 1833; married EDWARD EPENETER, February, 1858; he was born in Bingen, Germany. Resided in West Rochester, Vt. She died June 4, 1863, and he died June 1, 1864.

THEIR CHILDREN:

1. ADOLPH E., b. April 27, 1859, in Iowa City, Ia. Adopted by Dura Kinsman (192), his grandfather, about November, 1864.
2. FRANKIE MARIA, b. Jan. 1, 1861, in Iowa City, Ia. Adopted by George Washington Kinsman (197), her great-uncle, Nov. 12, 1864.

---

290. ROXA ARVILLA KINSMAN, daughter of Dura and Mary (p. 165), born in Rochester, Vt., Feb. 6, 1836; married WILLIAM P. WHITNEY, Sept. 22, 1852.

He was born in Goshen, Vt., Feb. 12, 1825, the son of Oliver and Rebecca (Nichols) Whitney. Residence, Rochester, Vt.

THEIR CHILDREN:

1. Hattie E., b. Nov. 30, 1853.
2. Ernest L., b. Jan. 23, 1855.
3. Arthur H., b. March 10, 1858.
4. Willie B., b. Dec. 11, 1860.
5. Luella E., b. June 4, 1866.

---

291. SARAH ALMEDA KINSMAN, daughter of Dura and Mary (p. 165), born in Rochester, Vt., Jan. 1, 1838; married Royal I. Laird. He was born in Rochester, Vt., Feb. 12, 1825, the son of Stephen and Hannah (Brink) Laird, and died Jan. 2, 1863. She married, second, Milton T. Crossman, Oct. 19, 1867. He was born in Pittsfield, Vt., Jan. 3, 1843, the son of Amos and Polly (Wheat) Crossman. Residence, Pittsfield, Vt.

HER CHILDREN BY ROYAL I. LAIRD:

1. Dura H., b. Jan. 15, 1858: d. March 14, 1858.
2. Nellie I., b. Aug. 9, 1859.
3. George E., b. April 5, 1861: d. Sept., 1863.

HER CHILD BY MILTON T. CROSSMAN:

4. Flora May, b. April 23, 1869.

---

292. ELVIRA DEAN KINSMAN, daughter of Caryl and Lydia (p. 165), born in Goshen, Vt., Aug. 18, 1835; married, in Rutland, Vt., Alonzo E. Lord, Jan. 24, 1856, the son of Henry and Ann Emeline (Kent) Lord. Residence, Brandon, Vt.

THEIR CHILDREN:

1. Lillian Alice, b. Jan. 23, 1857: d. April 6, 1861.
2. Minnie Janette, b. May 20, 1859.
3. Flora Alice, b. March 26, 1861.

293. CHARLES CARYL KINSMAN, son of Caryl and Lydia (p. 165), born in Brandon, Vt., April 28, 1840; married there, ABBY MANDANY ROSS, Oct. 18, 1864. She was born in Reading, Vt., April 13, 1841, the daughter of Ephraim and Sarah (Robinson) Ross. Residence, Rutland, Vt.

THEIR CHILDREN:

1. CARYL EPHRAIM, b. March 25, 1867.
2. FRANK ROSS, b. Oct. 18, 1870.

---

294. HENRY HARRISON KINSMAN, son of Philonas and Adaline (p. 169), born in Sherbrooke, Canada East, Sept. 16, 1840; married LYDIA MARTHA LEVERING, Nov. 21, 1867. She was born in Philadelphia, Penn., Oct. 7, 1835, the daughter of Nathan and Elizabeth Ann Levering. Residence, Philadelphia.

THEIR CHILDREN:

1. WILLIAM LEVERING, b. Oct. 4, 1868, in Pittsburg, Penn.
2. RICHARD BROCKWAY, b. April 23, 1871, in Philadelphia.
3. ELIZABETH NINA, b. Aug. 21, 1873, in Philadelphia.

---

295. SARAH ADA KINSMAN, daughter of Philonas and Adaline (p. 169), born in Lowell, Mass., Aug. 4, 1845; graduated at Evanston, Ill., June 27, 1867; married, in Beloit, Wis., Rev. EDWARD ARCHIBALD WANLESS, May 12, 1868. He was born in St. Andrews, Canada East, April 8, 1837, the son of Thomas and Elizabeth (Jones) Wanless. She went abroad as a missionary, and died in Rustchuk, Turkey, March 18, 1871. He is a Methodist minister in Wisconsin.

THEIR CHILD:

1. LAURA ADA THEODORA, b. Feb. 19, 1871, in Rustchuk, Turkey.

296. CLARA CROWNINSHIELD KINSMAN, daughter of Henry W. and Elizabeth (p. 174), born in Boston, Nov. 24, 1837; married GAMALIEL BRADFORD, Oct. 30, 1861. He was born in Boston, Jan. 15, 1831, the son of Gamaliel and Sophia R. Bradford. She died June 9, 1866. He resides in Boston.

THEIR CHILDREN:

1. GAMALIEL, b. Oct. 9, 1863.
2. CHARLES KINSMAN, b. March 26, 1866.

---

297. MARY McKINSTRY KINSMAN, daughter of Henry W. and Elizabeth (p. 174), born in Boston, March 10, 1839; married WILLIAM GARLAND HOWE, of Haverhill, July 28, 1862. He was born in Haverhill, Aug. 1, 1829, the son of Isaac R. and Sarah (Saltonstall) Howe. She died Nov. 12, 1867. He resides in Haverhill.

THEIR CHILDREN:

1. SARAH SALTONSTALL, b. July 8, 1863: d. Oct. 25, 1868.
2. HENRY KINSMAN, b. April 15, 1865: d. Nov. 15, 1868.
3. GURDON SALTONSTALL, b. Nov. 30, 1866.

---

298. DAVID N. KINSMAN, son of Bliss and Betsey (p. 181), born in Heath, Mass., May 3, 1834; married in Utica, O., ISABELLE L. STEVENS, July 22, 1857. She was born July 1, 1836, the daughter of Lemuel Baçon and Sarah (Chapman) Stevens.

He graduated at the Medical College of Ohio, in Cincinnati, in 1863. Is Professor of Diseases of Women and Children, in Starling Medical College, Columbus, Ohio.

Residence, Lancaster, O.

THEIR CHILDREN:

1. ALICE BERTHA, b. Jan. 16, 1863.
2. BELLE MCCREA, b. Dec. 5, 1865.
3. HENRY BLISS, b. July 30, 1868: d. Dec. 13, 1868.

---

299. MARIAN E. KINSMAN, daughter of Bliss and Betsey (p. 181), born in Heath, Mass., April 6, 1843; married JOHN A. DWIGHT, of Coleraine, Mass., Dec. 20, 1859.

THEIR CHILDREN:

1. EDGAR M., b. Feb. 13, 1861.
2. EMMA H., b. Feb. 4, 1863.
3. HENRY A., b. Sept. 15, 1870.
4. ALICE MARIA, b. June 28, 1874.

---

300. WALTER E. KINSMAN, son of Bliss and Betsey (p. 181), born in Heath, Mass., July 12, 1847; married CLARA J. BASSETT, June 5, 1872. Residence, Heath.

THEIR CHILD:

1. ERNEST EUGENE, b. April 27, 1873.

---

301. KATE E. KINSMAN, daughter of Bliss and Betsey (p. 181), born in Heath, Mass., July 29, 1853; married OSCAR A. SUMNER, Jan. 1, 1872. Residence, Heath.

THEIR CHILD:

1. ALICE BELL, b. July 15, 1874.

---

302. JOHN A. KINSMAN, son of Adnah B. and Asenath (p. 183), born in Ellington, N. Y., Feb. 8, 1838;

married in Gerry, N. Y., CYNTHIA J. BILLINGS, of that place, Oct. 18, 1865. Residence, Ellington, N. Y.

THEIR CHILDREN:

1. WINNIE MAY, b. Aug. 4, 1867.
2. FRANK W., b. Sept. 4, 1869.

---

303. ELLA M. KINSMAN, daughter of Adnah B. and Asenath (p. 183), born in Ellington, N. Y., Jan. 18, 1847; married CHAUNCEY CRUMB, of Cherry Creek, N. Y., Jan. 12, 1868. Residence, Chesterfield, Ohio.

THEIR CHILD:

1. WILLIE GLEN, b. Oct. 4, 1869.

---

304. GEORGE CHANDLER KINSMAN, son of Adnah B. and Asenath (p. 183), born in Ellington, N. Y., Aug. 22, 1850; married in Monroe, Mich., LORA S. CHRISTIANCY, March 5, 1873. She was born in Dundee, Mich., Dec. 17, 1852, the daughter of Hon. I. P. and Mary (Springer) Christiancy, of Monroe. Residence, Springfield, Ill.

THEIR CHILD:

1. CHARLES COLLINS, b. Dec. 14, 1873.

---

305. SARAH J. KINSMAN, daughter of John and Lucy (p. 184), born in Shrewsbury, Vt., Jan. 17, 1844; married HENRY O. WAITE, Feb. 24, 1866. He was born in West Stephentown, N. Y., March 4, 1840, the son of John and Laura (Coleman) Waite.

THEIR CHILDREN:

1. Colie H., b. Jan. 28, 1867.
2. Perley C., b. Aug. 12, 1868.
3. Mattie K., b. March 24, 1870.

---

306. HELEN N. KINSMAN, daughter of John M. and Nancy (p. 185), born in Potsdam, N. Y., March 1, 1844; married Henry D. Morgan, Oct. 21, 1864, and died in Potsdam, Oct. 13, 1865.

THEIR CHILD:

1. Frankie H., b. Aug. 16, 1865: d. Oct. 18, 1865.

---

307. JOSEPH JEROME KINSMAN, son of Elisha and Lydia (p. 186), born in Darien, Genesee Co., N. Y., March 4, 1832; married in Richfield, Genesee Co., Mich., Martha E. Fuller, Feb. 20, 1853. She was born in New York, Aug. 8, 1834, the daughter of Thomas and Margaret Fuller. He is a farmer in Richfield, Mich.

THEIR CHILD:

1. Emma Jennie, b. May 30, 1859.

---

308. JULIUS KINSMAN, son of Elisha and Lydia (p. 186), born in Bennington, N. Y., Nov. 18, 1836; married in Richfield, Mich., Maria Grove, Jan. 1, 1861. She was born in Clarence, N. Y., March 10, 1845, the daughter of Abraham and Fanny Grove. He is a farmer in Richfield, Mich.

THEIR CHILDREN:

1. Frank, b. March 18, 1862.
2. Bertie, b. Sept. 3, 1869.
3. Vernia A., b. April 28, 1871.

309. WILLIAM E. KINSMAN, son of Elisha and Lydia (p. 186), born in Darien, Genesee Co., N. Y., July 1, 1844; married CASSIE CHAPMAN, of Sparta, Kent Co., Mich., March 3, 1872. She was born in Harmony, Susquehanna Co., Penn., Nov. 11, 1852, the daughter of Abraham and Lavinia Chapman.

He enlisted in the 8th Michigan Infantry, Aug. 15, 1861, and was discharged for ill health Jan. 30, 1862; enlisted again in May, 1863, and served until the war closed. Residence, Grand Rapids, Mich.

---

310. HARRIET ADELIA KINSMAN, daughter of William M. and Sarah (p. 187), born in Novi, Mich., Sept. 30, 1845; married in Vernon, Mich., WILLIAM M. BROWN, Sept. 28, 1865. He was born in Vernon, May 22, 1838, the son of Benjamin and Eliza Brown. Residence, Vernon, Mich.

THEIR CHILDREN:

1. FRANKIE VERTNER, b. Nov. 29, 1867.
2. MYRTIE ALMA, b. Nov. 13, 1871.

---

311. ALMA MARIA KINSMAN, daughter of William M. and Sarah (p. 187), born in Novi, Mich., Nov. 14, 1848; married in Vernon, Mich., EDWARD NEUMAN, March 3, 1869. He was born in Orion, Mich., Feb. 26, 1845, the son of John and Fanny Neuman. Residence, Holly, Mich.

THEIR CHILD:

1. ORPHA ADELIA, b. Aug. 13, 1870.

312. WARREN DOWNE KINSMAN, son of Timothy W. and Joanna (p. 189), born in Fitchburg, Mass., Oct. 11, 1837; married ADDIE LOUISE DOWE, Feb. 16, 1865. She was born in Springfield, Mass., June 18, 1844, the daughter of Joseph T. and Wealtha A. (Higgins) Dowe. He is a merchant in Springfield.

THEIR CHILDREN:

1. ALICE LOUISE, b. Oct. 7, 1866.
2. HELEN ISABEL, b. Dec. 27, 1869.

---

313. THOMAS STEWART KINSMAN, son of Timothy W. and Joanna (p. 189), born in Fitchburg, Nov. 2, 1839; married EMILY ELIZA EATON, Sept. 17, 1861, the daughter of Abel and Sabra Eaton, of Fitchburg. She died in Fitchburg, Dec. 7, 1861, aged 21 yrs. 4 mos. He married, second, JOSIE D. SLADE, May 25, 1865, the daughter of Thomson and Dolly Slade, of Springfield. Residence, Springfield.

HIS CHILD BY JOSIE D. SLADE:

1. FANNY ESTELLE, b. Dec. 23, 1869.

---

314. HANNAH ELIZABETH KINSMAN, daughter of William L. and Eliza (p. 190), born in Fitchburg, July 14, 1841; married FRANCIS R. BILLINGS, June 15, 1857. Residence, Fitchburg.

THEIR CHILDREN:

1. LOTTIE ELIZABETH, b. April 6, 1859.
2. FRANK ISAAC, b. June 6, 1861.
3. CLARA ELDORA, b. April 5, 1864.
4. LURA ELIZA, b. Feb. 12, 1866.
5. GERTRUDE, b. Dec. 23, 1870.

315. OLIVE AMANDA KINSMAN, daughter of William L. and Eliza (p. 190), born in Fitchburg, April 9, 1844; married CALVIN A. BIGELOW, July 5, 1870. Residence, Fitchburg.

THEIR CHILD:

1. WILLIAM CALVIN, b. June 20, 1871.

---

316. GEORGE HAMILTON KINSMAN, son of Cyrus and Mary (p. 191), born in Leominster, Oct. 13, 1834; married MARY GOODALL, of Fitchburg. Residence, Fitchburg.

THEIR CHILDREN:

1. FREDDIE ALLEN, b.
2. WALTER ROBERT, b.

---

317. NANCY ELIZABETH KINSMAN, daughter of John S. and Sarah (p. 193), born in Troy, N. H., June 22, 1843; married in Keene, N. H., WILLIAM ARTHUR PARMENTER, of Marlborough, Mass., Aug. 25, 1868. He was born Nov. 8, 1844. Residence, Keene, N. H.

THEIR CHILD:

1. GEORGE ARTHUR, b. June 11, 1869.

---

318. GEORGE HERBERT KINSMAN, son of John S. and Sarah (p. 193), born in Fitchburg, April 21, 1845; married SARAH ANN TOLMAN, Nov. 13, 1866. She was born in Troy, N. H., March 4, 1847, the daughter of Elisha Harris and Rusina Beard Tolman. Residence, Keene, N. H.

THEIR CHILDREN:

1. MINNIE RUSINA, b. July 19, 1868.
2. JOHN SUMNER, b. Sept. 29, 1869.

319. SARAH AMANDA KINSMAN, daughter of John S. and Sarah (p. 193), born in Ashburnham, June 15, 1848; married in Keene, N. H., FRANCIS M. CARTER, of Marlborough, Mass., Sept. 17, 1868. He was born in Wayland, Sept. 27, 1843. Residence, Norwalk, Ohio.

THEIR CHILDREN:

1. EDITH EVELYN, b. July 31, 1869.
2. MABEL LOUISA, b. March 12, 1871.

---

320. ADELINE KINSMAN, daughter of John S. and Sarah (p. 193), born in Ashburnham, Feb. 27, 1850; married in Keene, N. H., SIDNEY E. TOLMAN, of Troy, N. H., Sept. 18, 1867. He was born Nov. 14, 1844, the son of Elisha Harris and Rusina Beard Tolman. Residence, Keene, N. H.

THEIR CHILD:

1. FRED ALBERT, b. March 19, 1870.

---

321. CYRUS KINSMAN, son of Lorenzo and Lydia (p. 193), born in Fitchburg, April 20, 1846; married ANGIE A. UNDERWOOD, the daughter of William G. and Emma A. Underwood, of Lowell.

THEIR CHILDREN:

1. HARVEY C., b. Dec. 8, 1867: d. Feb. 11, 1869.
2. LYDIA E., b. Jan. 1, 1869: d. April 6, 1869.

---

322. MARTHA A. KINSMAN, daughter of Lorenzo and Lydia (p. 193), born in Fitchburg, July 25, 1849; married ROBERT TAYLOR, Feb. 21, 1866. He was born in Quebec, Aug. 24, 1846.

THEIR CHILDREN:

1 LIZZIE JANE, b. March 1, 1867.
HANNAH, b. Oct. 18, 1868: d. March 23, 1869.
ALICE, b. Feb. 14, 1870.

---

323. LYDIA ANN KINSMAN, daughter of Simon B. and Elizabeth (p. 195), born in Ipswich, June 19, 1834; baptized Nov. 5, 1843; married Capt. CHARLES ANDERSON HOMANS, March 20, 1856. He was born in Beverly, May 6, 1830. Residence, Paramaribo, Surinam, S. A.

THEIR CHILDREN:

1. LUCY ROGERS, b. Dec. 23, 1856.
2. ALICE DOWNING, b. April 23, 1871.

---

324. SARAH MARIA KINSMAN, daughter of Willard B. and Harriet (p. 197), born in Ipswich, July 3, 1844; married JOSEPH AUSTIN STORY, May 19, 1868. He was born in Essex, Jan. 23, 1845. Residence, Salem.

THEIR CHILD:

1. MARION KINSMAN, b. Sept. 9, 1870.

---

325. WILLIAM HENRY KINSMAN, son of Oliver D. and Ruth (p. 199), born in Beverly, June 8, 1835; married CATHARINE COLEMAN JORDAN, Aug. 5, 1860. She was born in Nantucket, July 17, 1842, the daughter of Thomas and Jerusha Jordan. Residence, South Boston.

THEIR CHILDREN:

1. OLIVER AUGUSTUS, b. Aug. 26, 1865.
2. BENJAMIN FRANKLIN, b. Nov. 16, 1869.

326. JACOB KINSMAN, son of Oliver D. and Ruth (p. 199), born in Beverly, May 10, 1837; married Lydia Ann Smith, Sept. 14, 1862. She was born in Salem, April 27, 1844, the daughter of Thomas and Martha Smith, and died Nov. 17, 1865. He married, second, Sarah Elizabeth Thomas, Dec. 31, 1866. She was born in Salem, May 7, 1845, the daughter of Eli and Clarissa Thomas. Residence, Tewksbury.

HIS CHILDREN BY SARAH E. THOMAS:

1. Jacob Franklin, b. July 31, 1867.
2. Anna Lizzie, b. June 25, 1871.

---

327. RUTH AUGUSTA KINSMAN, daughter of Oliver D. and Ruth (p. 199), born in Beverly, June 25, 1844; married George Frederick Standley, Dec. 9, 1868. He was born in Beverly, Nov. 2, 1844, the son of Timothy Morgan and Anna Porter Standley. Residence, Beverly.

THEIR CHILD:

1. Willard Allan, b. June 19, 1870.

---

328. CHARLES FOSTER KINSMAN, son of Oliver D. and Ruth (p. 199), born in Beverly, May 31, 1847; married Hannah Jane Mears, March 19, 1868. She was born in Hamilton, Jan. 1, 1848, the daughter of Samuel and Sarah Ann Mears. Residence, Beverly.

THEIR CHILDREN:

1. Jennie Carlotta, b. Oct. 23, 1869.
2. Nellie Arlina, b. Oct. 25, 1870.

APPENDIX.

NO connection has been found in the foregoing records for the following family: —

CHARLES KINSMAN died about December, 1780, leaving a widow, who died in January, 1781.

THEIR CHILDREN:

1. PEREZ, b. : went to sea.
2. CHARLES, b. Dec. 25, 1780: m. Eleanor Jackson.

CHARLES KINSMAN, son of Charles, born in Bristol, R. I., Dec. 25, 1780; married ELEANOR JACKSON. She was born in Stout Water, Cape Elizabeth, Me., Aug. 21, 1776. After the death of his parents he lived with his two aunts; in 1802 he removed to Windham, Me., and in 1817 to Gardiner, Me. He died in Pittston, Me., April 9, 1847, and his widow died there Jan. 21, 1851.

THEIR CHILDREN:

1. ELIZA, b. January, 1804: m. Jesse B. Tosier.
2. JOHN, b. Feb. 14, 1807: m. Anna Nichols; Susan Cornish; Mary ——.
3. FRANKLIN, b. April 4, 1808: m. Eliza B. Waterhouse.
4. ABIGAIL, b. October, 1811: m. Luther Cole, 1831, in Gardiner, Me., and d. February, 1835, leaving no issue.
5. MARY, } Twins, { m. Rufus Blanchard.
6. HANNAH, } b. October, 1814: { m. Solomon Hatch; removed in 1853 to Minnesota, where he died, leaving two sons and two daughters.
7. CHARLES, b. Sept. 30, 1817: m. Mary A. Miles.

ELIZA KINSMAN, daughter of Charles and Eleanor, born in Windham, Me., January, 1804; married JESSE B. TOSIER, and resided in Gardiner, Me.

THEIR CHILDREN:

1. HARTSON KINSMAN, b. : m. Hannah L. Miles; is a physician, and resides in Mexico.
2. ELLEN, b. : d. unm. April, 1874.

JOHN KINSMAN, son of Charles and Eleanor, born in Windham, Me., Feb. 14, 1807; married in Louisville, Ky., ANNA NICHOLS, Aug. 25, 1830. She was born Dec. 14, 1808, and died Nov. 6, 1851. He married, second, SUSAN CORNISH, by whom he had no children. He married, third, MARY ——, of Lowell, Mass. In early life he went to sea; after his marriage he settled in Louisville, Ky., and removed, in 1851, to Kennebec, Me.

HIS CHILDREN BY ANNA NICHOLS:

1. MARY JANE, b. June 27, 1831: m. Frank Smith, Dec. 26, 1852; d. April 5, 1869.
2. CHARLES, b. Oct. 30, 1833: d. Jan. 7, 1839.
3. WILLIAM, b. Dec. 31, 1835: d. Aug. 8, 1836.

4. JOHN, b. Oct. 28, 1838: d. July 20, 1850.
5. EMMA P., b. May 3, 1840: m. Lycurgus Bean, May 19, 1858; d. Aug. 27, 1863.
6. SARAH ELLEN, b. May 30, 1842: m. John Mulligan, Aug. 24, 1862; d. Aug. 5, 1871.
7. THOMAS JEFFERSON, b. March 13, 1844: m. Lula V. Webb, Oct. 15, 1872; residence, Cincinnati, O.

FRANKLIN KINSMAN, son of Charles and Eleanor, born in Windham, Me., April 4, 1808; married ELIZA B. WATERHOUSE, of Dresden, Me. Lived in Gardiner and Pittston, Me.; removed to San Francisco, Cal., in 1849.

THEIR CHILDREN:

1. CHARLES WESTLEY, b. Jan. 19, 1830: m. ; residence, San Francisco, Cal.; has two children, Emma and Charles.
2. MARY ELLEN, b. Dec. 3, 1832: m. Charles Jordan.
3. JAMES W., b. July, 1836: m.
4. HANNAH MATILDA, b. May, 1838: m. W. H. Codington, of New York; residence, San Francisco, Cal.
5. ANN, b. m. John Spencer.

MARY KINSMAN, daughter of Charles and Eleanor, born in Windham, Me., October, 1814, twin with Hannah; married RUFUS BLANCHARD, of Hallowell, Me. Settled in Chelsea, Me., where she died in 1867.

THEIR CHILDREN:

1. ABBIE, b. : m. Lord.
2. MARY, b. : m. Lord.
3. ELIZA, b. : m.
4. MARIA, b. : m. Joseph Carew.
5. CHARLES, b. : m. Emma Blanchard.
6. JOHN, b.
7. EDWARD EVERETT, b.

CHARLES KINSMAN, son of Charles and Eleanor, born in Hallowell, Me., Sept. 30, 1817; married in Philadelphia, Pa., by Rev. Orson Douglas, pastor of the Mariners' Church, to MARY AUGUSTA MILES, Oct. 1, 1846. She was born Jan. 2, 1821, the daughter of Capt. Joseph and Hannah (Brown) Miles, of Concord, Mass. He was a shipmaster, and died June 9, 1866.

Residence, Chelsea, Mass.

THEIR CHILDREN:

1. MARY AUGUSTA, b. in the Downs, Straits of Dover, on board the bark "Mary Ellen," Oct. 28, 1849.
2. ADALIZA, b. Pittston, Me., Aug. 12, 1851: d. Chelsea, Mass., Dec. 21, 1874.
3. CHARLES, b. Concord, Mass., Oct. 17, 1853.
4. MARTHA ANNA, b. Concord, Mass., Aug. 9, 1857.
5. ARTHUR, b. Chelsea, Mass., Feb. 5, 1859: d. May 23, 1864.
6. CAROLINE, b. Chelsea, Mass., April 16, 1861: d. May 30, 1861.
7. JOSEPH MILES, b. Chelsea, Mass., April 4, 1865.

INDEX.

KINSMAN.

B.

F.

K.

N.

O.

INDEX.

NAMES OTHER THAN KINSMAN.

E.

M.

Q.

T.

www.ingramcontent.com/pod-product-compliance
Lightning Source LLC
LaVergne TN
LVHW010239110826
845151LV00004B/1334
* 9 7 8 1 4 2 5 5 2 4 4 0 1 *